Anthropological Reflections on Missiological Issues

Paul G. Hiebert

Baker Books

A Division of Baker Book House Co
Grand Rapids, Michigan 49516

Published by Baker Books
a division of Baker Book House Company
P.O. Box 6287, Grand Rapids, Michigan 49516-6287

Third printing, November 1999

Printed in the United States of America

Library of Congress Cataloging-in-Publication Data

Hiebert, Paul G., 1932–
    Anthropological reflections on missiological issues / by Paul G. Hiebert.
      p. cm.
    Includes bibliographical references.
    ISBN 0-8010-4394-8
    1. Missions—Theory. 2. Missions—Anthropological aspects.
    3. Christianity and culture. I. Title.
    BV2063.H46 1994
    266'.001—dc20
                                        94-22638

Cover: all photos by William Hebert.

For information about academic books, resources for Christian leaders, and all
new releases available from Baker Book House, visit our web site:
                        http://www.bakerbooks.com/

Anthropological
Reflections
on Missiological Issues

Paul G. Hiebert is professor of mission and anthropology and chair of the department of mission and evangelism at Trinity Evangelical Divinity School. He has written several books, including *Anthropological Insights for Missionaries* and *Cultural Anthropology*.

To: Michael, Byron, and Jane
Who have enriched our lives immeasurably.

Contents

Illustrations

Introduction

What can anthropology contribute to mission? This is a critical question, one that we must face squarely and answer carefully. Preparation for missionary service has traditionally included the study of Bible, theology, history, and other religions. In the last twenty-five years, cultural anthropology has become important—indeed essential—to the missiological enterprise. No one would be considered adequately trained for cross-cultural missions now without some understanding of cultural anthropology.[1]

Anthropology and Missions

The first connection between anthropology and missions came through descriptive linguistics, which found its vital role in Bible translation. H. A. Gleason, Kenneth Pike, Eugene Nida, William Reyburn, William Smalley, and Jacob Loewen were among those who made great contributions in applying linguistic theory to translation projects. Today, few question the value of such training for anyone involved in Bible translation. In recent years the focus has shifted to the study of a people's social and cultural contexts. The growing awareness of the fundamental differences between cultures has raised a host of new questions about cross-cultural communication, incarnational ministries, contextualization, and the relationship between theology and sociocultural contexts.

In many cases this emphasis on anthropology and the social sciences has led to a neglect of theology in the mission endeavor. A generation ago, most books and articles dealt with the nature of God's call, the lostness of humanity, the need for prayer and faithfulness, and the radical challenge of such old customs as widow burning and human sacrifice. Today publications deal with planning, leadership, cultural sensitivity, effective sociocultural strategies for evangelism, minimizing cultural dislocation in conversion, and how context determines meaning in the

---

1. Robert J. Schreiter, "Anthropology and Faith: Challenges to Missiology," *Missiology: An International Review* 19.3 (July 1991): 283–94.

contextualization of theology. Many in missions fear this invasion of missions by anthropology. Anthropology is, they note, a social science, built upon secular revelation rather than Scripture. To incorporate it into missions, they say, undermines the very foundations of missions by building them on sand.

The concern of these critics is well founded. On the one hand, if we uncritically accept anthropological teachings in missions we are in danger of replacing biblical foundations with secular ones. We soon will speak more of planning and strategies than of prayer and the leading of the Holy Spirit. We will look to human efforts more than to the work of God. In the short run we may generate a great deal of activity—but we will destroy the divine nature of the mission task.

On the other hand, we can cripple our work if we ignore the contributions anthropology can make to missions. Past missionaries often understood the Scriptures well, but not the people they served. Consequently, their message was often not understood by the people; the churches they planted were often alien and, as a result, remained dependent on outside support for their existence. Missionaries brought with them, not only the gospel, but also Western cultures, and often they failed to differentiate between the two. Many rejected Christ because they rejected the foreignness of the missionary message—not because of the offense of the gospel. Moreover, the people frequently equated Christianity with a set of explicit beliefs, but because these were erected on old pagan worldviews, those worldviews distorted these beliefs and subverted the gospel. To remain faithful, Christians must not only change their old beliefs and practices, but also their worldviews.

In missions we must study the Scriptures *and also* the sociocultural context of the people we serve, so that we can communicate the gospel to them in ways they understand.

Trialogue in Missions

How can we use anthropological insights, yet avoid captivity to the social sciences and a secular humanistic perspective?[2] Increasingly we are aware that systems of explicit human knowledge are embedded in worldviews. Our worldview is made up of our fundamental assumptions about the nature of reality. It is the way "things really are"—the picture of the world that we perceive to be true for everyone. It shapes

---

2. I am deeply indebted to Harvie Conn, *Eternal Word and Changing Worlds: Theology, Anthropology, and Mission in Trialogue* (Grand Rapids: Zondervan, 1984), and his stimulating discussion of the *trialogue* between theology, anthropology, and missions.

and integrates our various fields of knowledge: from theology, anthropology, and missions to physics and the culinary arts. Worldview governs everyday behavior.

To bring theology, anthropology, and missions together we must begin with a biblical worldview, one based on the affirmation that Scripture is God's revelation to us. This worldview, particularly as it manifests itself in the New Testament, is the norm whereby we understand and critique all realities. A Christian worldview begins with the reality that God has revealed himself in Scripture, in the person of Jesus Christ, and in the work of the Spirit in the church and the world. It includes

God's superintendence of history;

God's creation of perfect humans and their fall through sin;

God's work of salvation within those who believe in Christ—God himself among us; and

Christ's return to establish his kingdom of righteousness throughout the created universe.

These are part of a biblical worldview that defines for us the essential reality and history of the cosmos.

Self-Awareness through Trialogue

As we build our worldview on the careful study of the Bible, however, we recognize that our worldview is also shaped by a particular culture. So we constantly must reexamine any worldview, our own or someone else's, in the light of Scripture. It is here that the dialogue between biblical scholars, theologians, and anthropologists from different cultures can help greatly. Scholars from other cultures often are more aware than we of our Western culture biases. We can even learn from anthropologists when we see that they too color their views, of the Bible for example, according to Enlightenment presuppositions.

With such help we can begin to understand the parameters of worldview. We will begin to understand the ways our worldview shapes our theologies. We will also recognize the need for different theological approaches to help us better understand Scripture. *Systematic theology* is based on the study of the Bible, yet it answers questions of the origin and nature of the created order through the theories and methods of philosophy, which is dependent upon worldview. *Biblical theology*, with categories drawn from Scripture, uses a historical perspective to answer questions about God's purpose, design, and intention. And through these insights comes a biblical *anthropological theology*, in which observations about humans and their societies illumine how we understand Scripture.[3] We must, of course, test the categories, theories, and methods of these understandings to see that they are, in fact, compatible with a biblical worldview.

Insights into Scripture through Trialogue

If our systematic, biblical, and anthropological theologies are simply different approaches that are embedded in a Bible-centered worldview, their findings regarding Scripture should complement one another.[4] Just as we use different blueprints to describe different realities of a house—structure, plumbing, wiring—so the different approaches to the study of Scripture should add to, rather than conflict with, one another. That they complement one another means that we look at a reality from different points of view, not because reality is divided, but because of the limits of our human minds. Each view throws new light on the subject. Like binocular vision, the integration of the perspectives provides a refined understanding. This trialogue between systematic, biblical, and anthropological theology can help each of these fields study the Scripture more accurately.

However, since our theologies are based on the way our culture looks at reality, conflicts do arise among the different approaches for understanding Scripture. At such times we must reexamine our knowledge in each of these three approaches to see if it accurately interprets Scripture and human societies. We must see whether underlying theories and methods are indeed compatible with a biblical worldview. Conflicts among differing approaches to Scripture often yield benefits as they make us aware of cultural assumptions we unknowingly bring to the

3. Different systems of knowledge ask different questions, focus on different things, and use different methods. Synchronic theories focus on the structure and function of reality. For example, the discipline of medicine studies the systems of the human body: how they operate and how to fix them when things go wrong. Similarly, both systematic theology and anthropology in the West look at the structures of reality: the first at the ultimate structures, the second at human structures. Diachronic theories focus on the story and end of particular realities. For instance, a biography looks at the history of an individual, and a history views the story of a people. Biblical theology is a diachronic approach to the study of Scripture, and seeks to understand the overall story of God's acts in creation. Both synchronic and diachronic views are essential to understanding any reality. We need to understand how the human body operates, but we also need to understand the history of a people. Ultimately, more meaning is found in diachronic than in synchronic understandings of reality.

4. Complementarity is an essential part of a critical realist epistemology (see articles in this volume on epistemology). For a discussion of the theory of complementarity see D. M. MacKay, "Complementarity in Scientific and Theological Thinking," *Zygon* 9 (September 1974): 225–44; A. Grunbaum, "Complementarity in Quantum Physics and Its Philosophical Generalizations," *Journal of Philosophy* 54 (November 1957): 23–32.

text. Then we can set old views aside and find new insights on the meaning of the text.

Insights into People through Trialogue

The second step in missiology is to study the people we serve. Without knowing the people, we cannot effectively communicate the gospel to them, and the churches we plant will be cultural aliens.

Here we must bring our biblically shaped worldview, and our different perspectives to bear on the subject. The categories and theories of systematic theology show what the people are like as created in the image of God, fallen yet redeemable, objects of God's supreme love and sacrifice. The categories and theories of biblical theology show God's presence in the people's history, preparing them to hear the gospel and molding those who believe into the body of Christ. The categories and theories of anthropological theology show how the people's social and cultural systems expedite or impede their understanding of the Bible's message.

As noted above, this study of other humans, their beliefs and histories, makes us much more aware of the fact that we, too, are creatures in historical and sociocultural contexts, and that these contexts shape our way of seeing things. The self-understanding we gain from this process helps us to be aware of our biases and to read the Scriptures in fresh ways. The study of humans also helps us understand and communicate. We need to study other languages, social organizations, cultural beliefs, and worldviews. Moreover, we need to understand them not only from our own point of view *(etic analysis)* but also as the people understand themselves *(emic analysis)*. One major contribution of anthropology has been the awareness that all peoples have their own views of themselves and of reality and that we must comprehend these if we want to understand and communicate with them. Too often missionaries do not take time to understand the people they serve. We assume their beliefs and wordview will be displaced when they become Christians. Yet they can only understand our message in terms of their own philosophical categories and worldview. It will take time and the study of the Bible before they come to the point where they challenge their worldview.

Taken together, these different ways of looking at people and God's truth help us understand our mission task better. Unfortunately, in the past we used the approaches of systematic and biblical theology only to study Scripture, and anthropology only to study the people. We have missed valuable insights that anthropology can contribute to our understanding of the Bible, and that theology can give us concerning the fall and redemption of humans and their cultures.

Insights into the Kingdom through Trialogue

The third step in missiology is to evaluate the people, their societies and their cultures in the light, not of their culture or our culture, but of the kingdom of God. The goal is the transcendent cultural realities God intended for his creation. We must judge all culture painstakingly and critically, for our part in fulfilling the Great Commission in human lives is at stake. But we must do so with humility and love—with the mind of Christ, because the judgment is not ours, but God's. Moreover, this judgment should compel us to minister to the lost and broken world around us.

Insights into the Gospel Call through Trialogue

The fourth step in missions is to use all of our hard-won understandings from systematics, biblical theology, and anthropology to bear witness before the world to the good news of the gospel. The goal is not knowledge for knowledge's sake but the tools to help move people from old lives in natural fallenness to new lives in Christ.

> We begin with evangelism, with calling people to follow Christ as their Lord and Savior.
> We help nurture churches as covenant communities of love, righteousness, and reconciliation—living examples of God's transforming power.
> We call the world to God's justice and peace.

Missions is a process. We must begin where people are in their beliefs and lives, and then gently lead them to truth and righteousness (1 Thess. 2:7; 2 Tim. 2:24). Conversions to faith are often dramatic, but we cannot expect the people to instantly change their social systems, cultures, and worldviews. Through pastoral ministries we must help them work out the consequences of their new faith in their everyday lives. Throughout the process we must constantly remind ourselves that mission is God's work. Only secondarily is it our obedience to his call to announce to the world, "that God, Creator and Lord of the universe, has personally intervened in human history and has done so supremely through the person and ministry of Jesus of Nazareth who is the Lord of history, Savior and Liberator. In this Jesus, incarnate, crucified and risen, the reign of God has been inaugurated."[5]

This Jesus was at once the revelation in the flesh of what God is like,

---

5. David J. Bosch, *Transforming Mission: Paradigm Shifts in Theology of Mission* (Maryknoll, N.Y.: Orbis, 1991), 412.

and of what the kingdom of God is like. When we forget that missions is rooted in God and his reign, and make it a human activity that we carry out with our knowledge, we destroy it.

Anthropological Reflections

The articles in this book attempt to carry out the trialogue between philosophical, historical, and empirical approaches to the study of both Scripture and humanity. The process has often forced me to reexamine both the categories and theories I have used in theology, anthropology, and missions.

The chapters do not present a comprehensive missiology. They reflect specific issues that emerged on the missiological scene and my attempt to deal with them biblically and anthropologically. Many of them have appeared in journals in the past. Some are revised versions of earlier articles, and some are new additions to the collection.

Behind the trialogue lies a commitment to discovering a biblical worldview that can help us understand the world as God does. I certainly do not have a truly biblical worldview. In fact, the trialogue has made me aware of how deeply my Western worldview has colored not only my anthropological views but also my theological and missiological ones. It has forced me to study the Scriptures in new ways.

Mission is as essential to the life and vitality of the sending churches as it is to the newly planted ones. So too, the study of missions helps us not only to communicate the gospel more effectively to people around the world but also to understand ourselves, our contexts, and the gospel more fully. The reflections in this volume can help us both to communicate the good news of God's salvation to all more effectively and to better understand that great news ourselves.

Part 1

Reflections
on Epistemological
Foundations

1

Epistemological Foundations for Science and Theology

Christian theologies, like other systems of human thought, emerge in different historical and cultural contexts. To be sure, Christians seek to root their theologies in the revelation by God of himself in history, particularly as this is recorded in the Bible. But this does not preclude the fact that they are deeply influenced by the cultures in which they live.

It should not surprise us, therefore, that theologians of the nineteenth and twentieth centuries were influenced by modern science. The obvious successes of science had captured Western thought. Many, in fact, came to see theology as a kind of science. For example, Princeton theologian Archibald Alexander Hodge[1] defined systematic theology as "the science of religion." H. O. Wiley, Alvah Hovey, and W. G. T. Shedd define it similarly.[2] Lewis Sperry Chafer noted that "Systematic Theology, the greatest of the sciences, has fallen upon evil days."[3] A. H. Strong defined theology as "the science of God and of the relationships between God and the universe." He added, "If the universe were God, theology would be the only science. Since the universe is but a manifestation of God and is distinct from God, there are sciences of nature and

This chapter first appeared in *TSF Bulletin* 8.4 (March–April 1985): 5–10. Used by permission.

1. Archibald Alexander Hodge, *Outlines of Theology* (New York: Armstrong and Sons, 1891), 15.

2. H. O. Wiley, *Christian Theology* (1940; reprint, Kansas City, Mo.: Beacon Hill, 1969), 1:14–15; W. G. T. Shedd, *Dogmatic Theology,* 3 vols. (Edinburgh: T & T Clark, 1888–94).

3. Lewis Sperry Chafer, *Systematic Theology,* 8 vols. (Dallas: Dallas Seminary Press, 1947–48), v.

of the mind. Theology is 'the science of the sciences,' not in the sense of including all these sciences, but in the sense of using their results and of showing their underlying ground."[4] More recently, R. B. Griffiths has sought to show that theology is indeed a science.[5]

Often this definition of theology as a kind of science has meant no more than that theology was an orderly and systematic pursuit of knowledge. Theologians have long emulated philosophers in this. But in many instances there has been an attempt to build theology on the apparently solid epistemological foundations that seem to make science so certain and trustworthy. However we as Christians use the term *science*, its definition and nature are largely controlled by the modern natural sciences.

In the past few decades a radical change has been taking place in the epistemological foundations of science, a change in the way science itself is perceived. This shift holds profound implications for those seeking to integrate science and theology and, indeed, for theology itself. The epistemological crisis in the sciences raises questions about the epistemological foundations of theology and the relationship between science and theology. Since the crisis has not yet been resolved in the sciences, and because I am not a trained philosopher, what I present is more a set of questions than answers. Although it is easier for us to stay within our fields of specialization, this limits us to narrow questions and to piecemeal answers. We dare not avoid the big questions because we fear being wrong. The consequences of the current epistemological crisis will affect Christians, whether or not we examine them.

A word about my assumptions: I am committed to the full authority of the Scriptures and to an evangelical Anabaptist understanding of Christian theology. I am also an anthropologist and missionary seeking to understand our modern, pluralistic world, and to make Christ known within it.

The Crisis

In its early stages, science was based largely on an uncritical form of *realism*. While most philosophers and theologians argued from positions of *idealism*, scientists, with a few exceptions, "assumed that scientific theories were accurate descriptions of the world as it is in itself."[6]

---

4. Augustus H. Strong, *Systematic Theology* (1886; reprint, Philadelphia: Judson, 1973), 1.
5. R. B. Griffiths, "Is Theology a Science?" *Journal of the American Scientific Affiliation* (September 1980): 169–73.
6. Ian G. Barbour, *Myths, Models, and Paradigms: A Comparative Study in Science and Religion* (New York: Harper and Row, 1974), 34.

Scientific knowledge was seen as a photograph of reality, a complete and accurate picture of what is really real. In its positivistic forms it rejected metaphysics and transempirical realities. Consequently there was little room for theology. This stance seemed justified in view of the great strides made by science in its examination of nature.

The certainty of scientific knowledge and the optimism that marked its early years were undermined from within. There were three major attacks on the epistemological foundations of naïve realism, all reflecting the growing study by scientists of the scientific process itself. First, in the physical sciences, Albert Einstein in relativity, Niels Bohr in quantum mechanics, and others showed that the personal factor of the scientist inevitably enters into scientific knowledge. There is no such thing as totally objective knowledge. Second, social science began to study the psychological, social, and cultural factors involved in the scientific endeavor and demonstrated that there are no unbiased theories. Science is built on the cultural assumptions of the West and is deeply influenced by social and psychological processes. Third, such historians and philosophers of science as Michael Polanyi, Thomas Kuhn, and Larry Laudan found that science is not cumulative and exhaustive.[7] It is a sequence of competing paradigms or models of reality. But if theories taken as fact today are replaced by others tomorrow, what is the nature of scientific knowledge? Clearly we can no longer equate scientific knowledge about reality with reality itself. The old assumption that scientific theories have a one-to-one correspondence with reality has been shattered. We cannot have science without metaphysics. We must understand it within its historical, sociocultural and psychological settings. Whatever it is, science is not a photograph of reality.

Where To?

Forced to leave the comfortable certainty of naïve realism, scientists are now looking for a more stable epistemological foundation. What are their options? To answer this question, we need a taxonomy of epistemological systems, a meta-epistemological grid by which to compare various epistemological options. There are dangers, of course, in creating such a grid. Any taxonomy imposes biases on the field and overlooks nuances of the various positions. Moreover, it assumes that epistemo-

7. Michael Polanyi, *Personal Knowledge: Towards a Post-Critical Philosophy* (Chicago: University of Chicago Press, 1958); Thomas S. Kuhn, *The Structure of Scientific Revolutions,* 2d ed. (Chicago: University of Chicago Press, 1970); Larry Laudan, *Progress and Its Problems: Towards a Theory of Scientific Growth* (Berkeley, Calif.: University of California Press, 1977).

logical paradigms are comparable,[8] and that some mutual understanding among them is possible.[9]

There are, however, greater dangers in looking at various epistemological positions in isolation, or of assuming that they are incommensurable. If comparison between epistemological alternatives is impossible, rationality is undermined, and, with it, science and philosophy.

Figure 1.1 overly simplifies the various epistemologies, but it shows why there is a crisis in epistemology and hints at some possible solutions. In the last column the various epistemological answers are illustrated by a parable:

> Several umpires stood talking after a baseball game one day when a player asked them, "Why do you call a particular pitch a 'strike'?" Each of them gave a different response based on his epistemological position.

Idealism

Forced to abandon naïve realism, scientists are looking for a new epistemological foundation. Some, particularly in psychology and anthropology, advocate some form of *idealism*. Few go so far as Vedantic Hinduism, which denies the existence of an external world. Science, after all, began as an investigation of the world around us. Critical idealists argue that there may be external realities, but what really matters is the world we create within us. The order we perceive in the world is an order we impose on it by our categories and theories.

Most scientists, however, argue that to deny that the order we perceive does exist in nature itself and to abandon empirical observation as a method alters the scientific endeavor beyond recognition.

Determinism and Instrumentalism

Most scientists are too busy studying the world to give much thought to epistemology. They often use *deterministic models* to explain their observations, but they assume that their own theories are based on rational choice. Only recently has science become self-reflective enough to question this inconsistency.

A number of philosophers of science believe that we have no alternative but to accept some form of determinism. Feyerabend, for example, sought to found science on solid empirical and rational grounds. But he came to the conclusion that scientific decisions are based on politics and propaganda, in which prestige, power, age, and polemics

8. Contrary to Kuhn, *Structure*.
9. Douglas R. Hofstadter, *Godel, Escher, Bach: An Eternal Golden Braid* (New York: Random House, 1980).

Figure 1.1
A Taxonomy of Epistemological Positions

Position	Nature of Knowledge	Relationship between Systems of Knowledge	The Umpire's Response
Absolute Idealism	Reality exists in the mind. The external world is illusory (e.g., Vedantic and Advaita Hinduism).	Each system is an island to itself. Systems are incommensurable. Unity is possible only as everyone joins in the same system.	"My calling it makes it a strike. The game is in my mind."
Critical Idealism	Reality exists in the mind. The external world is unknowable. Order is imposed on sense experience by the mind.	Each system is an island to itself. Systems are incommensurable. A common ground is found in human rationality, which is assumed to be the same for all humans.	"My calling it makes it a strike. My mind imposes order on the world."
Naïve Idealism/ Naïve Realism	The external world is real. The mind can know it exactly, exhuastively, and without bias. Science is a photograph of reality. Knowledge and reality are equated uncritically.	Because knowledge is exact and potentially exhaustive, there can be only one unified theory. Various theories must be reduced to one. This leads to reductionism in the physical, psychological, or sociocultural sphere.	"I call it the way it is. If it is a strike I call it a strike. If it is a ball I call it a ball."
Critical Realism	The external world is real. Our knowledge of it is partial but can be true. Science is a map or model. It is made up of successive paradigms that bring us to closer approximations of reality and absolute truth.	Each field in science presents a different blueprint of reality. These are complementary to one another. Integration is achieved, not by reducing them all to one model, but by seeing their interrelationship. Each gives us partial insights into reality.	"I call it the way I see it, but there is a real pitch and an objective standard against which I must judge it. I can be shown to be right or wrong."
Instrumentalism (Pragmatism)	The external world is real. We cannot know if our knowledge of it is true, but if it "does the job" we can use it. Science is a Rorschach response that makes no ontological claims to truth.	Because we make no truth claims for our theories or models, there can be no ontological contradictions between them. We can use apparently controdictory models in different situations so long as they work.	"I call it the way I see it, but there is no way to know if I am right or wrong."
Determinism	The external world is real. We and our knowledge are determined by material causes, hence knowledge can lay no claim to truth (or to meaning).	There is no problem with integration, for all systems of knowledge are determined by external, nonrational factors such as infant experiences, emotional drives, and thought conditioning.	"I call it the way I am programmed to."

determine the choice among competing theories. He argued, "not merely that certain decisions between theories in science *have been irrational*, but that choices between competing scientific theories, in the nature of the case, *must be irrational*."[10] Carried to its logical conclusion, determinism renders human knowledge, including science, irrational and meaningless.[11]

Other philosophers of science, including Kuhn, argue for an instrumentalist epistemology. They see science as a "useful" way of looking at the world because it helps us solve problems. They affirm a real world, and mark a distinction between systems of knowledge and external realities. But they deny that science gives us a "true" picture of those realities. The criterion for evaluating science is pragmatism—"Does it work?" not "Is it true?" We must, therefore, live with scientific (and cultural) relativism. Ronald Sukenick writes,

> All versions of "reality" are of the nature of fiction. There's your story and my story, there's the journalist's story and the historian's story, there's the philosopher's story and the scientist's story. . . . Our common world is only a description . . . reality is imagined.[12]

But, as Marvin Harris notes, relativism destroys science as science.[13] And Peter Berger points out that relativism denies any concept of truth and in the end relativizes relativity itself, rendering it meaningless.[14]

A rejection of instrumentalism does not preclude scientists from creating and using models they know to be useful fictions. All scientists recognize that models for which no claims of truth are made sometimes can help sort out a problem. Those in the applied sciences, in particular, often use models simply because they work. The question is not whether *all* mental models depict reality, but whether *any* do.

Critical Realism

A number of scientists argue for a *critical realist* approach to science. Harold Schilling writes,

10. Laudan, *Progress*, 3 (italics in original).

11. See C. S. Lewis, *God in the Dock: Essays on Theology and Ethics*, ed. W. Hooper (Grand Rapids: Eerdmans, 1970), 129–46.

12. Ronald Sukenick, "Upward and Juanward: The Possible Dream," in Daniel Noel, ed., *Seeing Castaneda: Reactions to the "Don Juan" Writings of Carlos Castaneda* (New York: Putnam, 1976), 113.

13. Marvin Harris, *Cultural Materialism: The Struggle for a Science of Culture* (New York: Random House, 1980), 45.

14. Peter L. Berger, *The Sacred Canopy: Elements of a Sociological Theory of Religion* (Garden City, N.Y.: Doubleday, 1969), 40–42.

The interpretation I shall offer will be developed from the point of view of critical realism, as I believe it to be espoused by most scientists. . . . According to this view science actually investigates nature itself, not just its own ideas. It achieves much reliable knowledge about it. This knowledge is communicated through systems of theoretical models. . . . Science's descriptions of [nature] are . . . to be taken as "true," though not literalistically so in detail.[15]

Ian Barbour adds, ". . . the critical realist takes theories to be representations of the world. He holds that valid theories are true as well as useful."[16]

Like instrumentalism, critical realism makes a distinction between reality and our knowledge of it, but like naïve realism, it claims that knowledge can be true. Theories are not regarded as photographs of reality, but as maps or blueprints. Just as it takes many blueprints to understand a building, so it takes many theories to comprehend reality.

Truth in a map is different from truth in a photograph. Some is literal and some is symbolic. For example, a road map shows a road leading to an airport—a fact we can empirically verify. But the fact that the road on the map is colored red does not mean that the road itself is red in color. Nor is the city yellow. To be useful, a map must be selective. A road map must leave out information about underground pipes, overhead wires, buildings, trees, sidewalks, lawns, and the like. To put everything in one map clutters it and renders it useless. The choice of what to include and what to exclude depends on the purpose for which the map is to be used, for maps are not only symbols of reality but also guides for choosing a course of action.[17] Naïve realism has no room for metaphysics. Mental images are unincorporated photographs of reality. Determinism and instrumentalism accept metaphysics, but divorce mental images from external realities. Critical realism, as Laudan points out, restores metaphysics to a central place in science and postulates a complex dialectical relationship between realities and mental images.[18]

Critical realism is increasingly being accepted as a new epistemological base by the scientist. With the exception of a few social scientists, none are idealists. And with the exception of applied scientists, few are

15. Harold K. Schilling, *The New Consciousness in Science and Religion* (London: SCM, 1973), 99.

16. Barbour, *Myths, Models, and Paradigms*, 37.

17. Clifford Geertz, "Religion as a Cultural System," in William A. Lessa and Evon Z. Vogt, eds., *Reader in Comparative Religion: An Anthropological Approach,* 3d ed. (New York: Harper and Row, 1972), 168–69.

18. Laudan, *Progress.*

instrumentalists. Most are still convinced that they are in search of truth, and that their theories are more than useful fictions.

Epistemological Foundations for Theology

The epistemological crisis in the sciences raises important questions for theology, particularly where it tries to be a science. What are its epistemological foundations, and what is its relationship to science? These questions must be distinguished from questions regarding the content of theology, which must be dealt with on another level of discourse. We will limit ourselves here to the question of the relationship between theology as a system of thought and the Bible as a historical document.

Theology as Naïve Realism

Most Christians, like most scientists, do not examine their epistemological foundations. They assume that they understand clearly and without bias what Scripture has to say. Just as naïve realist scientists assume there is a one-to-one correlation between theories and a real world outside, they assume that their theology bears a one-to-one correspondence to the Bible. They reject the notion that their interpretations of Scripture are colored by their history and culture, their personal experiences, or even the language they speak. They are, in other words, either naïve realists or naïve idealists. It is hard to distinguish between the two, for both claim a one-to-one correspondence between knowledge and reality. Only when they are forced to leave a naïve realist/idealist position is the difference apparent. Naïve realists, in the end, move to some other form of realism; naïve idealists become critical or absolute idealists.

Because naïve realist/idealist Christians hold an exact correspondence between their theology and Scripture, they claim equal and absolute certainty for both. This raises problems when disagreements arise. Each claims that his or her own theology is full and certain truth; those who disagree, then, must be wrong. Both sides reject one another out of hand and separate. They believe that unity is possible only on the basis of complete theological agreement. But this is achieved only if people share the same historical and cultural contexts, or if they are willing to be followers of a single theological authority. This leaves little room for ordinary Christians to read and interpret the Scriptures for themselves. In the past, naïve realism/idealism provided us with the security of both a real world and certain knowledge, but it is no longer a tenable epistemological position.

Science has convincingly shown us that there is a human element in all knowledge.[19] Anthropologists have found that all languages have within them implicit cultural and theological biases. These biases are expressed in language categories that assume a particular worldview. Anthropologists have also shown that all human knowledge is molded in part by the cultural and historical context within which it is found.[20] Sociologists have shown that knowledge belongs to a community and is influenced by the dynamics of that community.[21] Psychologists have demonstrated that even so simple a task as reading and interpreting a written page involves a complex hermeneutical process that varies according to the level of mental development,[22] knowledge, and attitudes of the reader. There is, in fact, no knowledge in which the subjective dimension does not enter in some way or other.

The growing awareness of these findings has forced scientists to realize that science itself must be understood within its cultural and historical settings. If this is true of science, what about theology? Can we claim that no subjective factors enter our reading of Scripture? Certainly the Holy Spirit works in us, helping us to understand and interpret Scripture for our particular needs. But does he totally override our human thought processes?

If all knowledge has a subjective dimension to it, where is truth? What foundation can we trust? Where are absolutes? The answers we give to these questions will depend largely on the epistemological stance we take in theology.

Theology as Idealism

Forced to choose between human knowledge and the external world as the independent variable—the source from which the other is derived—many theologians opt for some form of idealism. In this, human thought is seen as foundational and empirical realities as contingent. The advantage of this, of course, is that we can have objective knowledge that is certain in every detail.

Idealists argue that this certainty rests on biblical revelation and reason. The Bible however, is a written document and a part of the external world we can know only through hearing and reading. This again raises

19. Charles A. Coulson, *Science and Christian Belief* (London: Fontana, 1955), 84–120.
20. Dell Hymes, ed., *Language in Culture and Society* (New York: Harper and Row, 1964).
21. Peter L. Berger and Thomas Luckmann, *The Social Construction of Reality: A Treatise in the Sociology of Knowledge* (Garden City, N.Y.: Doubleday, 1966).
22. Jean Piaget, *The Psychology of Intelligence* (Totowa, N.J.: Littlefield, Adams, 1960).

questions about the subjectivity of biblical knowledge. In the end, idealists must appeal to human reason as the arbiter of truth.

An idealist approach to theology does provide a viable way of looking
at reality. There are too many idealists in philosophy and theology to
write it off lightly. But it leaves several questions unanswered.

First, it assumes one uniform system of reason for all humans. This
assumption, however, is being increasingly challenged in the social
sciences. At the most fundamental level, all human minds work in the
same way. They all learn languages through common processes. They
are able to communicate and to understand one another, even when
those speaking to one another belong to different cultures. But there
are different types of formal logic. Mathematicians have shown that
we can construct many non-Euclidean geometries, each of which is internally consistent. More recently they have shown that fuzzy sets
("fuzzy algebra" and "fuzzy logic") provide us with a system of reason
in which the Western notions of either/or-ness and the law of the excluded middle do not hold.[23] If there are mental universals, and there
certainly are, they reside at a deeper level of thought than we once believed. Anthropologists have found different systems of logic used in
different societies.[24]

Second, an idealist theology has difficulty in accounting for communication. We cannot know another person's mind directly. All communication is mediated through external events. But if the meaning of
these events is what we make them to be, communication breaks down.
In extreme idealism, Vedantic Hinduism for example, we are left as islands of certainty within ourselves, with no real knowledge of one another apart from a mystical experience of oneness.

Third, an idealist theology leaves uncertain the question of discerning the work of the Holy Spirit. As Christians we hold that the Holy
Spirit is at work in the hearts and minds of his people, helping them to
understand the truth. But how can we test whether our understanding
has come from God, from our spirit, or some other spirit? We cannot
appeal to Scripture, for each person can claim to have had a divine revelation regarding its interpretation. We all face the danger of molding
Scripture to fit our thoughts.

Fourth, an idealist theology faces problems with disagreements. Because the final appeal is internal, there is no external reference point to
arbitrate between different theological positions. The resulting combat-

23. L. A. Zadeh, "Fuzzy Sets," *Information and Control* 8 (1965): 338–53.
24. Aleksandr R. Luria, *Cognitive Development: Its Cultural and Social Foundations*,
trans. M. Lopez-Morillas and L. Solotaroff (Cambridge, Mass.: Harvard University Press,
1976).

ive stance leads to divisiveness. The only real resolution lies in the conversion of one side to the position of the other. In the end we are in danger of worshiping human reason, where we become the final arbiters of truth, and those who disagree with us are wrong.

Fifth, an idealist theology undervalues the importance of history as the framework within which divine revelation takes place. It tends to be ahistorical and acultural. It has problems taking seriously the changing historical and cultural contexts of the Scriptures and of our times. In the extreme it leads to a Vedantic view in which the external world is *maya* or illusion, and history has no meaning. Mircea Eliade, E. Stanley Jones, and others have argued, however, that the Judeo-Christian tradition differs from tribal and Eastern religions precisely in its strong doctrine of the creation of a real world apart from, but contingent upon, God and in its strong sense of history as the arena within which God works. It is the *realist* epistemologies that take the external world seriously.

Sixth, it is well nigh impossible to integrate an idealist theology and a realist science. The two see knowledge in a different light. Consequently, in the end we are forced to choose between one or the other as our ultimate frame of reference.

Finally, as we will see in the next chapter, there are missiological questions. How does an idealist Christian theology relate to non-Christian religions, particularly to the great idealist religions of Hinduism and Buddhism? How does it affect evangelism?

Theology as Determinism or Instrumentalism

A deterministic approach to theology, like a deterministic approach to science, renders it meaningless. A few theologians may argue for a total divine determinism, but like scientists using deterministic models, they tend to exclude their own theologies from the picture.

Others, particularly such social scientists as Émile Durkheim, argue that theology is instrumental. It is a useful way of looking at things, whether true or false. It serves important functions in the society, giving it a sense of identity and encoding its values. As evangelicals we must reject an instrumentalist theology because it rejects the concept of truth. In the end it leads to theological and religious relativism.

Theology as Critical Realism

How would evangelical theology look in a critical realist mode? In the first place it would differentiate between theology and biblical revelation, ascribing final and full authority to the Bible as the inspired record of God in human history. The Bible would then be the source and rule for Christian faith and life, and the final criterion against which to measure theological truth. We would see in Scripture the definitive record of the person and work of Jesus Christ, who is our Lord.

Theology in a critical realist mode is our human understanding and interpretation of the Scriptures. Technically, we should speak of *theologies,* for each theology is an understanding of divine revelation within a particular historical and cultural context. Thus we would speak of the theology of Calvin or of Luther or of evangelicalism.

A critical realist approach to theology affirms the priesthood of all believers, and recognizes that they must and will apply the universal message of the Bible to their own lives and settings. It holds that the Holy Spirit is at work in all believers who are humbly open to his guidance, leading them through the Scriptures and the Christian community into a growing understanding of theological truth and its meaning for their lives.

This assumes that all theologies are partial and culturally biased, so that truth in the Scriptures is greater than our understanding of it. There is room, therefore, for growth in our theologies, but this means we must constantly test our theologies against the Scriptures and be willing to change them when we gain new understandings. Historical realities do not change, but our understandings of them do.

Does this not lead us into a morass of theological pluralism? Yes, in the sense that it recognizes that different people ask different questions when they go to the Scriptures and that their cultural and historical frameworks will color their interpretations. However, as Norman Kraus points outs, Paul makes it clear that the interpretation of the gospel is not ultimately the task of individuals, or even of leaders. It is the task of the church as a hermeneutical or "discerning community":

> Thus the Scripture can find its proper meaning as witness only within a *community of interpretation.* Principles of interpretation are important, but secondary. There needs to be an authentic correspondence between gospel announced and a "new order" embodied in community for Scripture to play its proper role as a part of the original witness. The authentic community is the hermeneutical community. It determines the actual enculturated meaning of Scripture.[25]

Similarly, the cultural biases of local churches must be checked by the international community of churches drawn from many cultures.

---

25. C. Norman Kraus, *The Authentic Witness: Credibility and Authority* (Grand Rapids: Eerdmans, 1979), 71.

There are three checks against theological error: First, all theology must be rooted in the Scriptures. Second, the Holy Spirit is at work in the hearts of God's people revealing the meaning of the Scriptures to individuals and churches in their particular settings. Third, believers and congregations must help one another discern the leading of the Holy Spirit. They must test one another's theology and be open to critique. Just as others see our sins more clearly than we do, so also they see our theological errors more clearly. The interpretation of Scripture within a hermeneutical community must, therefore, be carried out in a spirit of humility when speaking and with a willingness to learn.

Does this approach not lead us to instrumentalism and a consequent theological relativism? No. Historical and experiential facts remain the same in all times and cultures. And while our interpretation of history introduces a subjective dimension, the facts of history ensure a large measure of objectivity. Critical realist theology, like critical realist science, affirms that, while we see only in part, we do see. We can speak of theological truth in an absolute sense. We see clearly the great outlines of theology—creation, fall, and redemption. In the study of Scripture we see enough to lead us into faith and a growing discipleship. Too often it is not a lack of truth that holds us back, but our willingness to obey the truth we do have.

Epistemology and the Current Evangelical Scene

An understanding of the various epistemological positions can untangle some of the current debates among evangelicals, debates that often lead to confusion rather than to clarity. We must distinguish between debates over the epistemological foundations of theology and those over the content of theology (see fig. 1.2). Because we take our epistemological assumptions for granted, we do not debate them openly. Consequently disagreements on this level surface in debates over theological content and confuse the issues.

As I see it, many young evangelicals aware of the shifts now taking place in Western epistemology have moved from the old position of naïve realism to that of critical realism, while remaining evangelical in *theological content*. Seeing this move as a shift towards liberalism, other theologians have reacted by asserting the certainty of theology as a comprehensive, complete system of thought (not to be confused with the trustworthiness of Scripture as historical revelation). But in doing so they have been forced into an idealist epistemology that absolutizes ideas over historical realities (see fig. 1.1).

To be sure, the old debate over the content of theology between conservatives and liberals continues, and we must examine it with utmost

Figure 1.2
Types of Conflict on the Evangelical Scene

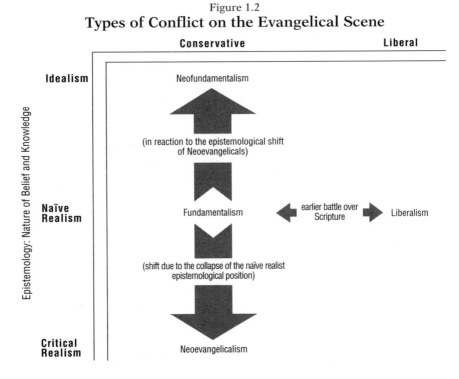

seriousness. It is here that we seek the content of truth. But this debate must not be confused with the debate over epistemology—over the nature of our understanding of the truth. There are naïve realist liberals who are just as dogmatic in declaring that they have a full knowledge of the truth as there are naïve realist evangelicals. There are also idealist liberals and idealist evangelicals. Some Christians have moved from a conservative naïve realist position to a more liberal critical realist position. But they must not be equated with those who have moved to a conservative critical realist position.

Biblical authority is one area in which the failure to distinguish between the epistemological foundations of theology and its content has created a great deal of confusion. For those who see human knowledge as a photograph of reality—bearing a one-to-one correspondence to it— all knowledge is considered factual and literal, and any difference between knowledge and reality is an error. For those who see knowledge as a map, some information may not literally correspond to the visible reality, but may communicate *another level of truth*. It is, therefore, not an "error." For example, freeways on a road map may be colored red and surface streets black. This does not mean the two are, in fact, red and black. It does mean that the roads are different in character and belong to different systems. Moreover, a map is not faulty if nonessential information is lacking. It is fully trustworthy and accurate if it serves the purposes for which it is intended.

A second area in which the confusion between epistemology and content has wreaked havoc has to do with focus. Idealism (naïve or critical) focuses on the ultimate unchanging structures of truth. Idealist theologians, therefore, emphasize systematic theologies (theologies of the balcony). Consequently they tend to be ahistorical and acultural. Realism looks at events in the real historical world within which we live and focuses on the nature of truth in specific situations. Realist theologians, therefore, emphasize biblical theologies that look at God's acts and self-revelation in specific historical and cultural situations (theologies of the road). As we shall see in the next chapter, we need both. As we read the historical record of God's revelation in the Bible, we all formulate implicit systematic theologies. The difference is that realists place greater emphasis on biblical theologies that focus on historical revelation and less on systematic theologies that look at the structures of reality.

Finally, the current confusion over epistemological foundations has lead to a breakdown in communication. When evangelical critical realist theologians and idealist theologians converse, they speak of the same things, but they have an uneasy feeling that something is amiss. The idealists accuse the realists of a lack of certainty, for the realists differentiate between their theology and Scripture. They tend to preface their remarks with "I believe," or "As I see it." Critical realists complain that the dogmatic certainty of the idealists does not take into account that all human knowledge occurs in the contexts of culture and history. Representatives of the two sides may, in fact, agree on the contents of theological truth but disagree on the epistemological nature of theology.

The breakdown in communication is most evident when disagreements arise. Idealists require agreement as the basis for harmony. Consequently, they tend to be conversionist and polemical in their approach to those holding other theological positions. They break with and attack those who refuse to accept their positions. Critical realists recognize that Christians will disagree in their understanding of Scripture and that unity lies in a commitment to the same Lord and to an obedience to the same Scripture. They tend to be confessional and irenic in their approach to those who disagree. Moreover, they are committed by their epistemological stance to continue discussion with other points of view.

When two idealists or two critical realists disagree, they at least share common assumptions. Communication of some sort occurs, whether in mutual attack or mutual dialogue, because they both are playing by the same rules. But when an idealist and a critical realist disagree, confusion sets in because one is playing chess and the other playing checkers on the same board.

As evangelicals, we need to distinguish epistemological issues from theological ones so that we do not waste our energies and so that we can work toward a resolution of our differences without misguidedly attacking a brother or sister. We need to guard against heresy. We also need to carry out the mission Christ has given us in this lost and broken world.

2

The Missiological Implications of an Epistemological Shift

The current epistemological crisis in science and philosophy has significant implications for Western theology.[1] It also affects the integration of theology and science, and our understanding of the missionary task. How we contextualize theology, how we respond to the theological pluralism now emerging in non-Western churches, and how we relate to non-Christian religions as systems of thought and to non-Christians as persons are all determined to a great extent by our epistemological premises. At the core is the question of how we interrelate two or more differing systems of knowledge.

Systems of Knowledge

When we talk of relationships among systems of knowledge, we must specify their level of abstraction (see fig. 2.1).[2] For our purposes, we will differentiate three levels.

Theories

The lowest level of abstraction is *theories*. Theories are limited, low-level systems of explanation that seek to answer specific questions about a narrow range of reality, using perceptions, concepts, notions of

This chapter first appeared in *TSF Bulletin* 8.5 (May–June 1985): 6–11. Used by permission.

1. See chapter 1; also Thomas S. Kuhn, *The Structure of Scientific Revolutions,* 2d ed. (Chicago: University of Chicago Press, 1962).

2. Cf. Kuhn, *Structure;* Harold K. Schilling, *The New Consciousness in Science and Religion* (London: SCM, 1973); Larry Laudan, *Progress and Its Problems: Towards a Theory of Scientific Growth* (Berkeley, Calif.: University of California Press, 1977); Douglas R. Hofstadter, *Godel, Escher, Bach: An Eternal Golden Braid* (New York: Random House, 1980).

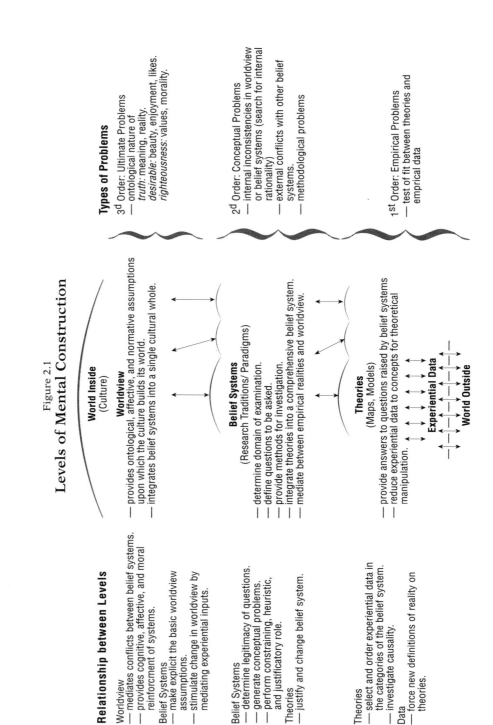

Figure 2.1
Levels of Mental Construction

causation, and the like. Alternative theories may arise that give different answers to the same set of questions. Theories themselves may be on different levels of generality, and broader theories may subsume more limited ones.

Belief Systems

Theories are imbedded in higher-level systems of knowledge that Thomas Kuhn calls *paradigms,*[3] Larry Laudan calls *research traditions,*[4] and I will refer to as *belief systems.* In the sciences these include physics, chemistry, and biology. In theology they include the disciplines of systematic theology and biblical theology. Belief systems select a domain of reality to examine, determine the critical questions to be investigated, provide methods for investigation, and integrate one or more theories into a comprehensive system of beliefs. They also mediate between each theory and the worldview of the culture within which it is embedded. In relation to theories, belief systems set the boundaries of inquiry and determine the legitimacy of the problems examined. They generate conceptual problems for theoretical investigation, set standards for how the investigation will be conducted and consider whether research models are justified.[5] Belief systems make explicit the implicit assumptions of the worldview within which they function and apply these assumptions to beliefs and behavior. They also change the worldview as they introduce new theoretical constructs and mediate the new experiences of those who hold the worldview.

The specialists who work in a belief system form a community that sets the standards, defines "proofs," and checks their research and teaching. This community also controls the training and entry of candidates into the discipline.[6] Other specialists apply the theories of a belief system to life. The engineers and technologists who work in the discipline of *applied* physics draw on the work of those involved in the belief system of *theoretical* physics. The general public may accept the word of such specialists as authority. Most Americans, for instance, are confident that physicists have a great deal of true knowledge about the real world. People see and use the technological fruits of the physicists' theories. The public is generally unaware of the theoretical debates taking place within a research tradition.

3. Kuhn, *Structure.*
4. Laudan, *Progress.*
5. Ibid., 78–120.
6. Barry Barnes, *T. S. Kuhn and Social Science* (New York: Columbia University Press, 1982), 10.

Worldviews

At the top level, a number of research traditions and a great deal of common-sense knowledge are loosely integrated into an overarching worldview. Worldviews are the most fundamental and encompassing views of reality shared by a people in a culture. The worldview incorporates assumptions about the nature of things—about the "givens" of reality. Challenges to these assumptions threaten the very foundations of their world. People resist such challenges with deep emotion, for such questions threaten to destroy their understanding of reality. As Clifford Geertz points out, there is no greater human fear than the loss of a sense of order and meaning.[7] People are even willing to die for beliefs that make their lives and deaths meaningful.

Relationship between Systems of Knowledge

In interrelating different systems of knowledge we must keep in mind the three levels—theories, belief systems, and worldviews. Although it is important to examine in detail how elements on one level relate to those on another (e.g., how theories relate to belief systems and belief systems to worldviews), we will only briefly examine how theories in a belief system relate to each other, how belief systems within a worldview relate to each other, and how worldviews relate to each other.

How we view the relationship between systems of knowledge on the same level is largely determined by our epistemological foundations (fig. 2.1). As noted in chapter 1, naïve realists and idealists hold that true knowledge must be precise, objective, and certain. Both basically hold to a one-to-one correspondence between human knowledge and reality, but for different reasons. Naïve realists see knowledge as a *photograph* or mirror of reality;[8] idealists believe knowledge *creates* reality. Consequently, both look for a single comprehensive system of knowledge that will encompass all of reality—a sort of "grand unified theory." They cannot accept as valid two differing views of the same reality. All photographs taken of a hill or tree from the same spot should be the same.

Because of this, naïve realist scientists are not willing to accept the validity of theology until it fits into the assumptions of science—hence the need to "demythologize" religion. Naïve realist or idealist theologians refuse to accept the findings of science if these challenge their

---

7. Clifford Geertz, "Religion as a Cultural System," in William A. Lessa and Evon Z. Vogt, eds., *Reader in Comparative Religion: An Anthropological Approach,* 3d ed. (New York: Harper and Row, 1972).

8. Jerry H. Gill, *On Knowing God: New Directions for the Future of Theology* (Philadelphia: Westminster, 1981), 34–36.

theologically based views of nature. A unified theory can be achieved in any of several ways. Competing theories can be modified to make them compatible with each other, a new theory or belief system can be formulated to replace the old one, or areas of conflict may be declared unimportant or handed over to another belief system.[9]

Naïve realists and idealists have taken two approaches to the integration of belief systems. One is to *separate them into nonoverlapping domains.* This has been most common in rationalism. For example, many Christians sought to integrate science and theology by assigning them to two realms. This was a legacy of the classical perspective, following Plato, in which reality was divided into two main worlds: the one natural, tangible, and transitory; the other transcendent, spiritual, and eternal. Augustine and Aquinas introduced this approach into theology.

The other approach, found particularly in empiricism, is *reductionism.* Gill notes: "Materialists claim that all intangibles are nothing but epiphenomena, positivists argue that all value judgments are nothing but expressions of emotion, behaviorists maintain that mind and spirit are nothing but conditioned behavior, and Marxists affirm that culture and society are nothing but reflections of material conditions."[10]

Reductionism has been used to integrate the sciences. For example, physical reductionism reduces all phenomena ultimately to fundamental particles (such as atoms, mesons, and quarks) and to forces. Galileo concluded that the physical world is a perfect machine whose future happenings can be fully predicted and controlled by one who has full knowledge and control of the present motions. This led nearly two centuries later to the famous remark of Pierre-Simon Laplace that a superhuman intelligence acquainted with the position and motion of the atoms at any moment could predict the whole course of human events.[11] The result, observes Harold K. Schilling,[12] was a world that was "closed, essentially completed and unchanging, basically substantive, simple and shallow, and fundamentally unmysterious—a rigidly programmed machine."

Similarly, psychological reductionism roots all human realities, including human societies and culture, in psychological theory. Sociological reductionism sees group dynamics as the foundation of all human beliefs and behavior, and leads to a formulaic approach to changing humans.

---

9. Laudan, *Progress,* 45–69.
10. Gill, *On Knowing God,* 29.
11. Edwin A. Burtt, *The Metaphysical Foundations of Modern Science,* rev. ed. (Garden City, N.Y.: Doubleday, Anchor, 1954), 96.
12. Schilling, *New Consciousness,* 44.

Figure 2.2
Characteristics of Epistemological Positions

	Mentalism	Dogmatic	Absolutes	Volitional
Idealism	(reality is in the mind)	(closed to change)	(affirms that truth can be known) ...un know in full	(humans reason and choose)
	• we know it with certainty	• declarative in stance		
	Realism	• ahistorical and acultural in nature		
Naïve Realism	(reality is the world including the mind) • tests knowledge against experience and history • knowledge is totally objective • photograph view of knowledge	• authoritarian • parent/child approach to others • learning = memorizing • teacher- and message-oriented • at times arrogant and combative • conversion is radical displacement	• can know in full • knowledge is totally objective	
		Affirmational		
Critical Realism	• tests knowledge against experience and history • knowledge is both subjective and objective • map or model view of knowledge	(open to change) • testimonial and irenic in nature • sees knowledge in cultural and historical contexts • adult/adult approach • concern for person and message • learner oriented • teaches students to think • more humble attitude • conversion = a new gestalt	• know only in part • knowledge is both objective and subjective	
			Relativism	
Instrumentalism	• knowledge is totally subjective		(denies that truth can be known) • pragmatism • test is usefulness: Does it work? • anti-conversion	
				Deterministic
Determinism				(no human reason or choice)

Given their commitment to what J. B. Conant has called "grand conceptual schemes," within which smaller theories are fit together, naïve realists and idealists cannot accept different, complementary views of the same reality.[13] Therefore, they do not speak of "different theologies." To them this is a contradiction in terms. And since they are certain about the truth and objectivity of their own views, they are often closed to changing them, and must attack other views as false. A summary of the characteristics of naïve realism and idealism, and the ways they resemble and differ from other epistemological positions, is given in figure 2.2.

Critical realists and instrumentalists, on the other hand, recognize the finitude of human knowledge and, therefore, are open to change and to the reexamination of their existing beliefs. Conflicting theories force them to test their assumptions further against empirical and rational criteria. Moreover, critical realists and instrumentalists allow for diverse views of reality, but on different premises. Critical realists claim truth for their systems of knowledge, while instrumentalists do not. This leads those of either mindset to relate differing systems of knowledge in different ways.

Critical realists see theories and belief systems as maps or blueprints of reality. Each may give us some truth about reality. None of them shows us the whole. To gain a comprehensive understanding of the complex nature of reality we need many blueprints that complement one another. For example, to understand a house, a simple photograph will not do. We need the blueprints of its wiring, plumbing, structural beams, and foundations, most of which remain unseen. Reality is far too complex for our minds to grasp in total. We need simplified maps through which we can comprehend its constituent parts.

At the heart of the integration of theories and belief systems for realists is the *theory of complementarity*.[14] Differing views of reality can be accepted as complementary so long as they do not contradict one another in those areas where they overlap. If there is disagreement, the discrepancy must be resolved, or one or the other must be rejected. We may see things in differing ways, but ultimately there can only be one truth within which there is no inconsistency. For instance, if the blue-

---

13. James B. Conant, *Modern Science and Modern Man* (New York: Columbia University Press, 1952).

14. William Austin, "Complementarity and Theological Paradox," *Zygon* 2 (December 1967): 365–81; A. Grunbaum, "Complementarity in Quantum Physics and Its Philosophical Generalizations," *Journal of Philosophy* 54 (November 1957): 23; Gerald Holton, "The Roots of Complementarity," *Daedalus* 99 (1970): 1015; Christopher Kaiser, "Christology and Complementarity," *Religious Studies* 12 (1973): 37–48; D. M. MacKay, "Complementarity," *Aristotelian Society Supplement* (1958): 32.

prints show wiring in a wall that does not exist in the structural blue-prints, one of them must be wrong.

A critical realist sees the various sciences as potentially complementary. Physics, chemistry, biology, psychology, sociology, and anthropology can all contribute insights into the nature of reality that the others do not provide. Each, in a sense, provides a level of analysis not found in the others. Schilling points out that physicists have found "that the newly discovered strange phenomena and entities (those of the microworld) differ so fundamentally and categorically from the more familiar ones (of the macroworld), known earlier, that no theory can possibly describe the newcomers adequately if its concepts and imagery are taken exclusively from the realm of the old. More than that, it became evident that theory in general could no longer be expected to describe reality pictorially, or in one-to-one correspondence to it"[15] He goes on to develop the theory of complementarity among levels of scientific analysis and suggests that to these can be added theological levels of analysis.

Because critical realists recognize the subjective dimensions of human knowledge, they are also aware that historical and sociocultural contexts influence systems of knowledge. At their deepest levels these context factors have to do with worldviews, so we will examine them later.

Instrumentalists see systems of knowledge as problem solving devices. Because neither theories nor belief systems make truth claims, there is no need to integrate them into a single grand conceptual scheme. Nor is there need for complementarity. Mutually contradictory theories and belief systems can be used so long as they "do the job." Thorough-going determinists, on the other hand, see all knowledge as epiphenomenal—as by-products of external forces. It is foolish, therefore, to speak of the integration of knowledge into single or complementary systems. Both of these views, obviously, are unacceptable to committed Christians because they deny any possibility of knowing the truth.

Integration of Theology and Science

Science and theology have emerged as separate belief systems in a Western worldview. How do they relate to each other? Again the epistemological question plays a key role in determining the nature of the relationship.

It is clear that no real integration can be achieved between an idealist theology and a realist science. The two are built on different foundations

15. Schilling, *New Consciousness*, 78.

and attempts to build a common structure upon them will inevitably lead to cracks. The two talk past each other, and in the end we are forced to choose one or the other as our fundamental frame of reference.

It is possible to seek an integration based on different types of realism. Many social scientists take a naïve or critical realist approach to their science and an instrumentalist approach to religion. They affirm the truth of their theories and belief systems, but see religion as a useful fiction created to hold human groups together. For Émile Durkheim, Marx, and others, religion symbolizes a group's authority over the individual. God is merely a projection of the group's power and values on the cosmic screen. Some theologians turn the tables and claim truth for theology and only practical utility for the sciences. In both cases, one party demeans the other by not taking it seriously.

As the record of the past one hundred years shows, integration between a naïve realist theology and science was difficult to achieve. Few problems arose in the areas of nuclear physics and chemistry where theology made no claims. The greatest conflicts arose in areas where the two overlapped, such as in theories about the origin of the universe, about humans, about miracles,[16] and about the meaning and forces behind history. Each claimed to offer a grand unified theory and attacked the other on points of disagreement. It is not surprising, therefore, that in a naïve realist framework no integration was achieved.

With the collapse of naïve realism, the picture has changed. There is a growing acceptance by critical realist and instrumentalist scientists and theologians of each other's disciplines. But the nature of integration differs greatly, depending upon the epistemological foundation used. Integration is unnecessary in an instrumentalist mode. Both science and theology are seen as pragmatic solutions to immediate problems; the only test is results. But instrumentalism undervalues both science and theology. Few scientists would agree that, although astronomy may do a better job than astrology in solving problems, it is no closer to the truth. Most scientist are convinced that they are discovering truth about nature. Similarly, no evangelical would hold a relativistic view of theology that affirms that Christ is not *the* truth, not even *a* truth, but only *a useful way of looking* at history.

What would integration look like in a critical realist mode? We must keep in mind that critical realism makes truth claims for its theories and belief systems. Therefore, it calls for a test to evaluate two or more theories that have been formulated to answer a set of questions. For example, we can determine which of two road maps is more accurate and complete. But, as we have seen, critical realism allows for complemen-

16. Colin Brown, *Miracles and the Critical Mind* (Grand Rapids: Eerdmans, 1984).

tary theories that examine the same reality in *different ways*—there may be several types of maps of the same city.

It is possible, therefore, to look for complementarity between theology and science, as long as they share the same worldview. This requires a theistic science that accepts the existence of God and seeks to examine the order in the universe he has created. We also need a realist theology that examines God's self-revelation in the history of that world. Both science and theology, then, are based on an examination of real events in history, but focus on different dimensions or levels of reality.

A second type of complementarity we need to explore is that between *synchronic* and *diachronic* systems of knowledge. Synchronic systems seek to understand how the structures of reality operate and the functions they serve. For example, a synchronic analysis of a human would include an analysis of the body—the circulatory, assimilative, digestive, and reproductive systems—and the way it thinks and moves. Synchronic analysis also would study the effects of various diseases upon the body. Diachronic systems look at the history of specific realities. A diachronic analysis of a person would examine her or his life story. It would look at various events in the lives of one or more individuals, the forces at work and the human responses to those forces.

This distinction helps us understand the sciences. Most, such as physics, chemistry, biology, psychology, sociology, and anthropology, are synchronic. They examine the structure of matter, life, persons, groups, and cultures. History, and to some extent astronomy, are diachronic. This distinction also helps us to understand theology. Systematic theology is synchronic. It examines the unchanging nature of God and the fundamental structures of creation. Biblical theology is diachronic. It looks at God's acts and revelation in specific cultural and historical settings. We need both synchronic and diachronic models. They complement each other. We begin with specific experiences in history, and from these we infer the basic structures of reality. And these structural models help us to understand and predict what is going on around us. Normally, if one model is in focus, the other model takes a subsidiary position. Synchronic models show us the universal order of things. They do not look at specific events. Consequently, exceptional cases and miracles are out of focus. Diachronic models, on the other hand, look at unique events. Synchronic models help us to understand *how* things operate, but *meaning* ultimately rests in diachronic models—in the story of the universe, of a specific people such as Israel, and of individuals.

When joined, the interplay of diachronic and synchronic belief systems in science and in theology provide a better understanding of reality (see fig. 2.3). But complementarity does not assure us of integration. We can deal with differing belief systems piecemeal and end with what Clifford Geertz calls a *stratigraphic approach* to reality.[17] For integration to take place we must learn how complementary belief systems relate to each other. When problems and contradictions arise we need to examine again our theologies against the biblical data and our sciences against observational data. The task of integrating the sciences and theology is not simple. But it is easier when we deal with complementarity rather than with grand conceptual schemes.

Figure 2.3
Complementary Belief Systems

	Diachronic Models	*Synchronic Models*
Theology	Biblical Theology	Systematic Theology
Science	Historical Sciences	Natural and Social Sciences

Epistemology and Christian Missions

What implications do epistemological stances have for Christian missions? There are six areas in which epistemology plays a particularly important part in missions thinking.

1. How the essence of the gospel is defined
2. How the relationship of gospel and culture are viewed
3. How Christians deal with the contextualization of theology and the resulting theological pluralism
4. How Christians view non-Christian religions
5. How Christians relate to non-Christians
6. How leadership develops in younger churches

For lack of space, we can touch on only a few of these.

Cultural Differences and Contextualized Theologies

One of the central problems facing all missionaries is how to deal with cultural pluralism—the fact that peoples put their world together in different ways that are affected by their cultural contexts. We must recognize the greatness of the early missionaries, their commitment to the gospel, and the sacrifices they made. However, for the most part, they were naïve realists and idealists. They were convinced that their

17. Eugene A. Hammel and William S. Simmons, eds., *Man Makes Sense: A Reader in Modern Cultural Anthropology* (Boston: Little, Brown, 1970), 50.

belief systems were true, and they failed to differentiate the gospel from their own cultural ways. Writing of them Juhnke says: "They were too confident of the wholesomeness and goodness of their own culture to see the pagan flaws in their own social and political structures. The mission was strongly influenced by nineteenth-century ideas of progress. . . . Missionaries believed themselves to be participating in a worldwide crusade of human advancement."[18] For them there could be only one theology. They assumed that their own theology was wholly biblical and that it was not biased by their cultural and historical contexts.

The consequences of these assumptions were damaging. First, the missionaries considered most local customs to be evil and sought to root them out. Little attention was given to the local culture and to the felt needs of the people. Consequently, the gospel was unnecessarily foreign. In a sense the gospel is foreign to every culture, for it is God's prophetic voice to sinners and the cultures they create. But to this was added the foreignness of Western culture with its dress, buildings, pews, hymns, leadership styles, and technology. Those who became Christians were often seen as agents of the West.

Second, the missionaries sought to transmit their theologies unchanged to the national church leaders. The relationship was that of parent to child. National leaders were expected to learn the missionary's theology by rote. Much was written about the three *selves*: Nationals were to become *self-propagating, self-supporting,* and *self-governing.* But little was said about the fourth *self: self-theologizing.* For the most part, national leaders were not encouraged to study the Scriptures for themselves and to develop their own theologies. Deviation from the missionary's theology was often branded as heresy. To young, nationalistically minded leaders this was theological colonialism.

Several forces have changed this picture.

The first was the *maturation of young churches.* First-generation national leaders were often simple tribal and village pastors, but the second and third generations grew up in Christian settings and included seminary-trained theologians.

The second was the *emergence of nationalism around the world.* Young national leaders threw off the colonial rule and trappings of the West. Young churches demanded self-rule and the right to study the Scriptures for themselves. This was particularly evident in the independent churches that emerged in many societies.

The third was the *rise of anthropological thought and the growing*

18. James C. Juhnke, *A People of Mission: A History of the General Conference Mennonite Overseas Missions* (Newton, Kans.: Faith and Life, 1979), 10–11.

awareness among missionaries of the impact of cultural contexts on Bible translations and theology.

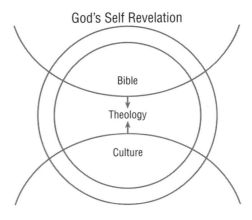

Figure 2.4
Theology: Understanding Scripture in a Cultural Context

Naïve realist approaches are becoming untenable in missions, not only because they are no longer intellectually credible, but also because they fail to resolve the problem of theological pluralism that has resulted from missions. Whether we like it or not, young theologians around the world are reading Scripture and interpreting it for their own cultures. To claim that only the missionaries' theology is correct leads to breaks in the relationships between Western missions and the churches they have planted around the world. It also denies the priesthood of all believers and the work of the Holy Spirit in non-Western Christians. Idealist theologies face the same problems, for they, too, are essentially ahistorical and acultural in nature. Moreover, they face the fact that different cultures use different systems of rationality to justify their beliefs,[19] so an appeal to universal human reason based on propositional logic is difficult—if not impossible—to make.

Critical realists, as realists, take the historical and cultural contexts of theology seriously. They see all theology as comprising human interpretations of the biblical revelation within specific contexts (see fig. 2.4). Consequently, different theologies are bound to emerge because different cultures ask different questions and view reality in different ways. For example, Indian Christians must discern a Christian response to the caste system and whether they can use such Indian terms as *deva, Brahman, avatar,* and *moksha* for God, incarnation, and salvation. These terms are used in Hinduism and normally have Hindu worldview connotations. Yet, to introduce Western or Greek and Hebrew terms makes the gospel unintelligible to the average Indian. Similarly, Latin American theologians must struggle with the biblical response to the oppression of peasants and the poor.

19. A. R. Luria, *Cognitive Development: Its Cultural and Social Foundations,* trans. M. Lopez-Morillas and L. Solotaroff (Cambridge, Mass.: Harvard University Press, 1976).

Because critical realists affirm truth in theology, they must deal with these differences. They cannot accept mutually contradictory theological positions. Theologies may differ and yet be complementary; they may address different needs and situations while resolving contradictions by examining the Scriptures. Critical realists also check for cultural biases. Just as we can more clearly see sin in the lives of others, so we can see how the cultural and historical settings of Christians in other lands affect their theology. Conversely, they see the cultural biases of our theology much more clearly than we do. Therefore, we need to see the church as an *international hermeneutical community,* in which Christians and theologians from different lands check one another's cultural biases. In the process, there can emerge out of the current diversity a metacultural and metahistorical theology that is largely freed from the influences of specific human contexts. This could benefit Western theology by freeing it from its cultural biases and restoring its prophetic voice in the face of modernity. As Linder and Pierard point out, Western Christianity is in danger of becoming a civil religion justifying Western cultural systems.[20]

All this affects the way critical realists view the training of national leaders. The first missionary task is to translate the Bible; the second is to train national leaders to read and interpret the Scriptures in their own cultural context. While the missionaries are deeply persuaded about their own theological understandings, they must accept the fact that the Holy Spirit also leads national leaders and that the message of the gospel must be discerned within the community of believers and their leaders, and not by outside leaders alone.

Christianity and Non-Christian Religions

How do epistemological positions affect our attitudes toward non-Christian religions? Idealists and naïve realists are compelled by their epistemologies to reject other religions as totally wrong, but for different reasons. Both seek to construct grand conceptual schemes, brick by brick, by analyzing discernible *parts*.[21] For naïve realists these are empirical facts; for idealists they are rational propositions. Consequently, other religions and cultures must be radically displaced, not only in their configurational whole, but also in their parts. Old customs, beliefs, and rituals must be destroyed and replaced by new Christian ones.

---

20. Robert D. Linder and Richard V. Pierard, *Twilight of the Saints: Biblical Christianity and Civil Religion in America* (Downers Grove, Ill.: InterVarsity, 1977).

21. Gill, *On Knowing God,* 20–25; Peter L. Berger, Brigitte Berger, and Hansfried Kellner, *The Homeless Mind: Modernization and Consciousness* (New York: Random House, 1973).

There is little room for reinterpreting them to fit Christianity. Christianity must, therefore, take a combative approach to other religions and seek to discredit them. The battle must be won on the basis of facts and reason. Conversion, in this epistemological mode, requires a radical change in beliefs and behavior in all details.

Instrumentalists, on the other hand, see all religions as useful, yet culture-bound, servants of their respective societies. Christianity may be shown to be the best of religions, but it is not unique. Consequently, Christian missionaries should not call for a radical displacement of the old. They should seek to help others better their old religions, and look for an evolutionary movement toward Christianity. Not conversion, but helping people to solve their life problems, is central.

Critical realists fall between the extremes of strict absolutes and relativism. On the one hand they affirm the uniqueness of a Christianity that is faithful to biblical revelation. Consequently, they hold to truth and to absolutes and reject religious relativism. They call for radical conversion to Christ.[22] They also recognize that such conversions take place within cultural and historical settings. Young converts cannot totally change the way they see the world. Converts come with their old categories of thought and old worldview assumptions. These must be changed through careful instruction after conversion. Conversion itself is not a change in propositional or factual knowledge. It is a change in the overall configuration or gestalt in which these are seen; it is a change of allegiance in which Christ is accepted as Lord and the center of one's life. On the synchronic level this means accepting Christ as Lord of all things. On the diachronic level it means accepting Christ as Lord of history and of the convert's everyday life. The implications for the new convert's beliefs, customs, and behavior must be worked out in daily living under the authority of the Scriptures. The process of sanctification cannot be divorced from that of justification.

Because people live in cultural contexts, the gospel must be translated into forms and meanings they understand. But this requires a deep knowledge of other cultures. Missionaries, therefore, must study other religions and dialogue with their leaders, not to create a new synthesis between Christianity and other religions, but to build bridges of understanding so that the people may hear the call of the gospel in ways they comprehend, without compromising the truth of the gospel. Because critical realists are deeply concerned about truth, they are aware of the dangers of syncretism and a false gospel.

22. C. Hendrik Kraemer, *The Christian Message in a Non-Christian World* (London: James Clarke, 1938).

Christians and Non-Christians

How do epistemological positions influence our attitudes towards non-Christians as persons? Because idealists and naïve realists claim certain truth, they often see evangelism as the proclamation of the truth and as an attack on the evils of other religions. This polemical stance seems arrogant to non-Christians, who resent the parent-child relationship implicit within it. Moreover, the emphasis idealists and naïve realists place on objectivity and right systems of belief, and their combative approach to other belief systems, often leads to accusations that they are more intent on proving correct doctrine than on winning persons. In both of these positions, emotions, social interaction, and other human factors are thought to contaminate reason and truth.[23] Instrumentalists recognize the subjective dimension of human knowledge and make no claims to truth. Consequently, they accept religious differences uncritically. Often for them, interpersonal relationships and open dialogue are more important than personal convictions.

Critical realists hold to objective truth, but recognize that it is understood by humans in their contexts. There is, therefore, an element of faith, a personal commitment in the knowledge of truth.[24] There are several consequences of this. Critical realists respect people of other beliefs as thinking adults and show respect for their convictions, yet realists have deep convictions about the truth of their own belief systems and bear testimony to these. Mission to non-Christians, then, begins in witness—declaring what God has done in the Christian's life through Jesus Christ. It begins with "I believe . . ." and shares with others a good news personally experienced (cf. Acts 26:16; 2 Tim. 1:12). Once people have accepted the gospel, missionaries can proclaim its authority. E. Stanley Jones, one of the great missionary evangelists of our time, wrote: "When I was called to the ministry, I had a vague notion that I was to be God's lawyer—I was to argue his case for him and put it up brilliantly." After describing his failure in this approach, he continues:

> This was the beginning of my ministry, I thought—a tragic failure. As I was about to leave the pulpit a Voice seemed to say to me, "Haven't I done anything for you?" "Yes," I replied, "You have done everything for me." "Well," answered the Voice, "couldn't you tell that?" "Yes, I suppose I could," I eagerly replied. So . . . [I] said, "Friends, I see I cannot preach, but I love Jesus Christ. You know what my life was in this community— that of a wild reckless young man—and you know what it now is. You

23. Gill, *On Knowing God,* 50–52.
24. Cf. Charles S. Peirce, *Philosophical Writings of Peirce,* ed. J. Buchler (1940; reprint, New York: Dover, 1955).

know he has made life new for me, and though I cannot preach, I am determined to love and serve him." . . . The Lord let me down with a terrible thump, but I got the lesson never to be forgotten: in my ministry I was to be, not God's lawyer, but his witness. That would mean that there would have to be living communion with Christ so that there would always be something to pass on. Since that day I have tried to witness before high and low what Christ has been to an unworthy life.[25]

It was on this basis that he later established his effective *round-table method* for witnessing to Hindus and Muslims.

Conclusions

I realize that in some ways I have painted a caricature of various epistemological responses to the key missionary questions of our day. But even a caricature can help us to cut through surface impressions to see what lies beneath. Clearly, in a postmodern world we need to reexamine our epistemological foundations to see how they affect our relationships to other people, cultures, theologies, and religions in a pluralistic world. I am convinced that critical realism is a biblical approach to knowledge (1 Cor. 13:12). I am also convinced it is the approach we must take in a postcolonial era in missions. We must deal with cultural, religious, and theological pluralism with deep conviction about the truth, but without arrogance and paternalism.

25. E. Stanley Jones, *The Christ of the Indian Road* (New York: Abingdon, 1925), 141–42.

3

Beyond Anticolonialism
to Globalism

Western missionaries and anthropologists, like all humans, have world-views, and when those worldviews change, their thinking is affected. I would like to examine two fundamental worldview shifts precipitated by the encounter of missionaries and anthropologists with other peoples and cultures. We will note the growing awareness of these professionals that they were in contact with something radically different from their own background. As Bernard McGrane points out, a world-view transformation was precipitated in the West by encounter with *others*—with people from other races, cultures, religions, and societies—and, at a deeper level, the transformation was precipitated by encounter with *otherness*.[1]

Shifts in worldview do not come easily for groups or individuals. Wilbert Shenk observes,

> Rapid transition brings trauma and disintegration. Old values appear obsolete to many people, and they reach for new but untried alternatives. Other people recoil and attempt to reinforce the traditions against encroaching [change]. . . . [A change in eras is a] moment in history when profound change occurs and we move from one order to another—a change in ethos, in values, in myths, in political relationships, in economic systems.[2]

This chapter first appeared in *Missiology: An International Review* 19.3 (July 1991): 263–82. Used by permission.

1. Bernard McGrane, *Beyond Anthropology: Society and the Other* (New York: Columbia University Press, 1989).
2. Wilbert Shenk, "The Changing Role of the Missionary: From 'Civilization to Contextualization,'" in C. Norman Kraus, ed., *Missions, Evangelism, and Church Growth* (Scottdale, Penn.: Herald, 1980), 34.

I suggest that there are three historical eras in the West's reaction to pluralism, particularly cultural pluralism, as Western traders, government officials, missionaries, and anthropologists encountered pluralism at increasingly deeper levels of awareness and relationship. Underlying each era was a worldview shift that profoundly shaped the way Westerners related to other people and the way they did missions.

In a secondary sense these are stages North American churches now experience as they encounter foreigners in their midst. We all experience such changes as individuals when we move into cultures different from our own.

As with all general schema, this one is simplistic, but all general maps must be simple if we are to make sense of an infinitely complex world. It is important to keep in mind that this is not a chronological history, but a schema of the development of worldviews in contemporary Western thought. In fact, many people and agencies still operate in a colonial mode, and others react to that paradigm. A few have begun the difficult task of moving on to deeper relationships of mutuality with those of other races and cultures.

This schema is presented as a tentative proposal that calls for further discussion and the formulation of other, more accurate, understandings of ourselves and our times.

The Colonial Era: First Encounters with an Other Kind

Aside from a few daring travelers who returned with strange tales, the first serious encounters of Westerners with people of radically different cultures began with the age of exploration and trade. Exploration and trade led to foreign settlements, missions, and eventually Western colonial rule. Encounter led to a growing awareness in the West of the *otherness* of peoples, cultures, and religions in other parts of the world.

Traders and Governments

The first response of Western traders and officials to these racial and cultural differences was a sense of personal superiority. Western science and technology were becoming increasingly powerful, and their superiority to the sciences and technologies of other cultures seemed self-evident. Moreover, Western governments were conquering other nations and making them colonies.

It is not surprising that in this context the idea of "progress" found ready acceptance as an explanation of cultural differences. Clearly the West was "civilized" and the rest of the world was "primitive." It was the "white man's burden," therefore, to educate the world.

Missions

Missionaries, too, were affected by the spirit of their times. They equated Christianity with Western culture, and the West's obvious superiority over other cultures proved the superiority of Christianity over pagan religions. Shenk notes,

> The seventeenth-century New England Puritan missionaries largely set the course for modern missions. They defined their task as preaching the gospel so that Native Americans would be converted and receive personal salvation. But early in their missionary experience these New Englanders concluded that Indian converts could only be Christians if they were "civilized." The model by which they measured their converts was English Puritan civilization. The missionaries felt compassion and responsibility for their converts. They gathered these new Christians into churches for nurture and discipline and set up programs to transform Christian Indians into English Puritans.[3]

In 1890, T. W. Pearce pointed out that merely introducing Christianity to China was not enough. Western civilization, in its entirety, had to "overcome" Chinese civilization.[4] Later, missionaries sought to end slavery and came to believe that commerce was the only lasting solution. Christianity, civilization, and commerce became the "threefold flag under which the missionary ship sailed for the next generations."[5]

During this era the missionaries stressed biblically defined needs: divine judgment of sin, repentance, and eternal salvation. They also introduced Western medicine, education, worship styles, architecture, and even dress. They translated the Bible literally, assuming that meanings were tied to forms. They measured communication by what they said, not by what people heard.

Missionaries often came as outsiders, living on compounds where they tried to recreate their Western, Christian cultures. Given the sense of racial superiority that pervaded their times, they often kept themselves apart from the national Christians. They also remained in charge of most things.

Most missionaries saw Christianity as true and other religions as false and "pagan." With some notable exceptions, missionaries saw no need to study the local cultures or to contextualize their message. Other religions had to be displaced, and because these religions pervaded every area of life, local cultures had to be changed.

3. Ibid., 35.
4. Jonathan Chao, "Indigenization of the Christian Movement in China IV: Deculturalization of the Chinese Church," *Missionary Monthly* 94 (August/September 1987): 12.
5. Shenk, "Changing Role," 36.

Anthropology

In this context of cross-cultural encounters, anthropology emerged as the science for the study of otherness. Like other scientists, anthropologists had a positivist view of their discipline. They believed their findings were objective truth. Moreover, like other scientists, they sought to construct one grand unified theory to integrate all data into a single system of knowledge.

Anthropologists believed that their theories were unaffected by their own historical, cultural, and personal contexts. Their truth was universal truth. The first anthropological theories had to do with the otherness of race. During the last half of the nineteenth century anthropologists tried to account for racial variations by the theory of biological evolution. Behind their search lay the assumption that the white race was superior to other races. This justified the segregation of whites from other races overseas and (before emancipation in England and the United States) slavery at home.

When scientific evidence did not support this assumption, anthropologists turned their attention to cultural differences. The result was the theory of cultural evolution. This theory affirmed the unity of humankind and of culture. Lewis Henry Morgan wrote, "The history of the human race is one in source, one in experience and one in progress."[6] Anthropologists spoke of "culture," not "cultures." Evolution, however, still accounted for cultural variations by arranging them along a scale from "primitive," and "prelogical" to "civilized" with the West at the top. It was assumed that, left to themselves, the lower cultures would eventually develop a Western sort of civilization. With help, however, this time could be shortened. Evolution enabled anthropologists to affirm both unity and diversity in one grand unified theory.

Theology

The Enlightenment divided human experience into two spheres: public and private.[7] The public sphere is the domain of universal, objective, rational truth. Here science and formal logic rule. The private sphere is the domain of subjective beliefs and emotions. Here the humanities and arts express their particularist views of reality.

During the colonial era, biblical scholars and theologians sought to give their disciplines credibility as objective truth by claiming the status

6. Lewis Henry Morgan, *Ancient Society* (New York: Henry Holt, 1877), vi.
7. Lesslie Newbigin, *Foolishness to the Greeks: The Gospel and Western Culture* (Grand Rapids: Eerdmans, 1986); idem, *The Gospel in a Pluralist Society* (Grand Rapids: Eerdmans, 1990).

of "sciences." Most systematic theologies written before 1950 began with the claim that theology is, in fact, the queen of the sciences. Like scientists, theologians had a positivist view of their work. It was objective truth encoded in formal statements and unaffected by the personality and culture of the theologian. Moreover, they sought to develop a comprehensive, systematic theology based on facts and reason. Disagreements led to heated arguments.

Like scientists, theologians focused their attention on universals. They gave little thought to the relationship of the gospel to the concrete particularities of the history and culture in which it was revealed or proclaimed.

Epistemology

At the worldview level, the epistemology that emerged during this era was positivism, or naïve realism, the belief that science was a new and unique type of knowledge. Its knowledge, carefully tested and proved, was assumed to be timeless, objective, universal truth. Other systems of knowledge (and many included religion among them) were superstitions based on prelogical thought. People in other cultures had no science. In positivism, scientific knowledge was thought to be an accurate photograph of reality. Scientists believed that, as new facts were added, the whole picture of reality would become clear. Disagreements often led to confrontations, because if one theory was right, others that conflicted with it had to be wrong.

Results

What did the colonial era produce? On the positive side, a great many people benefited from the medical, educational, and agricultural advances of the West. Colonialism reduced the number of internecine wars that plagued many parts of the world and introduced ideas of nationhood and the welfare state.

In missions, driven by deep convictions regarding the truth of the gospel, a small cadre of missionaries braved conditions that sometimes seemed impossible in order to plant churches in the most remote regions of the world. They translated the Bible into many tongues and laid foundations for the medical and educational systems of numerous young nations. The global church is a testimony to God's blessing of their work despite ways that were often colonial.

On the negative side, the colonial era engendered arrogance and segregation. Few Westerners took other cultures seriously or sought to understand them in their own terms. Many saw themselves as superior to the peoples they met.

In the end, the colonial era planted the seeds of its own demise. Education prepared people to run their own countries, and Westerners began to interact with people of other cultures in deeper ways that called their Western ethnocentrism into question. Westerners were forced to take others, and otherness, more seriously than they had before.

The Anticolonial Era: Taking the Other Seriously

Intense interaction with others produced a reaction in the West against colonialism and its arrogance and cultural oppression. Anticolonialism appeared first among sensitive missionaries and anthropologists who worked most closely with people in other cultures. It spread to governments and led to the collapse of the colonial empires after World War II. It continues to spread to business, education, theology, medicine, and other areas of life.

What is the nature of this anticolonial revolution, and how does it affect missions, anthropology, theology, and epistemology?

Missions

Early on, Henry Venn and Rufus Anderson called for the planting of indigenous churches that were self-supporting, self-governing, and self-propagating. These three "selves" became the watchwords for progressive missions and led to the development of autonomous churches around the world.

Since the 1970s the question of the *fourth* "self" has become the center of mission debates. Do churches in other cultures have the right—even the responsibility—to read and interpret the Scriptures in their own historical and cultural contexts? The *contextualization* of theology is a more explosive issue than the earlier question of *indigenization*, because it has to do with the very nature of the gospel itself. Is there one gospel or many? Do we speak of theology or theologies? Do other religions contain truth, or are they wholly false? Is Christianity unique, or is it one among many valid religions?

Reacting to earlier missionaries who equated Christianity with Western culture, theology with Western theology, and the church with the Western churches, missionaries began to encourage young churches to develop their own theologies. Some began to study other religions to find bridges of communication to them. A few sought areas of common faith, such as worship forms and beliefs in a transcendent God. They joined leaders in other religions to oppose secularism and other evils in the modern world. Those who opposed contextualization were labeled "colonial."

In the end, contextualization often became an uncritical process in which the good in other cultures was affirmed, but the evil in them was left unchallenged. Young churches were free to interpret Scripture as they saw fit, unchecked by the church in other parts of the world or its history. The emphasis moved to local theologizing.

In communication, the emphasis shifted from what the missionary said to what the people understood. It became clear that people reinterpreted messages in terms of their own cultural contexts. In Bible translation attention turned to dynamic equivalent translations. Here a distinction was made between the forms and the meanings of words. "Good translations" were those that preserved the meanings, even if this meant changing the forms. With the shift to context and receptor came an emphasis on "felt needs." The needs missionaries should address were now defined by the people being served, rather than by the missionary or even by the Scriptures.

In their encounter with other religions, missionaries began to move away from confrontation and radical displacement, which now seemed colonial and arrogant, to dialogue. Other religions were accepted as valid systems of belief, having their own internal logic and understandings of truth. It was important, therefore, for missionaries to understand and respect them. The anticolonial stance became essentially laissez-faire.

The emphasis was on dialogue, not proclamation. On one level, dialogue is a way to understand other religions so as to make the gospel known clearly to people in those religions. In anticolonialism, however, it came to mean the process by which we learn from other religions or seek a religious synthesis that eliminates our differences. Such a consensus is often found first in common worship services, spiritual exercises, and theologies of God and creation. What is sacrificed is the uniqueness of Christ and his salvation, because this is an offense to non-Christians.

Anthropology

In anthropology the serious acceptance of other people as fully human and other cultures as having their own logic and integrity began with British *structural functionalism* and the *new anthropology*, the latter emphasizing ethnosemantics, ethnomusicology, ethnohermeneutics, and so on. Each society was seen as an integrated whole. Each had its own culture or conceptual paradigm. No society had the right to judge another by its own values. To do so was cultural arrogance. Ethnocentrism became the cardinal sin and cultural relativism the acknowledged good.

Unwilling to judge other cultures by Western standards, and lacking any transcultural basis for making ontological judgments among cultures, anthropology was reduced to phenomenology—to describing and explaining societies in terms of their own truths and values. It focused on *emics*—on helping us understand other cultures from within. Moreover, lacking criteria for critiquing cultures, it no longer became an advocate for cultural change, particularly of change initiated from without.

Anthropology focused first on social, and then on cultural, diversity. Each society was seen as an autonomous group, with its own social organization. Its culture and worldview had an internal logic and had to be understood from within. Ethnographies and ethnosemantic studies of various peoples and cultures became the hallmark of sociocultural anthropology.

Carried to the extreme, human knowledge becomes totally subjective. Ronald Sukenick wrote, "All versions of 'reality' are of the nature of fiction. There's your story and my story, there's the journalist's story and the historian's story, there's the philosopher's story and the scientist's story. . . . Our common world is only a description . . . reality is imagined."[8] Societies and cultures, too, become islands of subjectivity. A true, deep understanding across cultural boundaries was seen as virtually impossible. In the end, some anthropologists argued that anthropology said more about the cognitive pilgrimages of the anthropologists than about other cultures.

This view of knowledge as culture-bound and subjective was reinforced by a theory of language that divided words and other symbols into forms and meanings, and saw the link between form and meaning as purely arbitrary. What was important was meaning, and it existed only in the minds of people.

Theology

Theology, too, was confronted by pluralism.[9] With the emergence of liberation theology, Indian theology, local theologies, and a multiplicity of other theologies, it became more difficult to speak of a single, comprehensive systematic theology. It also became more difficult to speak of truth and theological absolutes.

The anticolonial reaction led to a *deconstructionism* that tied theologies to specific cultural and historical contexts. They were seen as solu-

8. Ronald Sukenick, "Upward and Juanward: The Possible Dream," in Daniel Noel, ed., *Seeing Castaneda: Reactions to the "Don Juan" Writings of Carlos Castaneda* (New York: Putnam, 1976).

9. David Tracy, *The Blessed Rage for Order: The New Pluralism in Theology* (New York: Seabury, 1975).

tions to particular problems of oppression, racism, or sexism. It was important, therefore, to understand the contexts in which theologies emerged in order to understand the problems they addressed. Here the theologians turned to the social sciences for help. In some cases, theories of language, religion, and culture became the foundations for theological discourse.

But this deconstruction went further. Theologians soon realized that not only the questions, but the very categories in which a theology was cast, was determined by the cultural frame of the theologian. Theologizing was seen, therefore, as a subjective human process and theologies as human creations. The result was theological relativism. One could no longer speak of theology because there was no basis for judging among theologies to determine truth. The logical conclusion to the progression was the denial of the uniqueness of Christ as the only way to salvation.[10]

At the level of common folk, deconstruction reduced theology to problem solving. As Bibby points out, many Christians have no integrated theology by which to understand reality.[11] Rather, they have a toolbox of disparate theologies which they use to solve different problems in their lives.

Because theologies are seen as culture and person-specific, to seek to convert others to one's own is religious imperialism. Mutual affirmation and peaceful coexistence, not debate, are affirmed.

Epistemology

Underlying these shifts in anthropology, missions, and theology is a shift in epistemology—in how we look at systems of human knowledge. With the growing awareness of others and of the contextual nature of all human knowledge, it is hard to defend the positivism of the colonial era. To take others seriously, we have to take their beliefs seriously.

The epistemological foundation for anticolonialism was instrumentalism.[12] This allowed for a real external world but reduced knowledge to subjective speculations about that world, speculations shaped by our

10. S. Wesley Ariaraja, *The Bible and People of Other Faiths* (Maryknoll, N.Y.: Orbis, 1989); John Hick and Paul Knitter, eds., *The Myth of Christian Uniqueness: Toward a Pluralistic Theology of Religions* (Maryknoll, N.Y.: Orbis, 1988); Leonard Swidler, *After the Absolute: The Dialogical Future of Religious Reflection* (Minneapolis: Fortress, 1990). For a review of many recent works on the subject see Francis Clooney, "Christianity and World Religions: Religion, Reason, and Pluralism," *Religious Studies Review* 15.3 (1989): 197–204; Paul Knitter, "Making Sense of the Many," *Religious Studies Review* 15.3 (1989): 204–9.

11. Reginald Bibby, *Fragmented Gods* (Toronto: Irwin, 1987).

12. See chapter 1.

cultures and histories. There is no way to show that our knowledge is objectively true. At best we can say that it works and helps us solve our daily problems. The result is a pragmatic, rather than an ontological, approach to knowledge and life. In instrumentalism, knowledge is subjective, encased in Kuhnian paradigms.[13] It makes good sense to those operating in the paradigm but is largely unintelligible to those in another one. Because in Kuhnian thought all observers are locked in paradigms and have no external vantage point from which to see reality, there is no way they can test whether one or another paradigm is true or false. Such paradigms can be judged only from within.

True communication between Kuhnian paradigms is essentially impossible. Meaning is found in people's heads and in cultures. People can understand external messages only in terms of their own paradigms. Communication must, therefore, be measured by what the receptor understands, not what the sender means.

One consequence of instrumentalism is deconstructionism—giving up the search for one grand unifying theory of knowledge, and celebrating pluralism and diversity despite their incongruity and lack of coherence. Jean-Francois Lyotard and other postmodernists see the world as fragmented and unpresentable. They detest the idea of what Habermas called "the unity of experience"[14] and they celebrate pluralism and contradiction.[15] In this spirit Lyotard declares,

> It must be clear that it is our business not to supply reality but to invent illusion to the conceivable which cannot be presented. And it is not to be expected that this task will effect the last reconciliation between language games (which, under the name of faculties, Kant knew to be separated by a chasm), and that only the transcendental illusion (that of Hegel) can hope to totalize then into a real unity. . . . Let us wage a war on totality; let us be witnesses to the unpresentable; let us activate the differences.[16]

Linda Hutcheon notes, "Willfully contradictory, then, post modern culture uses and abuses the conventions of discourse. There is no outside. All it can do is question from within."[17] In postmodernity, there is no

---

13. Thomas S. Kuhn, *The Structure of Scientific Revolutions,* 2d ed. (Chicago: University of Chicago Press, 1970).

14. Jurgen Habermas, *Knowledge and Human Interests,* trans. J. J. Shapiro (Boston: Beacon Press, 1971).

15. Cf. David Harvey, *The Condition of Post-modernity: An Enquiry into the Origins of Culture Change* (Cambridge: Basil Blackwell, 1984); Jonathan Arac, ed., *Postmodernism and Politics* (Minneapolis: University of Minnesota Press, 1986).

16. Jean-Francois Lyotard, *The Postmodern Condition: A Report on Knowledge* (Minneapolis: University of Minnesota Press, 1984), 80–81.

17. Linda Hutcheon, *A Poetics of Postmodernity* (New York: Routledge, 1980), xiii.

basis for debate over truth. We must tolerate differences and celebrate diversity. To seek to convert others to our beliefs is arrogance.

Another consequence of instrumentalism is relativism and pragmatism. We do not choose theories on the basis of truth. Rather our choices are determined by historical accidents such as birth, by our participation in social groups that shape our thinking, and by our personal idiosyncrasies. The only rational basis for selecting theories is their usefulness to us.

Results

The anticolonial reaction was a necessary corrective. It called into question Western cultural arrogance, and it forced Western Christians to differentiate between the gospel and their culture.

In itself, however, anticolonialism does not move us from our initial prejudices to mutual respect. It leaves us as separate islands of subjective being. Furthermore, it lives in reaction, not proaction. Its agenda is to root out the last vestiges of colonialism, but this does little to help us work together to solve the global crises facing humankind.

Finally, anticolonialism brings theological relativism. Paul Knitter wrote that "in our contemporary world, in which we are aware of the presence of others and the absence of absolutes, Christian theology, to be *truly* Christian, can no longer be *only* Christian."[18] This leads us to deny the uniqueness of Christ and his salvation, and destroys the foundations of Christianity itself. It also undermines evangelism and missions and, in the end, precipitates the demise of missiology as a discipline of study.

The Global Era: Hard Love

Anticolonialism is a corrective to colonialism with its cultural arrogance, but it does not provide us with the foundations for working with or relating intimately to people different from ourselves.

There are two responses to anticolonialism. Some, sensing the void of relativism, turn back, looking for certainty in more subtle forms of neocolonialism. Others look forward, past the present relativizing experience of pluralism for deeper foundations beyond. Berger's metaphor is helpful. In positivism we stand on the firm ground of absolutes. When we enter the river of pluralism, the water rises to our necks. Some retreat in fear to the solid bank behind them. Some continue on and are swept away by the river. Some swim to the firm bank beyond. What is

18. Swidler, *After the Absolute,* back cover (italics in original).

that bank beyond? How does it affect missions, anthropology, theology, and epistemology?

Missions

What are the consequences of a global perspective for missions and for our relationship to other religions? First, a global perspective requires *reevaluation of mission history.* Colonial writers presented Western missionaries in a totally positive light. Anticolonial writers paint them as servants of colonialism and destroyers of cultures. In recent years such historians as Lamin Sanneh have begun to reinterpret mission history from a global perspective.[19] They see both the good and the bad in the modern missionary movement. They recognize that, despite its weaknesses, the movement did plant the church throughout the world.

Second, a global perspective requires *critical contextualization.* The response of colonial missionaries to other cultures was often one of radical displacement. Consequently, to become Christian, the people had to become Western. In reaction, anticolonial advocates called for contextualization. People should keep their cultures and social systems when they become Christian. This affirmation of other cultures and societies was an important correction, but carried too far, its uncritical contextualization compromised the gospel. Critical contextualization is an ongoing response that sees the gospel as outside culture.[20] It comes as the message of salvation, not from West to East, but from God to people in all cultures. For them to hear and believe, the gospel must be communicated in ways they understand and value.

The gospel calls us all to follow Christ. It also stands in prophetic judgment on all societies and cultures. It affirms what is good in each but condemns what is evil—our corporate idolatries and rebellions against God and our sins of oppression and injustice. As William Dyrness points out, our concern to communicate the gospel in culturally sensitive ways must be guided by two commitments: effective communication and fidelity to biblical truth.[21]

Third, a global perspective requires *double translation.* During the colonial era, Bible translation was formal. It was assumed that if one translated the forms, the meanings would follow. Further analysis showed that this assumption was not true. People reinterpret what they

19. Lamin O. Sanneh, *Translating the Message: The Missionary Impact on Culture* (Maryknoll, N.Y.: Orbis, 1989).
20. See chapter 4.
21. William Dyrness, *How Does America Hear the Gospel?* (Grand Rapids: Eerdmans, 1990).

hear in terms of their own cultures and worldviews. Care has to be taken if meanings are to be preserved in cross-cultural communication. This concern led to dynamic equivalence translations that sought to preserve meanings by changing forms. This view of symbols can reduce meanings to subjective perceptions in the heads of people. There is no objective reality against which to test meanings. Moreover, there is little recognition of the fact that changing forms to preserve meanings introduces another type of distortion of the message.[22]

The solution offered by the newly emerging field of semiotics is *double translation*. The translator seeks to preserve the connection between meanings, forms, and realities in the translation.[23] For example, information needed to make a passage clear to another culture may be added as a commentary note. As one instance, *shekels* is not translated *dollars;* rather a footnote gives the approximate value of a shekel in dollars for readers who have no idea of what a shekel is worth. In this way care is given to both form and meaning.

Semiotics, according to Charles Peirce, recognizes that forms and meanings are linked to realities and that meaning lies in our understanding of reality.[24] This is related to the correspondence between our mental maps and those realities. Communication, therefore, is not measured by what the sender means or the receptor comprehends, but by the *correspondence* between what the sender and the receptor experience and understand about reality.

Fourth, a global perspective requires *incarnational witness*. Given a global perspective, how do we respond to other religions? We cannot assume a colonial stance of prejudice and arrogance. Nor can we take the anticolonial position that all faiths are equally good. We must enter into dialogue with those of other faiths, balancing humility and sensitivity with critique and challenge.[25] The purpose of this dialogue is not a Hegelian search for a synthesis of faiths. Nor is it aimed at mutual understanding and communication. Ultimately, dialogue should point people to Christ, who stands neither on our ground nor on that of any other culture. Rather, he defines the reality of all other grounds. Our desire is not to win arguments but to persuade people to follow Christ.

22. Eugene Nida and William Reyburn, *Meaning across Cultures: A Study on Bible Translating* (Maryknoll, N.Y.: Orbis, 1981).
23. Kenneth L. Pike, *Linguistic Concepts: An Introduction to Tagmemics* (Lincoln: University of Nebraska Press, 1982).
24. Charles S. Peirce, *The Philosophical Writings of Peirce*, ed. J. Buchler (1940; reprint, New York: Dover, 1955).
25. John R. Stott, *The Authentic Jesus: The Certainty of Christ in a Skeptical World* (Downers Grove, Ill.: InterVarsity, 1986).

Incarnational witness goes where people are, speaks their language, and becomes one with them as far as we are psychologically able and our consciences allow. People need to hear the gospel in their heart language and see it lived out by us. Incarnational witness also means, however, that the gospel and its messengers stand outside their language and culture.

Fifth, a global perspective requires *recognition of both felt and real needs*. Colonial missions focused on the ultimate human need for salvation; anticolonial missions looked to the felt needs of food, material well-being, and self-esteem. Today we realize that we may need to start with felt needs, but we must move on from them to the ultimate needs of salvation, reconciliation, justice, and peace, which only the gospel addresses.

Anthropology

The anticolonial era in anthropology challenged the ethnocentrisms of earlier theories and led anthropologists to understand other cultures in greater depth. The emphasis on understanding cultures from within helped us see reality as people in those cultures see it. But in anticolonialism, truly understanding other people from within is impossible. Cultures are like Kuhnian islands. Only those raised on them know their way around. Outsiders, such as anthropologists, bring their own questions, categories, and other biases. Consequently, they never gain a complete or an accurate view of the local terrain. Carried to the extreme, this means anthropological fieldwork is not about understanding another culture, but about understanding our own mental response to the encounter of other cultures. Anthropology then is not an objective analysis of human cultures, but autobiographies of the personal pilgrimages of anthropologists entering other cultures.

This instrumentalist view destroyed any claims anthropology had to objective knowledge. Science, too, was reduced to one view among many. In the end, instrumentalism relativized not only cultures, but all systems of human knowledge. Since the 1970s, this has led to a rejection of anthropological relativism. The move has been so strong that Clifford Geertz, in his presidential address to the American Anthropological Association, reminded us that the theory of cultural relativism had been, in fact, a helpful corrective at one stage in the development of anthropological theory.[26] But what replaces relativism? The answer in anthropology is a semiotic view of symbols and a critical realist view of knowledge.

26. Clifford Geertz, "Anti-Relativism," *American Anthropologist* 86.2 (1984): 263–78.

Figure 3.1

The Nature of Symbols

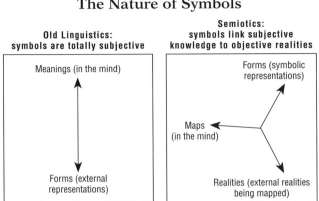

Old Linguistics:
symbols are totally subjective

Meanings (in the mind)

Forms (external representations)

Semiotics:
symbols link subjective knowledge to objective realities

Forms (symbolic representations)

Maps (in the mind)

Realities (external realities being mapped)

Semiotics

To forge a new global view of humanity we must reexamine the nature of symbols. In instrumentalism symbols are defined as forms and meanings, making knowledge totally subjective. In Peircean semiotics, symbols stand for realities and are defined in terms of realities *(objects)*, forms *(representamen)*, and meanings *(interpretants*, see fig. 3.1).[27] Semiotics begins with a real world with a real history and sees symbols as the links between that world and our mental maps of it.[28]

Symbols, therefore, have both objective and subjective dimensions. Truth and meaning lie not in the mind alone, but in the correspondence between our mental maps or models, and the reality represented. This means we must test our interior view of the symbol (and all knowledge comprises symbols) against the external reality by careful examination and independent verification. We must also recognize that our knowledge is partial and biased. We see through a glass darkly, but we do see. We are not totally blind.

27. Peirce, *Philosophical Writings*. The *object* is the objective reality (real trees, real books). The *representamen* are the signs we use to represent these realities (the spoken or written words *trees* and *books*). The *interpretants* are the mental images these signs stimulate (the category and mental image of trees or books). Representamen are indeed categories we create culturally, but they also reflect categories that exist *in nature itself* if they are to be of any value for living in a real world. They are shaped by both culture and reality. No people confuse cows with pigs or ducks with chickens. All societies make these basic distinctions. So we are forced to conclude that such universal distinctions reflect not only cultural variances, but real differences in nature itself.

28. Kenneth L. Pike, "Here We Stand Creative Observers of Language," in *Approches du Langage*, Colloque Interdisciplinaire, Publications de la Sorbonne, Serie Etudes, E. Reuchlin and Francois, eds., vol. 16 (1980), 9–45; idem, "The Relation of Language to the World," *International Journal of Dravidian Linguistics* 16.1 (1987): 77–98.

Complementarity

In a critical realist epistemology we recognize the *complementary* nature of human knowledge. Because our minds are incapable of comprehending the whole of reality at once, we must break our knowledge of it down into different maps or blueprints. Each of these asks its own questions and uses its own methods to examine reality. Each contributes to our understanding of the whole. Various maps help us see different things in reality, but because they map the same reality they cannot contradict one another.[29] Disagreements lead not to polemical debate but to further analysis to make whatever corrections are necessary to resolve the contradiction.

One area of complementarity in anthropology is the relationship between *emic* (inside) and *etic* (outside) analyses.[30] Emic studies help us understand how a person forms his or her mental maps in ways that may differ from those of other people elsewhere around the world. We need etic analyses to compare these maps with maps of other peoples and with the objective reality symbolized. We need good ethnographies and good comparative studies to understand variations in the mental maps through the range of human cultures.

Another area of complementarity is the relationship between anthropology, sociology, psychology, biology, the other sciences, and the humanities. Each contributes something to our understanding of humans. We need help from all of these disciplines to get a more complete picture.

As Christians we also recognize the need for theological insights into the nature of reality. Theology, however, is not simply a system of beliefs to be added alongside the others. It is the master blueprint on which all other blueprints are mapped. But we must go further. All systems of knowledge must be understood within the perspective of a biblical worldview. Divine revelation in Scripture ultimately defines the questions, provides the categories, and outlines the methods that help us to see reality. It is this world known by God, not the worlds we create, that is the real world. All other systems of knowledge, including the sciences, must emerge out of this biblical realism.

A third area of complementarity is insights from different cultures regarding humanity. Our Western perspectives are colored by our Western worldview, and there is much we can learn from other peoples.

29. See chapter 1.
30. John W. Berry, "Imposed Etics, Emics, and Derived Etics: Their Conceptual and Operational Status in Cross-Cultural Psychology," in Thomas N. Headland, Kenneth L. Pike, and Marvin Harris, eds., *Emics and Etics: The Insider/Outsider Debate* (Newbury Park, Calif.: Sage, 1990), 84–99.

Both our knowledge and theirs need to be tested against reality and biblical revelation.

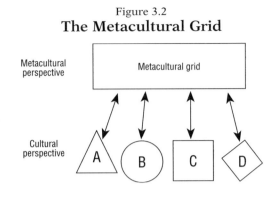

Figure 3.2

The Metacultural Grid

Metaculturalism

Critical realism in anthropology also affects our views of the unity and diversity of humankind. The colonial era stressed our common humanity with the other. The anticolonial era stressed the differences between us. Today anthropologists again emphasize the underlying oneness of human beings, while recognizing diversity. All share common mental processes and such human experiences as birth, maturation, and death. The ways these are understood and expressed, however, varies greatly from culture to culture.

We must reject the relativism of the anticolonial era, but on what basis can we pass judgment on cultures without falling back into a colonial ethnocentrism? Anthropologists are increasingly aware that true participation with others at a deep level changes us. As we learn to see the world through the eyes of two cultures, we are forced to develop a *metacultural* framework above these cultures that enables us to see both cultures from without, and to compare them. We become inside participants in, and outside observers of, the cultures. This "inside-outside" perspective enables us to translate from one to the other.[31] It also gives us a more objective vantage point from which to compare and judge them both (see fig. 3.2).

The development of a metacultural grid is the hallmark of anthropologists and other bicultural people. Having participated deeply in other cultures and having become both "empathetic insiders" and "comparing outsiders," they develop mental perspectives that enable them to relate to any number of other cultures.

Theology

What implications does a global view have for theology? During the colonial era theologians spoke of theology as a universal, objective system of truth. In the anticolonial reaction they speak of "theologies" as particularist, subjective understandings of truth. From a critical realist

31. Cf. ibid.

perspective, we must differentiate between God's revelation, and our understanding of it. Moreover, we recognize that God speaks to humans in specific contexts, but his message has universal truth and application. We must, therefore speak of both theologies and Theology.

In critical realism, communication is not simply the sharing of information. It calls for a response in a real world. So also, God reveals himself to us in the context of history and our histories. His purpose is not simply to give us information, but to call us to discipleship and obedience. Theology, therefore, is more than information. It calls us to a new life in Christ.

During the colonial era, scholars, missionaries, and pastors emphasized the text. They had little awareness of the ways cultural and historical contexts shaped the way they and their audiences understood the text, particularly in cross-cultural settings. During the anticolonial era they focused on the contexts, and were in danger of losing sight of the text. In a global perspective, we turn our attention again to the biblical texts, but seek to understand them in the contexts in which they occur, as well as their meaning in the many human contexts in which the words are communicated.

One important area of complementarity in theology is that between systematic and narrative theologies. The colonial era stressed the former. The anticolonial era reacted against systematics in favor of particular narrative theologies. In a global perspective we realize that in reading individual narratives we formulate universal and systematic views of reality. On the other hand, divorced from narrative realities, systematics can become arid. Globalism reminds us, however, that particular narratives have no ultimate meaning in themselves. They must be understood within one divine history that begins with creation, includes the fall and God's redemptive acts, and ends in eternity.

How do we resolve the tension between theological absolutes and theological pluralism—between Theology and theologies? The answer lies, in part, in developing a theology of how to do theology. This theology must recognize the fact that different persons and different cultures understand the Scriptures differently. It must also enable them to work toward a common understanding of the truth of Scripture.

Theologizing must begin with Scripture. It is God's revelation to us, not human reflections about God (although it contains these). It is God revealing himself to us from outside our human predicaments.

Theologizing must be led by the Holy Spirit, who instructs us in the truth. We need also to recognize that the same Holy Spirit at work in us is also at work in the lives of believers in other contexts. To deny them the right to interpret the Scriptures for themselves is to deny this fact.

This work of the Spirit guards us from cultural parochialism, and from theologies based on human reason alone.

Finally, theology must be done in the community.[32] It is ultimately the task not of individuals but of the church. This corporate nature of the hermeneutical task guards us against the privatization of faith and from our personal misinterpretations of Scripture. Just as others see our sins before we see our own, so Christians in other cultures see our cultural biases and the impact of those biases on our theology more clearly than we do ourselves.

Epistemology

Responding to Kuhn's subjectivism, Larry Laudan[33] and others argue for a critical realism that takes both the objective and subjective nature of human knowledge into account. They argue that human perceptions are tied to external realities, but not, like photographs, with a one-to-one correspondence. Rather, the relationship is one of limited correspondence and analogy, like maps and blueprints. Moreover, just as several maps are needed to help us understand reality, so different complementary theories are needed to help us understand reality.

As we have seen, in critical realism we speak of *the* Truth with reference to reality. We also speak of *a* truth—our partial understandings of that greater Truth. Our understandings are objective (to the extent they are tested against reality) and subjective (because they are ours as humans in our specific cultural and historical contexts).

Disagreements do not lead us into confrontation. On the other hand, we are not disinterested in contradictions. Dialogue between those with different understandings does not lead to a subjective Hegelian synthesis, but to an investigation to determine whose map or model fits reality and truth most closely. If our road maps vary, we drive the streets to determine which is correct.

Conclusions

Much has been written in recent years of the challenge of modernity to Christianity. It has led to a secularism that denies the existence of God, the deity of Christ, and the reality of the miracles recorded in the Bible. It has marginalized those who continue to hold religious convic-

32. C. Norman Kraus, *The Authentic Witness: Credibility and Authority* (Grand Rapids: Eerdmans, 1979).
33. Larry Laudan, *Progress and Its Problems: Towards a Theory of Scientific Growth* (Berkeley, Calif.: University of California Press, 1977).

Figure 3.3

Shifts in Western Thought

Missions:	Colonialism	Anticolonialism	Globalism
•other religions:	displacement	dialogue for consensus	dialogue to find the truth
•translation:	formal	dynamic equivalence	double translation
•symbols:	form = meaning (formal linguistics)	form/meaning (Saussurian linguistics)	form<–> meaning <–> reality (semiotics)
•contextualization:	noncontextualization	uncritical contextualization	critical contextualization
•need:	real need	felt need	real and felt needs
•message:	West to East	discovery from within	from above to all cultures
•missionary:	outsider	insider	incarnational
•attitude:	confrontational	nonconfrontational	hard love, non-Hegelian
Anthropology:	**Evolutionism**	**Functionalism**	**Postfunctionalism**
•culture & humanity:	unity (culture)	diversity (cultures)	unity/diversity
•view point:	etic	emic	etic/emic
•truth:	absolute	relative	absolute/relative
•communication:	sender oriented	receptor oriented	correspondence theory
•theory:	one comprehensive theory	particularistic theories	integration of several complementary theories
Theology:	**Theology**	**Theologies**	**Metatheology**
•nature:	systematic, comprehensive	deconstructionist, pluralist	metatheology leading to community-based theology
•focus:	text (theology)	context (social sciences)	text/context (theology/social sciences)
•hermeneutics:	literal	interpretive	double horizon
Epistemology:	**Positivism**	**Instrumentalism**	**Critical Realism**
•goal:	Truth	pragmatism & problem solving	Truth/truth & problem solving
•nature of truth:	absolute	relative, perspectival	absolute/relative, approximate
•knowledge:	objective	subjective	objective/subjective
•unity:	grand unified theory	deconstructionist & incommensurable Kuhnian paradigms	complementary models but interrelated, common human experience
•view of reality:	reductionist	reductionist	integrative
•perspective:	in culture A	in culture B	metacultural perspective

tions, because it relegates religion to the private sphere of personal opinions and feelings.

Today we face another challenge to Christian faith—*postmodernity*. Here spiritual experiences are no longer denied; they are all affirmed. The issue is not secularism but relativism and pragmatism. The debate centers about the uniqueness of Christ and his claim to be the only way to salvation (John 14:6). To deny this uniqueness, however, is to deny the truth of the gospel.

Many accuse us of religious arrogance when we proclaim Christ as the only Savior and Lord, but speaking the truth is not arrogance. Lesslie Newbigin notes, "To affirm the unique decisiveness of God's action in Jesus Christ is no arrogance; it is the enduring bulwark against the arrogance of every culture to be itself the criterion by which others are judged."[34]

We must be careful to proclaim the gospel, not our culture. We must also speak the truth in love (Eph. 4:15). Biblical love is not superficial sentiment. It is a deep commitment to be for the other. We affirm the full dignity of others as humans created in the image of God and care enough to confront them when we believe they are wrong. Above all, we must continue to point people to Christ as the way, the truth, and the life.

34. Newbigin, *Foolishness to the Greeks*, 166.

4

Critical
Contextualization

A great deal has been written on contextualization in the past few years.[1] I shall not summarize this literature or trace its development. Rather, I wish to propose a model, made up of three "ideal types" in the Weberian sense, that we can use to examine the ways in which Protestant missionaries have handled the problem over the past one hundred years. This is not a history of events, but an analysis of how missionaries dealt with the awareness of cultural pluralism that swept the West following the age of exploration.

I shall limit myself to the narrow question of how the missionaries responded to the traditional beliefs and practices of new converts—in other words, to the "old" culture. Missionaries do not enter cultural vacuums. The people to whom they go are members of ongoing societies and cultures. The people raise food and build houses. They arrange marriage for their young and bury their dead. They pray to their gods and propitiate the spirits. How did—and how should—missionaries who bring a new gospel respond to the old one?

The data will be drawn from the Indian scene, which has a long history of debates on the subject and with which I am most familiar. I believe, however, that the model applies to other parts of the world.

This chapter first appeared in *International Bulletin of Missionary Research* 11.3 (July 1987): 104–12. Used by permission.
1. See bibliographies in Stephen Bevans, "Models of Contextual Theology," *Missiology* 13 (1985): 185–202; David Gitari, "The Claims of Jesus in the African Context," *International Review of Mission* 71 (1982): 12–19; Krikor Haleblian, "The Problem of Contextualization," *Missiology* 11 (1983): 95–111; Millard C. Lind, "Refocusing Theological Education to Mission: The Old Testament and Contextualization," *Missiology* 10 (1982): 141–60.

Early Responses to the Question

There is a long history of answers given in missions to the question of what to do with traditional cultures. The early Roman Catholic missionaries struggled with the issue when they came to India. They were impressed with the sophistication of Indian culture. In many ways it was superior to that of Spain in the sixteenth and seventeenth centuries. But they sharply divided over the question of what to do with the existing culture. The Jesuits advocated accommodation and the retention of traditional Indian cultural forms. The Franciscans contended that the Jesuits were selling out the gospel.

Early Protestant missionaries, too, were impressed with Indian culture and its philosophical foundations. Many Protestants learned Indian languages well enough to produce dictionaries and write classical literature and hymnology, and to translate Indian sacred texts into German and English. These texts later played an important role in the rise of the Orientalist movement in the West. By the early nineteenth century, however, a major shift had taken place. With some notable exceptions, Protestant missionaries entered an era of noncontextualization.

The Era of Noncontextualization

Roughly from 1850 to 1950, most Protestant missionaries in India, and later in Africa, rejected the "pagan" beliefs and practices of the people they served. John Pobee observed that to his time "all the historical churches by and large implemented the doctrine of the *tabula rasa,* i.e. the missionary doctrine that there is nothing in the non-Christian culture on which the Christian missionary can build and, therefore, every aspect of the traditional non-Christian culture had to be destroyed before Christianity could be built up."[2] Consequently, the gospel was seen by the people as a foreign gospel. To become Christian one had to accept not only Christianity but also Western cultural ways.

In view of the earlier willingness to use traditional cultural forms, what had changed? Why this growing rejection of existing cultures?

The Rise of Colonialism

One reason was the emergence of colonialism, with its belief in the superiority of Western cultures. The expansion of the East India Trading Company in India came at a time when the Mogul and Vijayanagar empires were decadent and collapsing. By default the East India Trad-

2. John Pobee, "Political Theology in the African Context," *Africa Theological Journal* 11 (1982): 168–72.

ing Company became not only the economic but also the political master of much of India. The process was completed in 1858 when, because of the Indian Mutiny, the British government took control of India and made it its preeminent colony.

Colonialism convinced the people of the West of their own cultural superiority. Western civilization had triumphed. It was the task, therefore, of the West to bring the benefits of this civilization to the world. Old medical systems were seen as witchcraft and hocus-pocus and had to be stamped out. Old governments were seen as feudalistic and had to be replaced by modern, national governments. The result was direct rule in which the British sought to replace all Indian governmental structures.

For Christians, the parallel was the superiority of the gospel. Paganism had to be rooted out. Many missionaries, in fact, equated the two. Christianity, civilization, and, later, commerce (the three Cs) went hand in hand. Western civilization was spreading around the world, and it was assumed that people would become both Christian and "modern." There was no need, therefore, to study old cultures or to take them seriously. They were on the way out.

Not all rejection of traditional cultures, however, was rooted in a naïve equation of Christianity with Western civilization as Pobee suggests. Some missionaries developed a deep understanding of the local cultures. For example, in India, W. T. Elmore, H. Whitehead, and W. H. and C. V. Wiser wrote early ethnographies based on their lives in the villages. There they came face to face with Indian culture little changed by modernity and Christianity and saw the burning of widows, infant sacrifice to idols, the cruelties of untouchability, and demon worship.

These missionaries were profoundly aware that in peasant and tribal societies religion is at the center of culture and permeates most cultural forms. Food, clothing, house construction, marriages, markets, farming, fishing, hunting, festivals, music, dance, and drums all have religious significance in traditional cultures. In India even the direction in which the head faces when the person lies down to sleep has theological importance. If that is the case, they argued, religion and culture, forms and meaning cannot be arbitrarily separated. One cannot simply change the meanings of old forms in order to communicate the gospel, for the ties between them are rooted in social convention and cultural history. The only way to avoid syncretism is to bring radical changes into the whole of the culture.

The Theory of Cultural Evolution

A second reason for the rejection of non-Western cultures was the emergence of the theory of cultural evolution. If the political solution to the awareness of cultural pluralism created by the age of exploration was colonialism, the intellectual solution was evolutionism. Westerners could ignore other cultures by labeling them "primitive," "animistic," and "uncivilized." In fact, anthropologists until 1915 spoke of "culture" and "civilization," rather than of "cultures." They saw all cultures as different stages of development of the same thing; some were more advanced, and others more primitive.

After debates over the monogenetic versus polygenetic origins of human races had wracked anthropology in the last half of the nineteenth century, anthropologists united in emphasizing the commonness of all humanity. Differences, therefore, whether in race or culture, were seen as variations, not as different things.

Christians argued with secular biologists over biological evolution, but accepted cultural evolution. While biological evolution challenged the fundamental Christian tenet of the uniqueness and divine nature of human beings, cultural evolution was simply an updated version (along with Marxism) of the medieval paradigm that sought meaning in a universal history of humankind. Both science and Christianity sought meaning in diachronic (historical), rather than synchronic (structural), paradigms. Both saw history as directional—with an origin, a progression or regression, and a culmination in an ideal state, whether that state arrived through redemption or development.[3] There was argument over the causes of historical progression, but not over the fact that history was going somewhere.

Given this historical paradigm, noncontextualization made sense. Why contextualize the gospel in other cultures when they are in the process of dying out? It is only a matter of time before all people are civilized. What is important, therefore, is to bring the gospel along with civilization.

The Triumph of Science

A third factor leading to the rejection of other cultures was the triumph of science. When William Carey went to India, he was much impressed by its cultural sophistication. Certainly in the fifteenth to eighteenth centuries there was nothing in Europe comparable to the sophistication and technological advancement of the Mogul empire.

The rise of science changed all this. By the end of the nineteenth century, Western technology had conquered the world, and science had made giant strides in conquering nature. Faith in the final triumph of

---

3. Peter L. Berger traces the impact of this Christian paradigm on both the Western concept of development and the Marxist view of revolution in *Pyramids of Sacrifice: Political Ethics and Social Change* (New York: Doubleday, 1976).

science was widespread. As late as 1953, in his Reith Lectures for the British Broadcasting Corporation, Robert Oppenheimer could say without fear of contradiction: "Science has changed the conditions of man's life. . . . the ideas of science have changed the way men think of themselves and of the world."[4] Sir Francis Smith could write in the preface of his *The Neglect of Science:* "The world to-day is moulded, in the last resort, by scientific discovery. . . . whether we like it or not, science is forcing the pace."[5] C. A. Coulson wrote:

> It is important to realize that . . . the influences of a scientific view . . . have passed far beyond *mere* technology or gadgeteering. We may begin there, because this is about as far as the man-in-the-street, or the young apprentice at his lathe, can state his beliefs. But his unrecognized convictions go much deeper. For he knows that science grows, even though he may have no personal knowledge of any of its fundamental principles; and he knows that scientific controversy nearly always issues in a universal agreement, frequently very quickly. Science becomes the cohesive force in modern society, the ground on which may be built a secure way of life for man and for communities.[6]

F. S. C. Northrop of Yale added that "if one wants to understand the culture of the United Sates, one must not look at its departments of economics, sociology or politics, important as they are, but at its universal education in the natural sciences and their skills, its agricultural colleges, technological institutes and research laboratories."[7]

Underlying this optimism was a positivist (or, to use Ian Barbour's term, "naïve realist") epistemology.[8] This held that a careful examination of experience can lead us to the discovery of the "laws of nature," which upon further examination can be proved to be "true." Scientific knowledge was seen as objective (uncontaminated by the subjectivity of the scientist), cumulative, and true in an ultimate sense. In contrast to this, the knowledge of other cultures was thought to be subjective, piecemeal, and false.

The same epistemological foundations were widespread among many conservative Christians, including most missionaries. Only, here theology replaced science, and revelation replaced experience. Carefully crafted, theology could be totally objective and absolutely true. In the light of this, other religions were seen as highly subjective and to-

---

4. Charles E. Raven, *Science, Religion, and the Future* (1943; reprint, Cambridge, England: Cambridge University Press, 1953), 101.
   5. Francis Smith, *The Neglect of Science* (Oxford: Basil Blackwell, 1951), iv.
   6. Charles A. Coulson, *Science and Christian Belief* (London: Fontana, 1955), 20.
   7. F. S. C. Northrop, *The Taming of the Nations* (New York: Macmillan, 1952), 9.
   8. See chapters 1 and 2.

tally false. Consequently, Christians did not need to take other religions seriously, just as scientists refused to take other belief systems about nature seriously. The task of the missionary was to transmit his or her theology into new cultures unchanged.

The wedding of Christianity and science in the minds of missionaries in the eighteenth and nineteenth centuries is not surprising. Herbert Butterfield[9] and A. N. Whitehead[10] have shown convincingly that science grew up within a Christian tradition, and for many years it was not seen as a separate, secular endeavor. Robert Grosseteste, founder of the first department of science at Oxford University, was later the bishop of Lincoln. The British Royal Society counted among its members numerous bishops and ministers. And leading scientist such as natural philosopher Robert Boyle, John Ray (founder of systematic botany and zoology), Christopher Wren (astronomer and architect), and mathematician and scientific theorist Isaac Newton not only professed Christian faith but participated in theological debates.

The Intellectual Consequences of Noncontextualization

Colonialism demonstrated the superiority of Western civilization, evolutionism legitimized this in terms of history, and science and Christianity provided the intellectual foundations on which the whole was built. It is not surprising, therefore, that the period from 1850 to 1950 was anticontextualist in its approach.

This stance was essentially monocultural and monoreligious. Truth was seen as supracultural. Everything had to be seen from the perspective of Western civilization and Christianity, which had shown themselves to be technologically, historically, and intellectually superior to other cultures; and so those cultures could be discounted as "uncivilized." The missionary's culture was "good," "advanced," and "normative." Other cultures were "bad," "backward," and "distorted." Christianity was true; other religions were false.

In missions this had two consequences. First, Christianity was perceived in other cultures as a foreign religion identified with Western culture. Christian converts were expected to adopt Western ways. This cultural foreignness was a great barrier in the spread of the gospel.

The second consequence was more subtle. Old beliefs and customs did not die out. Because they were not consciously dealt with, they went underground. Young converts knew they dare not tell the missionary about their old ways lest they incur his or her anger. So these ways be-

---

9. Herbert Butterfield, *The Origins of Modern Science* (London: Bell and Sons, 1949).
10. Alfred North Whitehead, *Science and the Modern World* (Cambridge, England: Cambridge University Press, 1926).

came part of the new Christians' hidden culture. Public marriage ceremonies were held in the church, and then the people returned to their homes to celebrate the wedding in private. Amulets were hidden under shirts, and Christians did not admit to Christian doctors that they were also going to the village shaman. In India caste differences were denied in public, although Christians privately continued to marry their children along caste lines.

In the long run, this uneasy coexistence of public Christianity and private "paganism" has led to syncretism. Non-Christian beliefs and practices infiltrated the church from below. In India caste is becoming public in the church and destroying it with political strife and lawsuits. In Latin America, spiritism taught by nannies to upper-class children is becoming public and respectable in Kardicism and Umbanda.

From a Christian perspective this monocultural point of view has had its good sides. First, it affirmed the oneness of humanity and of human history. Second, it took history and culture change seriously. Third, it affirmed absolutes and universals, both in human cultures and in the gospel. It was concerned with preserving the uniqueness of the gospel and avoiding the syncretism that might result from the incorporation of non-Christian beliefs and practices in the church.

But it also had its bad sides. It was reductionist and acultural—it did not take other cultures and religions seriously. It was ethnocentric—it judged and found other cultures and religions wanting by its own standards, while assuming that its own ways were right. In the end it hindered the missionary task. The foreignness of the gospel was a barrier to evangelism and syncretism was not prevented. Far too often the missionaries ended as policemen, enforcing on the people what they believed to be Christian practices.

The Case for Contextualization

The picture began to change by the end of the nineteenth century. Colonial rule was expanding, but already the seeds of its destruction had been planted. These seeds bore fruit in the recognition that other cultures had to be understood and appreciated in terms of their own worldviews. The nature and supremacy of science itself also came into question.

Postcolonialism

By 1890 three important forces were at work that would bring about the destruction of colonialism and its intellectual foundations. The first of these was the growing cry against colonialism voiced in the West. As

Conrad Reining points out, by 1833 the Defense of the Natives League had been formed to oppose colonial oppression.[11] This was a loose coalition of humanists of various stripes, of evangelical Christians led by William Wilberforce, and of other fruits of the Wesleyan revivals. Shortly thereafter Henry Venn and Rufus Anderson articulated in the "three-self" formula the need for churches to be organizationally independent. Discussions about the contextualization of the gospel message in local cultural forms began soon afterward. Many missions continued to exercise authority, to use translated hymns, and to impose Western forms of church polity, but some encouraged the autonomy of young churches, the use of local music, and the adoption of indigenous forms of church organization. It was more than one hundred years, however, before the issue of the fourth self—self-theologizing—was raised.

The second force undermining colonialism was the very success of the colonial endeavor. In India the aim of colonialism was to bring "civilization" to the land. It is not surprising, then, that by the twentieth century there was a growing number of highly educated Indian leaders with a nationalist vision. By 1930 they had organized into an effective movement for independence. Culturally they bought into the ideas of the benevolent nation-state based on democratic principles, the British understanding of law, and modern science, health, and education. But socially they wanted Indians, not foreigners, to enforce the rights that British law affirmed. Therefore, the first area in which the Indian churches sought autonomy was self-rule.

Ironically, the third force weakening Western dominance was the introduction of "indirect rule." In India the British totally replaced the existing governmental structures from the village level to the national government. The expense of this, however, was prohibitive. Consequently, when they expanded their empire in Africa, they needed a less costly way of administering the colonies. The answer was indirect rule, in which British administrators provided the overarching government, under which indigenous political structures functioned in tribal matters. But indirect rule required that British administrators know something about the political, economic, and social structures of the people they ruled. Consequently, early anthropological research in Africa, often funded by the government, focused on indigenous forms of social organization.

Africa began to play a key role in the formation of anthropological theory. Unlike India, with its multilayered, interdependent, and un-

---

11. Conrad Reining, "A Lost Period of Applied Anthropology," in James A. Clifton, ed., *Applied Anthropology: Readings in the Uses of the Science of Man* (Boston: Houghton Mifflin, 1970).

bounded cultures, Africa presented anthropologists with discrete and autonomous social groups or tribes. Following the lead of Émile Durkheim and the research techniques of sociology, anthropology saw each of these societies as an organic entity with its own language, culture, and territory. Anthropologists no longer spoke of "culture" but of "cultures." And field work in non-Western societies became the hallmark of anthropological research.

Phenomenology, Structural Functionalism, Linguistics, and the New Anthropology

The impact of all this on anthropological theory was profound. In many universities, evolutionism's diachronic models were replaced by British *structural functionalism's* emphasis on phenomenology and synchronic analysis. The central questions no longer concerned origin, but rather the structure and integration of a society and the function of its various parts. Each society had to be understood in its own terms, not in comparison with Western society.

A parallel development was the emergence in North America of *descriptive linguistics*. Tribal cultures for the most part had no writing, so new methods had to be found to learn languages and reduce thought to writing. New linguistic methods enabled anthropologists to learn languages and also to analyze the structures and internal organization of these languages as an end in itself. Linguistics provided anthropologists with tools for recapturing images of cultures from aged informants and for reconstructing tribal histories.

The combination of British structural functionalism, with its emphasis on the social organization of tribes, and of the American interest in languages and cultures as cognitive maps led to the school of thought known as *ethnoscience*, or *new anthropology*. This theory, like those from which it was derived, emphasized the differences between cultures and the ways in which they see reality. Each culture was seen as an autonomous paradigm, with a worldview of its own. In the end, all three schools of thought (functionalism, linguistics, and new anthropology) were forced to acknowledge the cultural relativism that was the logical outcome of their theories. Obviously, if we take all cultures seriously and emphasize their differences, no one of them can be used to judge the others. Where, then, are moral and cultural absolutes?

Postmodern Science

Not only was belief in Western cultural superiority called into question, but the certainty and absolute nature of science itself was under attack. By the mid-twentieth century, the charge was led by the social scientists who began to apply their theories to an analysis of science itself. Psychologists began to examine the subjective nature of all human knowledge; sociologists showed that science was a community affair, influenced by normal social dynamics; anthropologists placed science into its larger cultural and worldview context; and historians of science showed that our textbook understanding of the nature of science was misplaced. Michael Polanyi's writings and Thomas S. Kuhn's *The Structure of Scientific Revolutions*[12] drew these strands together in their theories that science was not a lineal, cumulative progression of objective knowledge, but a series of subjective, competing paradigms. Old positivist science had received a mortal blow. But where would postpositivist science find its new epistemological foundations?

For phenomenologists, including many psychologists, sociologists, and anthropologists, and for Kuhn himself, the answer was *instrumentalism*. Since we could no longer show that one theory or paradigm or culture was better than another, we could no longer speak of absolutes or truth. At best, we could appeal to pragmatism. Any paradigm was adequate so long as it solved the problems humans faced.

The Implications for Contextualization

In such an intellectual milieu, it is not surprising that missionaries and missiologists came to place a great deal of emphasis on contextualization, not only of the church in local social structures, but also of the gospel and theology in local cultural forms.

First, on the positive side, this approach avoided the foreignness of a gospel dressed in Western clothes that had characterized the era of noncontextualization. The gospel message had to be communicated in ways the people understood. It avoided the ethnocentrism of a monocultural approach by taking cultural differences seriously and by affirming the good in all cultures. And it affirmed the right of Christians in every country to be institutionally and cognitively free from Western domination. The right of every church to develop its own theology began to be recognized.

Embracing an uncritical contextualization, however, had its problems. Obviously the denial of absolutes and of truth itself runs counter to the core Christian claims of the truth of the gospel and the uniqueness of Christ. Moreover, if the gospel is contextualized, what

---

12. Thomas S. Kuhn, *The Structure of Scientific Revolutions*, 2d ed., enlarged (Chicago: University of Chicago Press, 1970).

are the checks against biblical and theological distortion? Where are the absolutes?

Second, according to Mary Douglas the separation between form and meaning implicit in these theories blinds us to the general nature of tribal and peasant societies—in which form and meaning are inextricably linked. For example, names and shadows are tied to a person's identity, and religious rites are performances, not simply the communication of messages.[13]

A third problem has to do with the emphasis that contextualization places on the accurate communication of meaning, often to the point of ignoring the emotive and volitional dimensions of the gospel. We are in danger of reducing the gospel to a set of disembodied beliefs that can be individually appropriated, forgetting that Christianity has to do with discipleship, with the church as the body of Christ, and with the kingdom of God on earth. Here Charles Kraft's call for a "dynamic-equivalent" response to the gospel message is a healthy reminder that in the Bible "to believe" is not simply to give mental assent to something; it is to act upon it in life.[14]

A fourth area of concern is the ahistorical nature of most discussions on contextualization. Contemporary cultural contexts are taken seriously, but the historical context of the universal church is largely ignored. In each culture Christians face new questions for which they must find biblical answers. But in many areas, and particularly in biblical and systematic theologies, the example and answers developed in the past can be vastly helpful and a check against error. All Christians must develop theologies, either implicitly or explicitly, as diachronic and synchronic paradigms of Christian truth. The right to do exegesis and hermeneutics belongs not to individuals. The ministry of the Word is a function of the church as an exegetical and hermeneutical community. That community includes not only the saints within a single cultural context, but saints in other cultures and saints down through history. To become a Christian is to become part of a new history, and that history must be learned.

A fifth area of concern is that uncritical contextualization, at least in its more extreme forms, provides no basis for unity among churches in different cultures. Instrumentalism is built on the belief that different cultures and paradigms are incommensurable—there is no common thread by which to bind a mutual understanding. Each can be under-

13. Mary Douglas, *Natural Symbols: Explorations in Cosmology* (New York: Random House, 1970).
14. Charles H. Kraft, *Christianity in Culture: A Study in Dynamic Biblical Theologizing in Cross-Cultural Perspective* (Maryknoll, N. Y.: Orbis, 1979).

stood only in its own terms. But if this is so, there can be no real communication among Christians in different cultures, no comparison of their theologies, and no common foundations of faith. Christianity is composed of a great many isolated churches. For any of these to claim that its theology is normative is ethnocentric. There may be some common ground in common human experiences, but that is too limited to provide the basis for developing a common theology. The best we can do is to affirm pluralism and to forget unity.

Sixth, uncritical contextualization has a weak view of sin. It tends to affirm human social organizations and cultures as essentially good. Sin is confined largely to personal evil. But social systems and cultures are human creations marked by sin. In Scripture more than 75 percent of the occurrences of such Greek terms as *archē* and *archōn* (organizational power), *exousia* (authority), *dynamis* (power), and *thronos* (throne) refer to human institutions.[15] There is a need, therefore, to take a stand against corporate evil as well as against individual sin.

Finally, a call for contextualization without a simultaneous call for preserving the gospel without compromise opens the door to syncretism. William Willimon relates: "The persistent problem is not how to keep the church from withdrawing from the world but how to keep the world from subverting the church. In each age the church succumbs to that Constantinian notion that we can get a handle on the way the world is run."[16] The foreignness of the culture we add to the gospel offends and must be eliminated. But the gospel itself offends. It is supposed to offend, and we dare not weaken its offense. The gospel must be contextualized, but it must remain prophetic. It must stand in judgment of what is evil in all cultures as well as in all persons.

Contextualization That Is Postrelative

Where do we go from here? We cannot go back to the ethnocentrism and foreignness of noncontextualization. Nor can we accept the relativism and syncretism of more extreme forms of contextualization. Cross-cultural workers must move from monoculturalism through the river of relativism that comes when we take other cultures and systems of belief seriously to the firm bank of postrelativism that lies beyond. But what is this bank?[17]

15. Walter Wink, *Naming the Powers: The Language of Power in the New Testament* (Philadelphia: Fortress, 1984).

16. William Willimon, "A Crisis of Identity," *Sojourners* 15 (May 1986): 24–28.

17. Peter L. Berger and Thomas Luckmann, *The Social Construction of Reality: A Treatise in the Sociology of Knowledge* (Garden City, N. Y.: Doubleday, 1966).

Interdependence

As the battle against colonialism is won (and the battle in more sub-tle forms is not yet over), we must look beyond the reactionary stance of anticolonialism and recognize the need to build institutions and un-derstandings that take into account our common human context. We are rapidly becoming one world (though not one culture), and peace, prosperity, and survival depends on thinking and working together as different cultures, peoples, and nations. As E. Stanley Jones puts it, on the level of both the world and the church we must move beyond depen-dency and independency to *interdependency*.[18]

Theoretical Complementarity

In anthropology the move is away from relativism and purely emic approaches to complementary theories and metacultural[19] grids. Com-plementarity is rooted in a critical realist epistemology. In this, human knowledge is seen, not as a photograph of reality but, rather, as a map or blueprint that gives us real, partial understandings of reality.[20] Just as we need several blueprints to get a mental picture of what a house is like, so we need several complementary theories to show us the nature of reality. In anthropology a growing number of scholars use more than one theory or paradigm, depending upon the questions being asked and the reality being examined. For example, emic and etic models are seen as complementing each other.

There appears also to be a growing affirmation that anthropology can provide metacultural grids by which we can compare and translate between cultures. Certainly anthropology has its roots in Western cul-ture, and it is deeply molded by Western presuppositions. But in its

18. E. Stanley Jones, *Christian Maturity* (Nashville: Abingdon, 1957), 211.

19. The prefix *meta* in the word *metacultural* is used as Douglas R. Hofstadter uses it, as a position above two or more systems of the same level (*Godel, Escher, Bach: An Eternal Braid* [New York: Random House, 1980]). David Bidney discusses three uses of the term (*Theoretical Anthropology*, 2d ed. [New York: Schocken, 1967], 156–82). A. Comte, Émile Durkheim, and C. Levy-Bruhl saw it as the "prelogical" thought that characterized tribal societies. Others such as Malinowski saw metaphysics as stepping in where science fails. Finally, Henri Bergson, P. Sorokin, Northrop, and Hofstadter appeal to metacultural grids as conceptual frameworks that emerge out of and stand above different cultures, allowing us to compare their beliefs and translate between them. This position would re-ject Kuhn's suggestion that paradigms are incommensurable. Such a position, in any case, falls under its own weight, for it makes intercultural understanding impossible and provides no basis for explaining cultural change. It also renders anthropology meaning-less. In a sense any person who has lived in two or more cultures deeply becomes "bicul-tural." By this we mean that she or he has developed the ability to stand above these cultures and compare them. This "balcony" view is, in fact, a metacultural grid.

20. Coulson, *Science.*

analysis of, and dialogue with, other cultures it has begun to free itself of some of its theoretical ethnocentrism.

Beyond Postmodern Science

Huston Smith observes that we are moving beyond postmodern science and its instrumentalism and relativism. In his chapter on "The Death and Rebirth of Metaphysics" Smith argues that a "comprehensive vision, an overview of some sort, remains a human requirement; reflective creatures cannot retain the sense of direction life requires without it."[21] Critical realism is emerging as the epistemological foundation that affirms both the objective and the subjective nature of knowledge. We see through a glass darkly, but we do see.[22]

In critical realism theories convey limited information, but that information may be shown to be true by means of reality testing. Theories are not totally subjective, relative, and arbitrary. Moreover, theories, like maps, may be complementary. Contradictions, however, must be taken seriously. Finally, in critical realism theories and paradigms are not incommensurable. Larry Laudan and D. R. Hofstadter say that metatheoretical models can be developed to compare theories and paradigms and to translate meaning from one to the other.[23]

Critical Contextualization

What does all this have to say to the question of contextualization? Specifically, what does one do with traditional cultural beliefs and practices? Here I am indebted to Jacob Loewen[24] and the work of John Geertz, who developed a method of contextualization among the Wanana of Panama that is applicable in other cultural contexts.

Exegesis of the Culture

The first step in critical contextualization is to study the local culture phenomenologically. Local church leaders and the missionary lead the congregation in *uncritically* gathering and analyzing the traditional beliefs and customs associated with some question at hand. For example, in asking how Christians should bury their dead, the people begin by analyzing their traditional rites: first by describing each song, dance,

---

21. Huston Smith, *Beyond the Post-Modern Mind* (New York: Crossroad, 1982), 16.

22. Ian G. Barbour, *Myths, Models, and Paradigms: A Comparative Study in Science and Religion* (New York: Harper and Row, 1974); see also chapter 1.

23. Larry Laudan, *Progress and Its Problems: Towards a Theory of Scientific Growth* (Berkeley: University of California Press, 1977); Hofstadter, *Godel, Escher, Bach.*

24. Jacob A. Loewen, *Culture and Human Values: Christian Intervention in Anthropological Perspective* (Pasadena, Calif.: William Carey Library, 1975).

recitation, and rite that makes up their old ceremony, and then by discussing its meaning and function within the overall ritual. The purpose here is to understand the old ways, not to judge them.

If at this point the missionary shows any criticism of the customary beliefs and practices, the people will not talk about them for fear of being condemned. We shall only drive the old ways underground.

Exegesis of Scripture and the Hermeneutical Bridge

In the second step, the pastor or missionary leads the church in a study of the Scriptures related to the question at hand. In the example of burial practices, the leader uses the occasion to teach the Christian beliefs about death and resurrection. Here the pastor or missionary plays a major role, for this is the area of his or her expertise.

The leader must also have a metacultural framework that enables him or her to translate the biblical message into the cognitive, affective, and evaluative dimensions of another culture. This step is crucial, for if the people do not clearly grasp the biblical message as originally intended, they will have a distorted view of the gospel. This is where the pastor or missionary, along with theology, anthropology, and linguistics, has the most to offer in an understanding of biblical truth and in making it known in other cultures. While the people must be involved in the study of Scripture so that they grow in their abilities to discern the truth, the leader must have the metacultural grids that enable him or her to move between cultures. Without this, biblical meanings will often be forced to fit local cultural categories, distorting the message.

Critical Response

The third step is for the people corporately to critically evaluate their own past customs in the light of their new biblical understandings and to make decisions regarding their response to their new-found truths. The gospel is not simply information to be communicated. It is a message to which people must respond. Moreover, it is not enough that the leaders be convinced that changes may be needed. Leaders may share their personal convictions and point out the consequences of various decisions, but they must allow the people to make the final decision in evaluating their past customs. If the leaders make the decisions, they must enforce these decisions. In the end, the people themselves will enforce decisions arrived at corporately, and there will be little likelihood that the customs they reject will go underground.

To involve people in evaluating their own culture in the light of new truth draws upon their strength. They know their old culture better than does the missionary and are in a better position to critique it, once they have biblical instruction. Moreover, their involvement helps them to grow spiritually through learning discernment and applying scriptural teachings to their own lives. The priesthood of believers works in practice within a hermeneutical community.

A congregation may respond to old beliefs and practices in any of several ways. Many past beliefs and practices they will keep, for these are not unbiblical. Western Christians, for example, see no problem with eating hamburgers, singing secular songs such as "Home on the Range," wearing business suits, or driving cars. In many areas of their lives Christians are no different from their non-Christian neighbors. As they retain these practices they reaffirm their own cultural identity and heritage.

Other customs will be explicitly rejected by the congregations as unbecoming for Christians. The reasons for such rejection may not be apparent to those outside, who often see little difference between the songs and rites the people reject and those they retain. But the people know the deep, hidden meanings and associations of their old customs. On the other hand, at some points the missionary may need to raise questions that the people have overlooked, for they may fail to see clearly their own cultural assumptions.

Sometimes the people will choose to modify old practices by giving them explicit Christian meanings. For example, Charles Wesley gave Christian words to the melodies of popular bar songs. Similarly, the early Christians modified the style of worship found in Jewish synagogues to fit their beliefs.

At points the Christians may substitute symbols and rites borrowed from another culture for those in their own that they reject. For example, the people may choose to adopt elements of the funeral practices of the missionary rather than to retain their own. Such functional substitutes are generally effective, for they minimize the cultural dislocation created by simply removing an old custom.

Sometimes the church may adopt rites drawn from its Christian heritage. In becoming Christians they enter into a second new history. The addition of such rituals as baptism and the Lord's Supper not only provides converts with ways to express their new faith, but also symbolizes their ties to the historical and international church.

Finally, the people may create new symbols and rituals to communicate Christian beliefs in forms that are indigenous to their own culture.

New Contextualized Practices

Having led the people to analyze their old customs in the light of biblical teaching, the pastor or missionary must help them to arrange the practices they have chosen into a new ritual that expresses the Christian meaning of the event. Such a ritual will be Christian, for it explicitly seeks to express biblical teaching. It will also be contextual, for the church has created it, using forms the people understand within their own culture.

Checks against Syncretism

What checks assure us that critical contextualization will not lead us astray? We must recognize that contextualization itself is an ongoing process. The world in which people live is constantly changing, raising new questions to be addressed. Moreover, our understandings of the gospel and its application to our lives is partial. Through continued study and spiritual growth, we should, however, come to a greater understanding of the truth.

First, critical contextualization takes the Bible seriously as the rule of faith and life. Contextualized practices, like contextualized theologies, must be biblically based. This may seem obvious, but we must constantly remind ourselves that biblical revelation is the standard against which all practices are measured.

Second, this approach recognizes the work of the Holy Spirit in the lives of all believers open to God's leading.

Third, in critical contextualization the church acts as a hermeneutical community.[25] The priesthood of believers is not a license for theological "Lone-Rangerism." We need each other to see our personal biases, for we see the ways others misinterpret Scriptures before we see our own misinterpretations. Along the same line, we need Christians from other cultures, for they often see how our cultural biases have distorted our interpretations of the Scriptures. This corporate nature of the church as a community of interpretation extends not only to the church in every culture, but also to the church in all ages. To say that exegesis and hermeneutics are corporate processes does not (as some sociologists of knowledge, such as Karl Mannheim and Maurice N. Richter, Jr., suggest) reduce them to social determinism.[26]

Fourth, there is a growing discussion among evangelical theologians from different cultures and, one hopes, a growing consensus on essential theological points. One can often see the sins of others better than his or her own, and theologians can often detect the cultural biases of theologians from other cultures better than they can critique themselves. Out of the exercise of the priesthood of believers within an international hermeneutical community should come a growing under-

25. Cf. C. Norman Kraus, *The Authentic Witness: Credibility and Authority* (Grand Rapids: Eerdmans, 1979).
26. For a good critique of the sociology of knowledge with regard to science, see Laudan, *Progress.*

standing, if not agreement, on key theological issues that can help us test the contextualization of cultural practices as well as theologies.

Critical contextualization does not operate from a monocultural perspective. Nor is it premised upon the pluralism of incommensurable cultures. It seeks to find *metacultural* and *metatheological frameworks* that enable people in one culture to understand messages and ritual practices from another culture with a minimum of distortion. It is based on a critical realist epistemology that sees all human knowledge as a combination of objective and subjective elements, and as partial but increasing approximations of truth. It takes both historical and cultural contexts seriously. And it sees the relationship between form and meaning in symbols such as words and rituals, ranging all the way from an equation of the two to simply arbitrary associations between them. Finally, it sees contextualization as an ongoing process in which the church must constantly engage itself, a process that can lead us to a better understanding of what the lordship of Christ and the kingdom of God on earth are about.

5

Metatheology: The Step beyond Contextualization

As G. W. Peters has pointed out, missions are revolutionary. Not only do they lead to the planting of churches in new social and geographical settings, but they also shatter the comfortable parochialisms of the sending church by forcing it to deal with the pluralism of the world outside. The early church found this to be true. So long as converts came from the Jewish community, questions of history and culture did not arise. Both Christian and non-Christian Jews had these in common. Even when such Gentiles as Cornelius and his household entered the church by ones and twos, they could be absorbed as proselytes who had learned Jewish ways.

But when the Gentiles began to flood the church, problems arose. The first difficulty had to do with social organization. How should Jewish Christians relate to Gentile Christians? Should they form separate churches or should they form one body? The second had to do with theology. As Gentiles heard the gospel they reinterpreted and applied it in their own cultural context. In this process they discarded many of the Old Testament customs symbolized by circumcision that Jewish Christians believed were essential to the gospel.

More recently, the missionary movement has also raised profound questions regarding the nature and limits of Christian theology. As churches were planted in new cultures, their leaders began to question whether their people had to wear Western clothes, sit in pews, and sing translated songs when they became Christians. They also began to read the Scriptures for themselves and formulated African, Indian, Latin

This chapter first appeared in Hans Kasdorf and Klaus Müller, eds., *Reflection and Projection: Missiology at the Threshold of 2001* (Bad Liebenzell, West Germany: Verlag der Liebenzeller Mission, 1988). Used by permission. This is a collection of essays honoring George W. Peters.

American, and Chinese theologies that challenged the widespread assumption that the theology developed in the West was normative and complete for the church everywhere. Even in evangelical circles the question was raised, and books with such titles as *The Bible and Theology in Asian Contexts*[1] and *Christian Alternatives to Ancestor Practices*[2] appeared. The result has been a growing confusion in the field of theology.[3] If now we must speak of "theologies" rather than of "theology," have we not reduced Christian faith to subjective human agreements and thereby opened the door for a theological relativism that destroys the meaning of truth?

As a result of the modern missionary movement, Western churches are being forced to leave their well-established Christian paradigms and to build houses large enough to accommodate Christians from a thousand different languages, cultures, and peoples. What will the new international church look like?

Here we will deal only with the second question raised above, the rise of theological pluralism and the search for a supracultural theology that transcends cultural differences. Without such a theology we are in danger of relativizing Christianity and reducing it to a subset of Hinduism, in which all theological roads lead to God and everyone may choose the road he or she finds best suited. The growing pluralism in Christianity raises, as it did in the early church, the question of absolutes and unity.

Paradigms of Theological Unity

As we trace the historical development of the church, there emerge several paradigms relevant to our subject.

The Theological Process of the Early Church

With the rapid spread of Christianity in the Gentile world, the question of theological absolutes became a pressing issue in the early church. The first great church council, held in Jerusalem (Acts 15), was called to resolve the debate between missionaries Paul and Barnabas and the conservative wing of the established church. It is interesting that the council said more about what the gospel is *not* (circumcision, diet, Mosaic laws) than about what it is. This does not mean that early

1. Bong Rin Ro and Ruth Eschenaur, eds. (Taichung, Taiwan: Asia Theological Association, 1984).
2. Bong Rin Ro, ed. (Taichung, Taiwan: Asia Theological Association, 1985).
3. David Tracy, *Blessed Rage for Order: The New Pluralism in Theology* (New York: Seabury, 1975).

church leaders were uninterested in theological orthodoxy. Paul (Gal. 4:9; 1 Tim. 1:3; 6:3, 20; 2 Tim. 4:3), Peter (2 Peter 2:1–22; 3:17), and John (1 John 2:18–23; 4:1) make correct doctrine a clear concern in their warnings against heresy. Rather, it reflects a willingness on their part to accept a range of theological interpretations (1 Cor. 1:11–12) centered around the key affirmation of the lordship of Christ (1 Cor. 12:3; 1 John 2:22–23), his death and resurrection (1 Corinthians 15), and the historicity of God's acts in human history. These affirmations were the "givens," the implied information shared by early Christians who lived in primary, face-to-face communities, in which much of the information was shared through oral communication. In such a setting the question was one of theological limits. How far were Gentile Christians allowed to contextualize the gospel in their own cultural settings?

The early church responded to this question of limits more by establishing theological processes than by forging dogmatic statements. All theologies had to be tested against the gospel as it had been revealed in Scripture and given to the apostles and elders. The test was made by the church and its leaders acting as a hermeneutical community.[4] Paul checked his message with the apostles (Gal. 2:2). The Jerusalem conference was an example of such a process.

The Medieval Synthesis

A second paradigm of theological unity emerged after Constantine and the merger of church and state. The kingdom of God had come to be equated with the Roman Empire. Orthodoxy was defined in precise theological propositions, defined by leaders in the ecclesiastical bureaucracy and enforced by the might of the state. Heresy was punishable by law.

Underlying this unity was the assumption that the church could and should define theology in cultural and historical terms. This assumption resulted in a great deal of investigation that contributed much to our understanding of the theological assumptions underlying Christian faith. The great debates on Christology and salvation fleshed out much that was assumed or implicit in the oral tradition of the early church. They also dealt with the difficult issue of how to make Hebrew understandings of the nature of God and of Christ understood in essentially Greek cultural categories. We can still learn much about the Christian life through the writings of Augustine, Francis of Assisi, Thomas à Kempis, and other writers of the Middle Ages.

---

4. C. Norman Kraus, *The Authentic Witness: Credibility and Authority* (Grand Rapids: Eerdmans, 1979).

But the medieval church was largely unaware of the profound cultural differences to be found around the world, or of their own worldview. With some notable exceptions, such as the Jesuits after they were founded in the 1600s, Western Christians avoided questions raised by cultural and theological differences. People from other cultures were labeled "savages," "uncivilized," and "pagans." They did not have to take the beliefs of these others seriously. The resulting unity was based on a theological synthesis rooted in Western cultural assumptions and ways of thinking.

Timeless and Universal Forms

Contacts with the Arab world through the crusades, the rediscovery of Greek thought, and the Renaissance to which these gave rise undermined the great medieval synthesis. The Reformation was not only a reaction to the excesses and nominalism of the Roman Church. It sought also to deal with the changes taking place in Western culture: the rediscovery of Greek philosophies; individualism and emphasis on the world here and now; science, and the discovery of the earth's tremendous cultural diversity. In principle the Protestant churches affirmed diversity by advocating the *priesthood of all believers*. In practice this principle was applied to economics, rather than to theology.[5] Protestant entrepreneurialism played an important role in the rise of capitalism. Reformed theologians, on the other hand, sought unity in specific theological formulations, which they held to be historically unchanging and culturally universal.

There was a great deal of theological diversity among John Calvin, Martin Luther, Ulrich Zwingli, and the later puritans, pietists, liberals, fundamentalists, and evangelicals. Each of these groups held its formulations to be true and other formulations to be false, so schisms continued to rend the church over issues of orthodoxy and orthopraxy. And when these movements became missionary, they sought to impose their own theological formulations on churches in other parts of the world.

The Paradigm of Self-Theologizing

Today, as young churches develop their own theological formulations, these churches face a theological crisis. Not only must they deal with new theological issues raised by churches abroad, but also with the theological fact itself—with African, Latin American, Indian, Chi-

5. Cf. Max Weber, *The Protestant Ethic and the Spirit of Capitalism* (New York: Charles Scribner's Sons, 1958).

nese, and other theologies. If unity is based on a specific theological formulation, how are they to deal with this diversity?

For the most part, evangelicals answered this question by requiring churches abroad to hold to the doctrinal systems of the older church in the West. Already in the eighteenth century there was a growing awareness that young churches had a right to be independent and that Western missions had to reject colonialism and its controls. The three selves—self-government, self-support, and self-propagation—were widely affirmed and implemented. The fourth self—self-theologizing—however, was rarely discussed.

Do young churches have a right to read and interpret the Scriptures in their own cultural contexts? Theoretically, most Protestant missionaries would admit that they do. But in practice most evangelical missionaries and sending churches are deeply threatened when national leaders begin to develop their own theologies. This is understandable. For evangelicals, theology lies at the heart of their being and their missionary endeavors. When truth is defined in terms of a specific theological formulation, to tamper with that formulation is to undermine the whole task. The priesthood of believers was good theology, but in practice did it not open the doors to all kinds of heresy? In the end, the priesthood of believers was confined to the missionaries and the sending churches.

Increasingly this theological hegemony is being called into question. As young churches gain organizational independence, they begin to formulate their own theologies. Severe tensions often develop between daughter and parent churches. But the young churches can no longer turn back. If they are to make the gospel relevant to their own people, they must contextualize it within their cultural settings. The attempts to export theologies developed in the West and to preserve them unchanged have, to a great extent, failed.

If this is so, where are theological absolutes? We hold the Scriptures to be true, for they are God's revelations. But how can we preserve that truth if we allow all believers to read and interpret the Scriptures in their own cultural settings? Has the internationalization of the church turned the Bible into a Rorschach inkblot into which every church can read its own beliefs? Must we agree with philosophers who argue that all knowledge is merely pragmatic, and that we can no longer speak of truth?[6] How can we speak of truth when we must recognize the subjective and culture-bound nature of all human knowledge?

6. Thomas S. Kuhn, *The Structure of Scientific Revolutions*, 2d ed., enlarged (Chicago: University of Chicago Press, 1970); Larry Laudan, *Progress and Its Problems: Towards a Theory of Scientific Growth* (Berkeley, Calif.: University of California Press, 1977).

The Metatheological Approach

With some exceptions, Anabaptists have not sought to define and pre-serve truth in specific theological formulations. Strong oral theologies have served as their confessions of faith, and recently some of these have been written down. But rarely do these define orthodoxy. How then have they defined truth? In a sense, they have done so in terms of *meta-theological truth*, the methods by which legitimate theologies could be developed, and the processes for setting limits to theological diversity.

The Bible and Theology

Most theologians and missionaries of the nineteenth and early twen-tieth centuries were positivists.[7] They assumed that human knowledge, carefully formulated, could be totally objective and, therefore, true in an absolute sense. Moreover, knowledge was cumulative and poten-tially exhaustive. Consequently, they sought to ever more precisely state final truth.

The Anabaptists, on the other hand, were critical realists. They af-firmed that there is objective reality and objective truth (reality as God sees it—as it really is). They recognized, however, that all truth as per-ceived by humans is partial and has a subjective element within it. Human knowledge exists in people. Therefore, it must be understood in terms of the social, cultural, and historical contexts in which people live.

In part, this epistemological stance grew out of a radical application within the church of the priesthood of all believers. Pastors were often laypeople, called from the ranks of the church. Furthermore, people were encouraged to read and interpret the Scriptures for themselves. But when everyone did so it was apparent that these interpretations were colored by personal biases.

This awareness led the Anabaptists to make a sharp distinction be-tween God's revelation as recorded in Scripture and human under-standings expressed in theology—a distinction not often drawn by pos-itivist theologians, who saw theology as an objective statement of biblical truth unaffected by the personal biases of the theologian. For positivist theologians, theological propositions were thought to have a one-to-one correspondence to biblical revelation. Therefore, they had the same truth value as the Scripture itself.

Like others in the Reformation, the Anabaptists affirmed the objec-tive truthfulness of the Bible. They saw theology, however, as a human

7. For a brief analysis of epistemological positions see chapters 1 and 2.

understanding of the Scriptures. To the extent a theology was rooted in Scripture, it contained objective truth, but because it was a human understanding, there was also a subjective element in it. It was truth "seen through a glass darkly." Theological truth was derived from biblical truth, but it was partial and colored by personal biases. To them the authority of Scripture meant that they constantly had to go to the Scriptures to test their beliefs and behavior. As Peters constantly pointed out, they were "people of the Book."[8]

The failure of the Anabaptists to formulate and publish formal systematic theologies was both a strength and a weakness. As we have noted, they did have strong convictions regarding theological absolutes. Moreover, in the reading of Scripture they could not help but formulate ideas about the fundamental nature of God, humans, sin, salvation, and eternity. They were, however, afraid theology might replace the Bible as the ultimate source of truth. In their failure to formally articulate their theologies and metatheological approach to Scripture, they were susceptible to influences from the theological systems with which they came into contact. This has been particularly true in North America since the emergence of paid clergy.

Theology in Human Contexts

This recognition of the objective and subjective nature of human knowledge, including theology, had two important consequences. First it related theology directly to human life. The purpose of theology, for the Anabaptists, was not to formulate an abstract system of unchanging truth detached from the problems of everyday life. That place was reserved for the Scriptures. Theology was the application of biblical truths to the situations in which the people found themselves. It was the dynamic process of applying the unchanging truths of the gospel to real life issues. It was not uncommon for Anabaptists to debate how Jesus would have acted in a given situation if he were a parent, teacher, farmer, or businessman.

Second, it led the Anabaptists to define faith as discipleship more than as mental affirmation. Faith was not simply giving intellectual assent to theological truth on the level of cognition. Nor was it mainly positive feelings of worship towards Christ and Christ's presence in the

8. Among the most vivid and prized experiences of those, like myself, who sat under Dr. G. W. Peters's instruction in the Mennonite Brethren Biblical Seminary was his course on Old Testament revelation, in which he unfolded for us the development of theological truth in the Old Testament. He constantly reminded us that the Mennonites rooted their beliefs in the Bible rather than in a theology, and that "they were a people of the Book."

believer on the affective level. Faith was the human response to both of these—it was to follow Christ as Lord in life. In conversion, cognitive and affective changes had to lead to evaluative changes—to changes in basic allegiance. As C. S. Peirce put it, faith is that upon which people act. For the Anabaptists the presence of faith shows in the transformation of a person's life.

This view led Anabaptists to take a humble view of theology. They held strongly to their theological convictions; many died for them.[9] But they readily admitted that their understanding of truth was partial, biased, and possibly wrong. They were, therefore, willing to test their convictions by returning to the Scriptures. This constant appeal to biblical passages in support of their beliefs was the hallmark of their theologies. It also led them to place a higher priority on biblical theology that traces God's revelation in specific historical settings, than on systematic theology that looks for ahistorical absolutes.

But the recognition of both the objective and subjective nature of theology raised critical questions. How could one differentiate in theological formulations between objective truth and personal bias? Did not the recognition of subjective elements in human knowledge condemn us forever to live with an uncertainty about truth?

The Anabaptist response to this question was not to formulate a systematic theology held to be absolute. Rather, it was to develop processes whereby theological opinions could be tested for error. There were three such tests. First, was the idea espoused based on the Bible? To the extent it was not, it was suspect. As we have seen, the Anabaptists affirmed the authority of the Scriptures, and the Bible declares many things clearly, such as the virgin birth and the death and resurrection of Christ. Second, was the interpreter of Scripture responsive to the leading of the Holy Spirit? In other words, was he or she approaching Scripture with a spirit of humility and a willingness to listen and learn rather than with dogmatic self-assurance? Third, was the person open to the checks of the Christian community?

Interpretation and application of Scripture in everyday life was not just a personal matter. Ultimately the church as a whole acted as a hermeneutical community. Believers needed others to help them detect their personal biases, of which they themselves were often unaware, just as they needed others to help them see the sins they did not want to admit to themselves. This appeal to the community as the basis for interpreting Scripture does not reduce its interpretations to social determinism, as some sociologists of knowledge might argue (Émile

9. Cf. Tieleman Janszoon van Bracht, *The Bloody Theater: Or Martyr's Mirror*, trans. J. F. Sohm (1837; reprint, Scottdale, Penn.: Herald, 1979).

Durkheim, Karl Mannheim, and others).[10] Rather, the corporate nature of hermeneutics serves to check the personal biases of individual interpretations of the Bible.

The answer of the original Anabaptists to theological unity and diversity, then, was not to formulate an unchanging systematic theology but to develop a *metatheology*—a set of procedures—by which different theologies, each a partial understanding of the truth in a certain context, could be constructed. These had to be rooted in the Scriptures, particularly in the person of Jesus Christ; they had to arise out of the questions of everyday life, for faith had to find its expression in discipleship; and the limits of understanding were set by the community of believers.

Metatheology and the Missionary Scene

Early Anabaptists did not face the tremendous cultural diversity we see in the church today. They did, however, seek to deal with the pluralism implicit in the priesthood of all believers through a metatheology that gave this diversity a center and a limit. Is it possible that the *metatheological* approach can solve the missiological problems of contextualization and theological pluralism where traditional *theological* approaches have failed? What would theology on the international scene look like if these approaches were taken? The fact is, Mennonites have been among the first to work with such indigenous church movements as the African Independent Churches.[11]

Contextualization

To take such an approach we would need from the start to recognize the right and responsibility of the church in each culture and historical setting to interpret and apply the Scriptures in its own context. This is to apply the priesthood of believers, not only to individuals, but also to churches in different cultural settings.

There are several levels at which contextualization takes place. First, the Bible needs to be translated into new languages. This involves much more than simply replacing old words and sentences with new ones. Built into every language are the implicit assumptions of the cul-

10. Émile Durkheim, *The Elementary Forms of the Religious Life*, trans. J. W. Swain (New York: Macmillan, 1915); Karl Mannheim, *Ideology and Utopia: An Introduction to the Sociology of Knowledge* (London: K. Paul, Trench and Trubner, 1936). For a good discussion of the relationship of rationality, truth, and the sociology of knowledge, see Laudan, *Progress*, 196–222.

11. Cf. Edwin Weaver and Irene Weaver, *From Kuku Hill: Among Indigenous Churches in West Africa* (Scottdale, Penn.: Herald, 1975).

ture—the worldview of the people. There is no theologically unbiased language, no philosophically neutral worldview. This task requires technical expertise, but the principle of community check applies even here. Individual translators often translate passages in ways that conform to their own personal theological positions, rather than to the text itself.

Second, old customs must be dealt with. Christians can always keep much in their culture. Cultures are human creations. Because humans are created in the image of God, they can create what is good and beautiful. But humans are also sinners, so sinfulness is found in every culture. The culture lies under the wrath of God. As Wink points out, more than three-quarters of the Bible's references to "powers" and "authorities" (*archē, archōn, exousia, dynamis,* and *thronos*) refer to human institutions—to corporate social structures.[12]

Third, the church is to be a new sociocultural order. This order should not be a reflection of the native culture of the missionary. Rather, it should increasingly manifest the kingdom of God within that sociocultural context.

Finally, the church in sociocultural settings must develop its own theology by applying biblical truth to the day-to-day issues it faces. In India it must struggle with the caste system and poverty; in Africa it must deal with tribalization and polygamy; in China it must wrestle with ancestor veneration; in North America it must responsibly come to terms with secularism, materialism, and affluence in a poverty-ridden world.

Beyond Contextualization to a Supracultural Theology

The goal of theology is not simply to apply the gospel in the diverse contexts of human life. Theology's nature also revolves around the goal to understand the unchanging nature of the gospel—the absolutes that transcend time and cultural pluralism. If theology is to become more than a Rorschach inkblot into which we project our own cultural prejudices, we need a standard against which to test our theologies. Here again we can apply principles used by the Anabaptists to test the orthodoxy of theologies. One principle is that the primary test is the Scripture itself—the divinely superintended record of God's acts in history. Another principle is that humility and the willingness to be led by the Spirit are vital to the reading of Scripture. The final principle is that the hermeneutical community checks interpretations and seeks consensus.

---

12. Walter Wink, *Naming the Powers: The Language of Power in the New Testament* (Philadelphia: Fortress, 1984).

Just as believers in a local church must test their interpretations of Scriptures with their community of believers, so the churches in different cultural and historical contexts must test their theologies with the international community of churches and the church down through the ages. The priesthood of believers must be exercised within a hermeneutical community.

As the church in a given sociocultural setting seeks to contextualize the gospel, it is keenly aware of the needs the gospel must address within its setting and the foreignness of Christian forms that have been introduced from without. It is often unaware, however, of its own cultural biases, which it projects into its understanding of the Scriptures. Believers in other cultures are generally more aware of these. Consequently, churches in specific cultural settings need the check of the international community of churches to test where theologies are too strongly influenced by cultural assumptions.

Ironically, this metatheological process, carried out on the international level, may lead us to what Western theologians have long sought—a growing consensus on theological absolutes. It may bring us closer to the formulation of a truly supracultural theology. But such a formulation must be an ongoing process; for as the world and its cultures change, so do the problems theology must address.

In fact, this process of internationalizing theology has begun. Conferences of theologians from different parts of the world are beginning to deal with such issues as ancestry veneration and the caste system. And non-Western theologians are beginning to call into question the cultural biases of Western theologies. For the moment this will disturb Western churches that see their theological formulations as complete and final. In the end, however, it can help us in the West see where we have sold out to our cultures and where Christianity is in danger of becoming a Western civil religion. It will remind us that the kingdom of God is always prophetic and calls all cultures toward God's ideals, and that citizens of that kingdom are to form living communities that manifest the nature of that kingdom. In such communities, understanding the Word of God must be an ongoing and living process that leads to discipleship under the lordship of Christ in every area of life.

Part 2

Reflections
on Planting
Churches

6

The Category *Christian* in the Mission Task

Can a nonliterate peasant become a Christian after hearing the gospel only once? If so, what do we mean by conversion?

Imagine, for a moment, Papayya, an Indian peasant, returning to his village after a hard day's work in the fields. His wife is preparing the evening meal, so to pass the time he wanders over to the village square. There he notices a stranger surrounded by a few curiosity-seekers. Tired and hungry, he sits down to hear what the man is saying. For an hour he listens to a message of a new God, and something he hears moves him deeply. Later he asks the stranger about the new way, and then, almost as if by impulse, he bows his head and prays to this God who is said to have appeared to humans in the form of Jesus. He doesn't quite understand it all. As a Hindu he worships Vishu, who incarnated himself many times as a human, animal, or fish to save humankind. Papayya also knows many of the 330 million Hindu gods. But the stranger says there is only one God, and this God has appeared among humans only once. Moreover, the stranger says that this Jesus is the Son of God, but he says nothing about God's wife. It is all confusing to Papayya.

The man turns to go home, and a new set of questions flood his mind. Can he still go to the Hindu temple to pray? Should he tell his family

Portions of this chapter first appeared in "Conversion, Culture, and Cognitive Categories," *Gospel in Context* 1 (October 1978): 24–29; "Sets and Structures: A Study of Church Patterns," in *New Horizons in World Missions: Evangelicals and the Christian Mission in the 1980s*, ed. D. J. Hesselgrave (Grand Rapids: Baker Book House, 1979), 217–27; "The Category 'Christian' in the Mission Task," *International Review of Missions* (July 1983): 421–27.

about his new faith? And how can he learn more about Jesus—he cannot read the few papers the stranger gave him, and there are no other Christians in a day's walk. Who knows when the stranger will come again?

Conversion and Cultural Differences

Can Papayya become a Christian after hearing the gospel only once? Our answer can only be yes. If a person must be educated, have an extensive knowledge of the Bible, or live a good life, the good news is only for a few.

But what essential change takes place when Papayya responds to the gospel message in simple faith? Certainly he has acquired some new information. He has heard of Christ and his redemptive work on the cross, and a story or two about Christ's life on earth. But his knowledge is minimal. Papayya can not pass even the simplest tests of Bible knowledge or theology. If we accept him as a brother are we not opening the door for "cheap grace" and a nominal church?

To complicate matters further, Papayya understands the knowledge he does have in a way radically different from how Christians in other parts of the world would perceive it. For example, the English speaker talks of *God*, but, being a Telugu speaker, Papayya speaks of *devudu*. *Devudu*, however, does not have the same meaning as does the English word *God*, just as the English word does not correspond exactly to the word *theos* used in the Greek New Testament.

Ordinary English speakers divide living beings into two basic domains (see fig. 6.1). In the first domain *supernatural* beings are counted: God, angels, Satan, and demons. The second domain is *natural* beings and things. This domain is broken down into different categories: human beings, animals, plants, and such inanimate objects as sand and rocks. In this system of classification God is categorically different from human beings, and humans are categorically different from animals, plants, and lifeless matter. *Incarnation* means that God crossed the categorical difference between himself and humans.

Telugu speakers do not differentiate among different kinds of life (fig. 6.1). All forms of life are thought to be manifestations of a single vital force; gods, demons, humans, animals, plants, and even what appear to be inanimate objects all have the same kind of life. To be sure, the gods have more of this life than humans, and humans more than animals or plants. But there is no categorical difference between gods and humans, or between humans and animals. After death, good humans are reborn as gods, and sinful gods as animals or ants. Moreover, gods repeatedly come to earth as *avatars* (loosely translated *in-*

Figure 6.1

A Comparison of American and Indian Views of Life

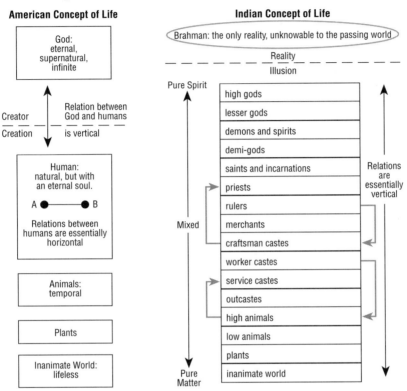

SOURCE: Paul G. Hiebert, "Missions and the Understanding of Culture," in *The Church in Mission*, ed. A. J. Klassen (Fresno: Board of Christian Literature, Mennonite Brethren Church, 1967), 254–55. Used by permission.

carnations) to help humans, just as rich people stoop to help their servants.

To make matters worse, gods in Hinduism are not the ultimate reality. They are parts of creation, or, technically, manifestations of the ultimate reality, which is a force or cosmic energy field. There is no word in Telugu for ultimate reality as a being. The fact is, each language gives expression to a worldview. No language is philosophically or theologically neutral.

Now we must ask, not only what knowledge must Papayya have to become a Christian, but also whether this knowledge must be perceived in a particular way, from a particular worldview. Must Papayya learn the English or the Greek meaning of *God* before he can become a Christian, or can he be saved even if he has a very imperfect understanding of the concept of God?[1]

Since it is hard to measure a person's beliefs and concepts, would it not be better to test his conversion by looking for changes in his life? Can we not define a Christian as a person who goes to church on Sunday, and who does not drink liquor or smoke? Here, too, Papayya's change at conversion may not be dramatic. There is no church for him to attend. The circuit preacher comes only a dozen times a year. Papayya cannot read the Scriptures. His theology is found in the few Christian songs he has learned to sing. To be sure, he no longer worships at the Hindu temple; instead he offers incense to a picture of Christ. But otherwise his life is much the same. He carries on his caste occupation, smokes an occasional cigarette, and lives as most other villagers do. Is he then not a Christian?

Types of Categories

What does it mean to be a Christian? Before we can answer this question we must look more closely at how we form categories such as *Christian* and *church*. These words, like many other nouns in English, refer to sets of people or things that we group on the basis of one reason or another. They refer to categories that exist in our minds. But how we form the categories influences profoundly what we see.

Current studies in mathematics show that we can create categories in several different ways, each of which has its own structural characteristics and logic. Here we will examine four ways to form categories, and examine how each affects our views of conversion, the church, and Christian mission.

Two variables are essential to defining a category. The first has to do with the basis on which elements are assigned to a category:

> *Intrinsic sets* are formed on the basis of the *essential nature of the members themselves*—on what they are in and of themselves. For example, *apples* are objects that are "round, red or yellow edible fruits of the *rosaceous* tree."[2] Most nouns in English, and most sets in modern algebra, are intrinsic sets.

1. The worldview of many Western Christians, and the Greek worldview on which it is based, are sub-Christian in character. In the biblical worldview, to put God together with angels and demons in the same category (supernatural beings, as against natural beings such as humans and animals) is the ultimate sacrilege. Angels and demons are part of "creation." God is alone as "Creator."

2. "Apple," in *Random House Dictionary of the English Language*, 2d unabridged ed. (New York: Random House, 1987).

Extrinsic, or relational, sets are formed, not on the basis of what things *are,* but on their relationship to other things or to a reference point. For example, a *son* and a *daughter* are *children* of a *father and mother.* If they are children of the same parents they are *brother* and *sister,* not because of what they are intrinsically, but because of their relationship to a common reference point.[3]

The second variable in forming categories has to do with their boundaries:

Well-formed sets have a sharp boundary. Things either belong to the set or they do not.[4] The result is a clear boundary between things that are inside and things that are outside the category.

Fuzzy sets have no sharp boundaries. Categories flow into one another. For example, day becomes night, and a mountain turns into a plain without a clear transition.[5]

If we combine these two variables, we have four types of categories (see fig. 6.2). Each of these types of categories reflects and creates a certain view of reality and a certain logic—in short, a distinct worldview. As Christians, we need to know these worldviews and how they cause us to understand and to misunderstand the Scriptures. As missionaries, we need to know how the categories people use affect such questions as the nature of Christianity, contextualization, and the relationship between religions.

Intrinsic Well-Formed (Bounded) Sets

The German mathematician Georg Cantor was the father of intrinsic well-formed set theory, one of the greatest achievements of nineteenth-century mathematics. His essential point is that a collection of objects can be regarded as a single entity (a whole) if the objects share properties that define a whole.[6] Well-formed sets are those in which it is pos-

---

3. It is difficult to find examples of extrinsic categories in English because it, like modern mathematics, is based on a Greek worldview that sought to define reality in terms of the essence of things.

4. Well-formed sets are digital sets in which X can be only 0 or 1 [$x : x = f (0, 1)$]. Consequently a thing cannot belong to the categories A and *not-A* at the same time. This is the "law of the excluded middle."

5. Fuzzy sets are analogical sets in which X may have any value from 0 to 1, such as .015, .289, or .683751 [$x : x = (f) 0 \rightarrow 1$]. Consequently the boundary is an infinite set of points between in and out. A member may therefore belong to the sets A and *not-A* at the same time. The law of the excluded middle does not apply to fuzzy sets.

6. Robert R. Stoll, *Set Theory and Logic* (San Francisco: W. H. Freeman, 1963), 2.

Figure 6.2
A Typology of Sets

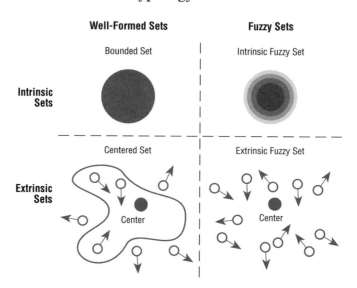

sible to determine whether any object is, or is not, a member of the set. Well-formed sets are the basis of modern algebra and geometry.

Characteristics of Bounded Sets

Bounded sets have certain structural characteristics—they force us to look at things in certain ways. The category *apple* can be used to illustrate some of these:

1. The category is created by listing the essential characteristics an object must have in itself to belong to the set. For example, an apple is (1) a kind of *fruit* that is (2) usually round, (3) red or yellow, (4) edible, and (5) produced by a *rosaceous* tree. Any fruit that meets these requirements (assuming we have an adequate definition) is an *apple*.
2. The category is defined by a clear boundary. A fruit is either an apple or it is not. It cannot be 70 percent apple and 30 percent pear. Most of the effort in defining the category is spent defining and maintaining the boundary. Not only must we say what an *apple* is, we also must clearly differentiate it from *oranges*, *pears*, and other similar objects that belong to the same domain but are not apples. The central question, therefore, is whether an object is inside or outside the category.

3. Objects within a bounded set are uniform in their essential characteristics—they constitute a homogeneous group. All apples are 100 percent apple. One is not more apple than another. Either a fruit is an apple or it is not. There may be different sizes, shapes, and varieties, but they are all the same in that they are all apples. There is no variation built into the structuring of the category.

4. Bounded sets are essentially static sets. An apple remains an apple whether it is green, ripe, or rotten. The only change occurs when it emerges from the flower, and when it ceases to be an apple (e.g., by being eaten). The only structural change is a move from outside to inside the category, or vice versa.

5. Bounded sets, as we use them in the West, are ontological sets. They have to do with the ultimate, changeless structure of reality, which is defined in terms of unchanging, universal, abstract categories. This view leads us to an abstract-analytical approach to logic. For example, in an IQ test with a picture of three adults and a child, we exclude the *child* because it does not belong to the abstract category *adult*.

Western Culture as a Bounded Set

We in the West are most familiar with bounded sets. They are the basis of our culture. In English our nouns, such as *apples*, *oranges*, *pencils*, and *pens*, are basic building blocks of our reality. Most of them are intrinsic well-formed sets. A dog is a dog because of what it *is*, and a cat is a cat. Moreover, there is no half-dog-half-cat, or three-quarters-dog-one-quarter-cat.

We use fuzzy sets, but as qualifiers (such as adjectives and adverbs) to modify nouns: green, greener, greenest; fast, faster, fastest. But we perceive the fundamental reality of nature in terms of bounded-set nouns. For example, at the supermarket we ask for *apples*. When asked what kind of apples we want, we say, "half-ripened" or "fully-ripened" apples.

Bounded sets are fundamental to our understanding of order. We want uniform categories. In the kitchen we put forks in the fork bin, knives in the knife bin, and spoons in the spoon bin. We want our walls to be uniform in color. In the yard we want grass lawns with no dandelions, tulips, or other "weeds."

We use bounded sets in classical music. There are seven notes, and five half-steps in the scale. Each has a fixed pitch, defined in terms of lengths of the sound waves it produces. Good musicians can hit the notes precisely and make clear runs.

Maintaining boundaries is essential in a bounded-set world, otherwise categories begin to disintegrate and chaos sets in. In the West, we do this by using borders. We put frames around pictures, windows, doors, and blackboards. We use moldings to cover cracks between panels on walls and to mark the boundaries between walls. Men wear ties to cover the joining of the fabric down the front of dress shirts. We edge our sidewalks so that the grass does not creep onto the cement. We use curbs to mark the edge of the street. On our highways we have solid lines to separate traffic lanes and to differentiate between traffic lanes and the highway's shoulders.

We define *cleanliness*, to a considerable extent, in terms of order. "Dirt" on a floor becomes "earth" when it is thrown out on the ground. Flowers in the lawn are "weeds." Walls, clothes, and cars are "dirty" if they are discolored. In all of these, cleanliness has more to do with order than sanitation.

Scholars have noted that we in America tend to think in terms of opposites: in terms of good versus bad, of rich versus poor, and of friends versus enemies.[7] In philosophy we follow the law of the excluded middle, which holds that something cannot belong to the category *A* and *not-A* at the same time.

This bounded set view of reality is based on a Greek worldview. Greek philosophers were interested in the intrinsic nature of things, and the ultimate, unchanging structure of reality.[8] They defined this reality in terms of sharply defined categories.

In modern science we create endless taxonomies of plants, animals, elementary particles, diseases, kinship systems, personality types, and what-not, as if these taxonomies form universal types. We also are concerned about impersonal objectivity in scientific knowledge. Subjectivity—the involvement of the knower in what is known—is seen as contamination. We separate objective knowledge from feelings and values, and exclude the latter because they are relational in nature.

Westerners view law as an impersonal set of norms that apply equally to all humans. Lying is wrong, not because it undermines a relationship, but because it violates a universal principle. The offender is guilty of breaking the law and must be punished, even if the punishment destroys relationships and harms other innocent people. We de-

7. Conrad M. Arensberg and Arthur H. Niehoff, *Introducing Social Change: A Manual for Community Development* (Chicago: Aldine, 1971).

8. E. J. Dijksterhuis traces this search for the ultimate intrinsic nature and structure of reality back to the Greeks. See *The Mechanization of the World Picture: Pythagoras to Newton*, trans. C. D. Dikshoorn (Princeton, N.J.: Princeton University Press, 1986), especially chapter 2.

fine justice and righteousness as living within the law, not as living in harmony with others.

Christian as a Bounded Set

What happens to our concept of *Christian* if we define it as a bounded set?

First, we would classify a person as a Christian on the basis of what she or he *is*. Because we cannot look into the hearts of people, we must focus on external characteristics that we can see or hear.

We usually begin with a test of orthodoxy, with a verbal affirmation of belief in a specific set of doctrines, such as the deity of Christ and the virgin birth. We often add tests of orthopraxy or right behavior. We look for evidences of faith in the changed lives of the people. A Christian is one who does not smoke, drink alcohol, and so on.

Let us return for a moment to Papayya. If we think of *Christian* as a bounded set, we must decide which beliefs (at both the explicit and the worldview levels) and practices will identify him as a Christian and set him apart from a non-Christian. If we make the list long enough to maintain the orthodoxy and purity of the church, it is impossible for Papayya to become a Christian that night or that year. It will take years of careful training for him to understand our theological tests in terms of a biblical worldview. If we make the list short to open the door to Papayya, with his simple, distorted understanding of the gospel, we offer "cheap grace" and open the door to a church full of people with little knowledge of the Scriptures. Having made the list, we then must test Papayya to make sure he has acquired *all* the characteristics we require of a Christian. If he has, there is no essential need for him to change further, because he already is fully a Christian.

Second, if we make *Christian* a bounded set, we would draw a sharp line between Christians and non-Christians. Moreover, we would work to maintain this boundary, because the boundary is critical to maintaining the category. We would seek to differentiate clearly between those who are truly Christian, and those who are not. Our central question would be whether a person is inside or outside the circle of faith.

Third, we would view all Christians as essentially the same, whether they are old, experienced Christians or young converts. We would not distinguish among them on the basis of their spiritual maturity. Once a person is a Christian, he or she is 100 percent Christian.

Fourth, we would put great emphasis on conversion as the one essential change all people must experience to be saved. We would see conversion as a point, a single dramatic crossing of the boundary between being a *non-Christian* and being a *Christian*. We would expect all believers to enter by the same door, share the same basic theological doctrines, and behave in the same basic way. Sanctification—growing in faith—is not a part of the set. It is good, but not essential. Bringing people to faith in Christ is essential; discipling them in Christian maturity can be left to others.

Fifth, we would see *Christian* as a state of ontological being acquired when one is declared righteousness before the law. The focus, therefore, is on the intrinsic nature of the person, on who she or he is.

Church as a Bounded Set

How does bounded-set thinking affect the way in which we view and organize the church?

First, we would see the church as a gathering of Christians. If Christians are all the same in essence, it would be a uniform, homogenous group. All would agree to the same doctrines, and all would observe the same behavior. Its unity would be based on uniformity—all Christians would think and act alike.

Other churches with different membership requirements would be seen as *other* sets. A critical question would be whether they are truly "Christian." Walls between churches and denominations would be important and high because boundaries define the ultimate nature of reality.

Bounded-set churches would act like clubs—voluntary associations of like-minded people who share a common interest, that of meeting specific personal needs. Other people would be permitted to join if they acquired the characteristics of the association, and if the people in it were willing to admit them.

The church would view theology as ultimate, universal, and unchanging truth and define it in general propositional statements. It would divorce theology from the historical and cultural contexts in which it is formulated.

Second, we would take care to maintain clear boundaries. We would require clear membership rolls, and limit participation in business meetings and church offices to members of the congregation. We would also seek congruency between church membership and the category *Christian*, and we would exclude non-Christians from the church.

Third, we would take a democratic approach to church membership. All members would have an equal say in running the church. Each would have a single vote and all votes would be of equal value—whether from an experienced elder or a new convert. Because the church would be built upon a common identity and task, its formal organization would be mechanical.[9] We would look for clearly defined roles, explicit rules, well-planned programs, management by objectives, and performance measured in quantitative terms and bottom lines. The church would function like a club or corporation.

Fourth, we would stress evangelism as the major task of the church—getting people into the category. Conversion would be the means by which people enter the church. Structurally, there would be no difference among Christians once in the circle of faith. Spiritual growth would not help define the set. Consequently, discipling new converts, organizing living churches, and manifesting the signs of the kingdom—while good in themselves—would not be essential to the central task of bringing people to faith in Christ.

Fifth, building the church would be seen as an end in itself. Church gatherings would focus on maintaining the identity of the church and its organization. Because identity is intrinsic, its greatest danger would be secularism—worship of the group, of the corporate self.

Missions and Bounded Sets

How would we view our mission task and other religions from a bounded-set perspective?

First, we would seek to win the lost to Christ, but we would be careful not to baptize them until they know and affirm our creed and follow our practices, such as monogamy and abstinence from evil habits. Consequently, baptism would normally take place years after a person turned to Christ in faith.

Second, because each religion is an intrinsic, defined set we would stress the radical difference between them. We would tend to view everything in Christianity as true, and everything in other religions as pagan and false.

In mission we would fear incorporating into Christianity ideas and practices found in other religions, lest these compromise its uniqueness. We would call for a radical displacement of all the elements of the pagan religion, fearing syncretism.

Third, we would define Christianity primarily in terms of our own beliefs and practices and require young churches in other cultures to conform. The danger is that we would bring the gospel in the garb of whatever culture originated it—historically that garb has been Western.

---

9. Peter L. Berger, Brigitte Berger, and Hansfried Kellner discuss this form of organization extensively in *The Homeless Mind: Modernization and Consciousness* (New York: Random House, 1973), as does Jacques Ellul in *The Technological Society* (New York: Random House, 1964). Eugene H. Peterson looks at the consequences of this view of organization on the Christian ministry in *Under the Unpredictable Plant: An Exploration in Vocational Holiness* (Grand Rapids: Eerdmans, 1992).

Fourth, because our theological position would be definitive, we would have to train native leaders who can maintain this position unchanged. Because this requires extensive education, we would be slow to appoint native leaders to positions of significant authority in the church.

Intrinsic Fuzzy Sets

Lofti Asker Zadeh, an Egyptian professor at the University of California in Berkeley, introduced the concept of "fuzzy" sets in 1965.[10] Noting that in everyday life most categories do not have exact boundaries, he wrote,

> In classical two-valued systems, all classes are assumed to have sharply defined boundaries. So an object is a member of a class or it is not a member of the class . . . mortal or not mortal, dead or alive, male or female, and so forth. . . . But most classes in the real world do not have sharp boundaries. For example, if you consider characteristics or properties like tall, intelligent, tired, sick, and so forth, all these characteristics lack sharp boundaries. Classical two-valued logic is not designed to deal with properties that are a matter of degree.[11]

The same fuzziness applies to categories such as day and night, sea and land, and trees and bushes. Even death, which at first glance seems to be definite, turns out to be fuzzy; some organs in the body, and some cells in the organs, are still alive after others have mortified. Nor can this fuzziness be removed by more careful definitions and better measurements.

Fuzzy sets are mathematical sets which have no sharp edges. Instead, there are degrees of inclusion. Things may be one-quarter, one-half, or even two-thirds in the set. For example, a mountain merges into the plain without a clear boundary, and the color red into orange. Fuzzy sets are analogical, rather than digital, in nature.

An example of the difference between fuzzy and well-formed categories is our view of race. Americans use well-defined sets to divide people sharply into different races, such as blacks, whites, and Latinos. In reality, races blend into one another along continuums of intermarriage. A person may have one, two, three, or four great-grandparents from one race and the rest from another. Ancestors may come from three or more races. There are no "pure" races. Seen in fuzzy-set terms, races form continua between poles, so sharp lines cannot be drawn.

10. Lofti Asker Zadeh, "Fuzzy Sets," *Information and Control* 8 (1965): 338–53.
11. R. R. Yager, et al., eds., *Fuzzy Sets and Applications: Selected Papers by L. A. Zadeh* (New York: Wiley, 1987), 17.

Fuzzy sets provide us with not only another way of viewing the world but also a new system of logic. Along with fuzzy-set theory have emerged fuzzy algebra, fuzzy geometry, and fuzzy logic.[12]

Fuzzy sets may be defined either intrinsically or extrinsically. We will examine intrinsic fuzzy sets here.

Characteristics of Intrinsic Fuzzy Sets

Intrinsic fuzzy sets have these characteristics:

1. As in bounded sets, membership in a set is based on the intrinsic nature of the members—on what they are. An apple is an apple because of what it is in itself.
2. The boundaries of categories are fuzzy, with degrees of inclusion in the set. Things may be 30 percent or 55 percent or 91.467 percent in the category. The result is a world of continuums in which everything flows into everything else, not a world sharply divided by *either-or* thinking. In this, fuzzy sets differ radically from bounded sets.
3. Because the boundary is fuzzy, a thing may belong to two or more sets at the same time. A paint may be mixed using three different pigments. A person may be one-quarter African-American, one-quarter white, and one-half Hispanic. There is, therefore, no excluded middle in fuzzy-set algebra or fuzzy-set logic. A thing may belong to both the sets *A* and *not-A* at the same time.
4. Change in intrinsic fuzzy sets is a process, not a point. Fruit becomes ripe by degrees, and night creeps up by stages. The process may be rapid or slow, but the fuzziness of the boundary remains.
5. Ontologically, a fuzzy-set world sees reality as continuums and fields that flow into one another. The underlying unity of reality is the common field or domain in which the categories exist. For example, in the illustration of racial identity, bounded-set thought would speak of different "races," and fuzzy-set thought of different variations within the one "race"—humanity.

Because there is no sharp distinction between right and wrong or truth and non-truth, fuzzy-set worlds tend to be relativistic.

---

12. Cf. Hans-Jurgens Zimmerman, *Fuzzy Set Theory and Its Applications* (Boston: Kluwer-Nijhoff, 1985).

Intrinsic Fuzzy Sets in Indian Culture

All cultures use both well-formed and fuzzy categories, but they seem to focus on one or the other as the basic building blocks for constructing their world. As we have seen, American culture places a premium on clear, well-bounded sets: on well-defined roads with curbs and marked lanes, well-edged lawns with no weeds or flowers in the grass, paint and glass well separated in the windows, and fixed prices.

Indian culture is built primarily on fuzzy sets. As we have seen, gods, humans, animals, plants, and matter are not seen as different kinds of life, but as variations of the same life. All gods are seen as manifestations of the same God, and all religions as different roads leading to the same end. In Indian philosophy, things may belong to the sets *A* and *not-A* at the same time, and contradictions are resolved by moving to a higher level. For example, good and evil are opposites on earth, but behind them is the one reality out of which both emerge.

Many Indian nouns are fuzzy nouns, modified by well-formed adjectives. For example, a woman at the market may ask for some "half-ripes." When the merchant asks what kind of half-ripe she wants, she says, "a banana half-ripe," or "an orange half-ripe." What she really wants is something that can be eaten tomorrow.

In everyday life there is little concern for sharp boundaries and uniform categories. Paint flows onto the window glass, and different colors are used on the same wall with little thought for boundaries. Traffic on traditional Indian streets is based on flexible lanes.[13] The center line is unmarked, and moves back and forth to equalize the flow of traffic as needed.

Indian music has sixty-four micro steps between each of the seven notes on its scale. Beginners play the main tones. Experts go from three sixty-fourths above, to five sixty-fourths above, then to two sixty-fourths below, before hitting the note. To Westerners the melody sounds like one continuous slide rather than precise scales.

Christian as an Intrinsic Fuzzy Set

If we define *Christian* in fuzzy-set terms, we would find the following:

First, as in intrinsic well-formed sets, a Christian would be defined in terms of beliefs and/or practices. We would need to make a list of all the characteristics a person would need to be a Christian. The list would

13. Paul G. Hiebert, "Traffic Patterns in Seattle and Hyderabad: Immediate and Mediate Transactions," *Journal of Anthropological Research* 32.4 (Winter 1976): 326–36.

be long or short, depending on whether we focus on maintaining the purity of the church or on reaching out to win the lost.

Second, membership in the set would be one of degree. A person might affirm half the necessary beliefs to be a Christian, and so be a half-Christian, or three-quarters of them and be a three-quarter-Christian.

Third, conversion to Christianity in fuzzy-set terms would rarely be a decisive event. Normally it would be seen as a gradual movement from outside to inside the set, based on the gradual acquisition of the necessary beliefs and practices or on a series of small decisions. There would be no point in the process where the person suddenly becomes a Christian.

Fourth, because there would be no sharp boundary between Christians and non-Christians, people could belong to two or more religions at the same time. They could participate in both Hindu and Christian services and be Hindu-Christians, or Christian-Hindus. They would not understand or accept the exclusive claims of any one religion to be the one true way.

Fifth, there would be little emphasis on evangelism. There would be the sharing and teaching of Christianity, but no call to make a clear choice between it and other religions.

Church as an Intrinsic Fuzzy Set

What would the church look like in fuzzy-set terms?

First, as in bounded-set thinking, we would formulate the creeds and practices a person needs to acquire to be regarded as part of the category *Christian*. We would assume these to be universally applicable and unchanging. But we would recognize that church members vary greatly in their affirmation of these beliefs and in their practices. Some accept a few, and are half-Christians. Others are full-Christians.

Second, we would not seek to maintain sharp boundaries for the church, such as a membership list. Moreover, we would resist efforts to draw such boundaries. We would encourage seekers and part-Christians to participate in the church in order to win them to full faith. We would, therefore, tolerate a wide diversity of beliefs and practices in the church, including non-Christian ones, with little critique. We would differentiate less sharply between ourselves and churches with other creedal positions.

Third, we would accept great diversity in the church on essential matters of faith and practice, while helping members to accept the official teachings of the church. We would distinguish between full-Christians and those still in the process of conversion. Elders or ordained clergy entrusted with defining and maintaining orthodoxy and ortho-praxy would come from those regarded as full-Christians.

There would be greater willingness to enter ecumenical discussions, not only with other Christians but with people of other religions. We would readily cooperate with others who differ from our church in matters of faith and practice.

Fourth, the church would not call for conversions, but for a growth or evolution into the essentials of Christian faith. Stress, therefore, would be on dialogue and education as the means of evangelism.

Fifth, because the set is based on shared intrinsic characteristics, the church would see itself as a body of believers sharing the same beliefs and practices. It would stress fellowship. In the end it would face the danger of worshiping its corporate self and of sliding into theological relativism.

Missions and Intrinsic Fuzzy Sets

How would thinking in terms of intrinsic fuzzy sets affect our view of missions?

First, we would not draw a sharp line between Christianity and other religions, and would recognize truth in all religions. We would, therefore, be less likely to affirm the uniqueness of Christ as the only way of salvation.

Second, we would not stress the proclamation of the gospel, or call for people to convert. We would not attack other religions as false or pagan, but encourage people to find the truth in their religions. Rather, we would dialogue with them to find a common ground for understanding and faith. We would recognize that all religions seek to meet the basic human needs, although we might affirm the superiority of Christianity as a way to God.

Third, we would encourage people of other faiths to find Christ in their own religions and cultures, and resist a radical displacement of their old beliefs with new ones. We would face dangers of relativism and nihilism.

Extrinsic Well-Formed (Centered) Sets

Another way to form sets is to use *extrinsic* rather than *intrinsic* characteristics to define membership in a category. We could group things on the basis of *how they relate to other things,* not on what they are in and of themselves.

Most kinship terms are extrinsic sets. *Sisters* are females related to one another through common parents. The *lion clan* in a tribal society is composed of people descended from a common ancestor—*Old First Lion.*

Phil Krumrei gives us an excellent example of the difference between extrinsic relational, or centered, sets and fuzzy sets.

> All the Ph.D. theses on microfilm in L. M. Graves Memorial Library bought in the year 1980 is a bounded set. The boundary is based on characteristics which all members of the set share, and there is a sharp boundary between what is and what is not part of the set.
>
> All the books from L. M. Graves Memorial Library which are checked out by student x form a centered set because it is defined by the relationship of "being checked out" to "student x" who is the center of the set. Books can change from not being checked out to being checked out, or from being checked out by student y to being checked out by student x. And there are different levels at which books can be checked out (two hour reserve, normal, due, past due).
>
> All students of Harding Graduate School of Religion who look like the author, form a fuzzy set because looking like someone means being somewhat the same in a great many separate features (height, weight, build, hair color, etc.).[14]

Extrinsic sets, like intrinsic ones, can have sharp or fuzzy boundaries. We will first examine those in the *relational well-formed* category and refer to them by way of shorthand as *centered sets*.[15]

Characteristics of Centered Sets

What are some of the characteristics of extrinsic well-formed, or centered, sets?

First, a centered set is created by defining a center or reference point and the relationship of things to that center. Things related to the center belong to the set, and those not related to the center do not.

Kinship groups, such as families, clans, and tribes, are relational categories. The Smith family consists of the John and Mary Smith who define the family, as well as their children, grandchildren, and those brought into the family through marriage or adoption; all bear some relationship to John and Mary Smith. Geographic reference points, too, are relationally defined. Forty degrees north means forty degrees north of the equator. Thirty degrees east is thirty degrees east of Greenwich, England.

---

14. Phil Krumrei, "An Analysis of Set Theory and Its Application to Christian Faith" (Unpubl. ms., Harding Graduate School of Religion, n.d.).

15. Theoretically, centered sets form only one type of intrinsic relational category. In some relational sets, members do not relate to a common center but to each other in a common field. I have chosen to discuss that type of relational set in which members are defined by their relationship to a common center, because this, I believe, fits a biblical view of the nature of Christianity and the church.

In science, many operational definitions are relational. In a box full of sand and iron filings, we define *iron* as those particles attracted by a magnet.

Another way to look at centered sets is in terms of elements moving in a field. In a centered set, members are things that move toward a common center or reference point. Nonmembers are things moving away from it.

Second, while centered sets are not created by drawing boundaries, *they do have sharp boundaries* that separate things inside the set from those outside it—between things related to or moving towards the center and those that are not.

Centered sets are well-formed, just like bounded sets. They are formed by defining the center and any relationships to it. The boundary then emerges automatically. Things related to the center naturally separate themselves from things that are not.

In centered-set thinking, greater emphasis is placed on the center and relationships than on maintaining a boundary, because there is no need to maintain the boundary in order to maintain the set.

Third, there are two variables intrinsic to centered sets. The first is membership. All members of a set are full members and share fully in its functions. There are no second-class members. The second variable is distance from the center. Some things are far from the center and others near to it, but all are moving toward it. They are, therefore, equally members of the set, even though they differ in distance from the reference point. Things near the center, but moving away from it, are not a part of the set despite their proximity to it.

Fourth, centered sets have two types of change inherent in their structure. The first has to do with entry into or exit from the set. Things headed away from the center can turn and move toward it. Or, to switch metaphors, a person may be adopted by a couple and become their child, or he or she may form a relationship with another person. We can call this change a conversion, because it is a radical transformation in the relationships of the person.

The second type of change has to do with movement toward or away from the center. Distant members can move toward the center, and those near it can slide back while still headed toward it. To switch to the relational metaphor, a person may rise in rank in the court as his or her relationship to the ruler grows in strength and intimacy or fall if that relationship grows cold. Relationships are constantly changing because they are continually renegotiated.

Hebrew Culture as a Centered Set

A strong case can be made for the idea that the Hebrew worldview of the prophets and of Christ was essentially extrinsic and well-formed in character. While the Greeks saw God in intrinsic terms, as supernatural, omnipotent, and omnipresent; the Israelites knew him in relational terms, as Creator, Judge, and Lord. They also referred to him as "the God of Abraham, Isaac, and Jacob, our forefathers." During the Exodus, the people camped around the tabernacle where God dwelt. In Palestine the people came three times a year to the "house of the Lord."

The Israelites saw themselves as people in a covenant relationship with God, and therefore as people-in-community. They were to marry insiders, not outsiders. The blessings of the faithful, and the punishments of the unfaithful were passed on to their descendants. The primary values were relational in character: justice, *shalom*, love, and mercy.

The teachings of Christ and Paul are primarily about our relationships to God and to one another. When Jesus says, "But you know him, for he lives with you and will be in you" (John 14:17b), and Paul writes, "I want to know Christ" (Phil. 3:10), they are not talking about objective knowledge of God, but about knowing him intimately as one person knows another. Paul makes it clear that our reconciliation to God through Christ is more fundamental than keeping the law. The New Testament writers must be understood within the Hebrew relational worldview, rather than the Greek structural worldview.

Christian as a Centered Set

What happens to our concept of *Christian* if we define it in centered-set terms?

First, Christians would be defined as followers of the Jesus Christ of the Bible, as those who make him the center or Lord of their lives.

Clearly, following Jesus requires some basic knowledge about him. The Jesus we follow is not the creation of our minds, but the Jesus of history as recorded in Scripture. But mental assent to the facts of biblical history does not make us Christians. We need to know Jesus personally, in the biblical sense of knowing another person (Deut. 34:10; Judg. 2:10; John 17:3). This is what Martin Buber means when he differentiates between an *I-it* and an *I-Thou* relationship.[16] The latter involves self-disclosure and listening. It is a covenant commitment to the other as a person, not a contract to join forces to accomplish a task.

Second, there would be a clear separation between Christians and non-Christians, between those who are followers of Jesus and those who are not. The emphasis, however, would be on exhorting people to follow Christ, rather than on excluding others to preserve the purity of

16. Martin Buber, *I and Thou*, 2d ed., trans. R. G. Smith (New York: Scribners, 1957).

the set. Salvation is open to everyone, no matter who they are, what they know, or what baggage they bring with them, if they become followers of Jesus Christ.

Third, there would be a recognition of variation among Christians. Some are close to Christ in their knowledge and maturity, others are immature and need to grow to attain an adequate understanding. Some might understand the suffering of Christ more deeply, and others are more deeply cognizant of his power. But all are Christian, and all are called to grow into the fullness of Christ.

Fourth, two important types of change would be recognized in centered-set thought. First there is conversion, entering or leaving the set. In centered-set terms this means to turn around and head in the opposite direction. This is the meaning of *sûb* in the Old Testament. Salvation includes both the turning away from evil and the turning to righteousness.[17] It means leaving other gods and following Jehovah (Deut. 4:10; 1 Sam. 7:3; Isa. 55:7). It also means becoming reconciled with someone who was one's enemy (Josh. 20:6; Judg. 21:14).

People may come to know Christ in many different ways. Some know him first as their Savior from sin. Others learn to know him first as the Great God, once estranged but now reconciled to them. Regarding the explosion of the church in Buganda, John V. Taylor writes,

> The message which was received and implanted, and upon which the church in Buganda was founded, was primarily news about the transcendent God. "Katonda," the unknown and scarcely heeded Creator, was proclaimed as the focus of all life, who yet lay beyond and above the closed unity of all existence. This was in itself so catastrophic a concept that, for the majority of hearers, it appeared to be the sum of the new teaching. . . . The fact that they did hear it, and did not at this stage, for the most part, hear the message of the Saviourhood of Christ or the power of the Spirit, though these were the themes that were being preached, suggests that this was the Word of God to them, and it was independent of the word of the preacher.[18]

Others meet God as their Great Physician, or Deliverer from oppression. He, in fact, is all these and much more, as all these people will learn in their lives.

There would also be differences in the nature of their conversion. Some know Christ well from childhood, and conversion is not the ac-

---

17. Walter Eichrodt, *Theology of the Old Testament*, 2 vols., trans. J. A. Baker (Philadelphia: Westminster, 1961–67), 2.466.

18. John V. Taylor, *The Growth of the Church in Buganda: An Attempt at Understanding* (London: SCM, 1958; reprint, Westport, Conn.: Greenwood Press, 1979), 252–53.

quisition of new knowledge, but the quiet turning of their lives over to him. Some are in rebellion against Christ and their conversions are dramatic. But all become followers of the same Lord.

The second change is movement towards the center, or growth in a relationship. A Christian is not a finished product the moment he or she is converted. Conversion, therefore, is a definite event followed by an ongoing process. Sanctification is not a separate activity, but the process of justification continued throughout life.

We need, therefore, to bring people to Christ, but we must also disciple them in Christian maturity—in their knowledge of Christ and their growth in Christ-likeness. Stress on growth means that every decision a Christian makes, not only the decision to become a Christian, must take Christ into account. Every decision moves a person towards Christ or away from him.

By recognizing variance in the set and the need for growth, a centered-set approach avoids the dilemma between offering cheap grace that allows new believers to become Christians but leads to a shallow church or costly grace that preserves the purity of the church but keeps them out of the kingdom.

If we define *Christian* in centered-set terms, the critical question regarding Papayya is not what he knows factually (although he obviously needs some knowledge) but whether he has made Jesus Christ his God, the center of his life. Is he willing to follow Christ to the extent he knows him, and does he desire to know Christ more fully?

Church as a Centered Set

How does centered-set thinking affect our view of the nature and ministry of the church?

First, the church would be defined by its center, the Jesus Christ of Scripture. It would be the set of the people gathered around Christ to worship, obey, and serve him. Precisely because they follow him, they form a covenant community characterized by righteousness, *koinonia*, and *shalom*.

Because membership in the church would be based on relationship to Christ, not on knowledge or behavior, we would see the church first as a place of worship—a place where we corporately declare our allegiance to Christ through praise and service. Communion with Christ would be the central focus in the life of the church. Instruction in doctrine and behavior would follow.

Because the church would be made up of the followers of the same Lord, it would be one family. Therefore, it also would be a place of fellowship. We could not exclude from the congregation those who are true disciples but who differ from us in race, class, gender, or theological view. Because membership is not at stake, differences in personality, language, culture, and worship style would be affirmed so long as these do not divide or discredit the family.

The church would focus on people and relationships of love and mutual submission, more than on programs and the maintenance of order.[19] But relationships are inherently chaotic. We would, therefore, seek consensus in the running of the church and mediate conflicts.

We would also encourage one another to use our spiritual gifts creatively, rather than demand conformity to dead tradition. In this encouragement, however, we should understand that creativity is chaotic. Eugene H. Peterson writes,

> Mess is the precondition of creativity. . . . Creativity is not neat. It is not orderly. When we are being creative we don't know what is going to happen next. . . . In any creative enterprise there are risks, mistakes, false starts, failures, frustrations, embarrassments, but out of this mess—when we stay with it long enough, enter it deeply enough—there slowly emerges love or beauty or peace. . . . We cannot nurture life of Spirit in a parishioner while holding a stopwatch. We cannot apply time management techniques to the development of souls.[20]

Second, we would make a clear distinction between Christians and non-Christians and recognize the priesthood of all believers. We would, however, recognize differences in spiritual maturity among Christians, in the degree of closeness to the center that defines the church. This means we must first carefully define that center in spiritual and theological terms. It is, first, the person of Christ and, second, our corporate theological and behavioral understanding of his teaching. These are the tenets we believe mature Christians hold and immature Christians should learn.

We would recognize the leadership of spiritually mature persons and hold them more accountable in their high office. We would be more tolerant with young believers, recognizing that they still are immature and are growing in faith and knowledge.[21] We would recognize that they struggle with different areas of growth in their lives. Some need to learn about Christ, others his healing power, his call to servanthood, his com-

19. This is reflected in many of the younger churches around the world in the terms they use for one another. They reject any title that places one member above another, such as "reverend" or "doctor." Rather, they call each other "sister" and "brother."

20. Peterson, *Under the Unpredictable Plant*, 163–64.

21. We see this attitude in the high standards Paul sets for church leaders in 1 Tim. 3:1–13, and in his gentleness with the immaturity of weak brothers and sisters in 1 Cor. 8:9–13 and Gal. 6:1.

passion for the poor, or his love of his enemies. None of them has a fully biblical worldview. This does not mean, however, that they are not Christians. They have turned to Christ and are seeking to grow in their understanding of him and obedience to his Word.

In church polity everyone's voice would be heard, but not all voices would carry equal weight. The spiritually mature, who win the trust of the people by putting aside their own self-interests and serving the group, would be the elders who formulate decisions on the basis of the discussions of the body.

The church would exercise discipline on members whose thought and behavior run contrary to Scripture as the church understands it, but the church's goal would be to restore them to faithfulness, not to ostracize them.

Because the church is not defined by its boundaries, there would be less concern about maintaining strict membership rolls. A number of stages or levels of participation might be recognized: seekers, believers, baptized members, and elders. There would also be less need to exclude those not truly Christian from fellowship in the church. Rather, the emphasis would be on pointing them to Jesus Christ.

Third, the church would stress evangelism—calling people to turn and follow Christ. This would not simply mean giving mental assent to the truths of the gospel, or feeling love for Christ. It would be surrendering one's self to Christ as Lord and becoming obedient to his leading.

The church would see discipling new believers to be as essential as conversion. Consequently, equal effort would be given to helping new believers grow and mature in their spiritual lives. Justification would not be separated in church life from sanctification.

Fourth, the primary task of the church would be to uphold Christ, so that he might draw all people to himself. Its second task would be to build a community of faith that incorporates new believers, and manifests Christ's reign on earth. Its third task would be to invite people to follow Christ, and to join the church, the outpost of his kingdom on earth.

Theology, too, would belong to the church, not to a few individuals. The church would be a hermeneutical community guided by a metatheology in interpreting and applying Scripture to its particular historical and sociocultural settings.[22] The global church also would be a theological community that helps local churches see and correct their own cultural biases.

Fifth, if secularism is the cardinal danger of bounded sets, idolatry is the greatest evil in centered sets (Exod. 20:1–5). This occurs when hu-

---

22. See chapter 5.

mans place anything but God at the center of their lives. Idols include false gods, such as the Baals and Ashtoreths (Judg. 2:11–14), Satan (Luke 4:6–8), and self (2 Tim. 3:2).

Probably the most subtle form of idolatry in the church is the worship of the leader. According to Peterson, "The pastoral paradigm that culture and denomination gave me was 'program director.' This paradigm, in America virtually unchallenged, powerfully and subtly shapes everything the pastor does and thinks into the religious programmatic. The pastor is in charge. God is marginalized."[23] What we need, he says, is a paradigm shift in which "the place occupied by the pastor is no longer perceived as a center from which bold programs are initiated and actions launched but a periphery that faces a center of clear kerygma and vast mystery."[24]

Missions and Centered Sets

How would a centered-set view of the world shape our concept of missions?

First, we would make a sharp distinction between Christianity and non-Christian religions and would affirm the uniqueness of Christ as the only Lord and Savior. Our primary aim would be to invite people to become followers of Jesus, not to prove that other religions are false. We would stress our personal testimonies of what Christ has done for us more than argue the superiority of Christianity.[25]

Second, we would be willing to baptize those who make a profession of faith and not wait until they had shown signs of Christian maturity and perfection. For example, a mission with a bounded view of Christianity baptized only a few dozen "converts" after twenty years of ministry in a West African city. Another, with a centered-set view of conversion, baptized two hundred in the first year of its ministry in the same city.

Third, we would recognize that evangelism involves both a point of decision and a process of growth. We would recognize that this is true, not only for young believers, but also young churches in new cultural contexts. Consequently, we would encourage young churches to do their own theologizing based on the Scripture, while sharing with them the theological insights gained by the church down through history and around the world.

23. Peterson, *Under the Unpredictable Plant*, 174.
24. Ibid., 176.
25. Examples of this are the round-table and ashram methods of evangelism used by E. Stanley Jones in India (*Christ at the Round Table* [Cincinnati: Abingdon, 1933]), and the use of banquet evangelism by the Eagles Communication team in Singapore.

Fourth, we would turn leadership over to national leaders from the beginning. We would not wait until they had acquired a thorough theological training, but rather choose natural leaders who demonstrate the power of God in their lives. We would then train from among them theologians and other leaders to provide long-term direction to the church.

Extrinsic Fuzzy Sets

The fourth type of set is the extrinsic fuzzy set. Less study has been given to this way of forming categories, so less will be said about it.

Characteristics of Extrinsic Fuzzy Sets

Extrinsic fuzzy sets combine the extrinsic nature of centered sets, and the fuzzy boundaries of fuzzy sets.

First, membership in a category is based, not on the intrinsic nature of a thing, but on its relationship to other things and/or a defining center.

Second, unlike centered sets, the boundary is fuzzy. The defining relationship shades from one to zero, from close to nonexistent, from being in the set to being outside the set, with no sharp point of transition between one and the other. Changing metaphors, things move towards and away from the center, and in all directions in between.

Third, there are two variables pertaining to extrinsic fuzzy sets. The first is degrees of membership. Things range from full membership to non-membership and all points between. The second is distance from the center—differences in the strength of the relationship.

Fourth, the relational aspect of extrinsic fuzzy sets views conversion as a process of changing directions, not as an instantaneous about-face.

These sets lead to relativism, because things move in many directions. Even things moving in the direction of the center may move independently from that center and pass by it on their own trajectory to some higher goal.

Extrinsic Fuzzy Sets in the World

It is harder to find examples of cultures that live on the basis of extrinsic fuzzy sets.[26] Totemic societies seem to do so. In them the bound-

---

26. A strong case could be made that Indian culture, particularly in the area of religion, is extrinsic-fuzzy in nature. This is particularly true in *bhakti*, in which all roads lead to God. In *advaita*, however, even God is *maya* or illusion, and the ultimate reality is the cosmic field out of which one emerges, not a being to which one relates. The New Age movement, too, operates in fuzzy-relational terms.

aries between humans, animals, plants, and nature are fuzzy, and be-hind all of these is one life force. Things have more or less of this force. In some of them there is no sharp boundary between members of their tribe and nonmembers. Marriages to people of neighboring communi-ties are common.

The modern parallel would be an evolutionary view of nature. All life is seen as evolving in different directions. Because everything is seen as descending from the same life source, the boundaries between objects are fuzzy. Apes are thought to be more closely related to humans than are horses or trees, but all are thought to share a common origin.

Christian as an Extrinsic Fuzzy Set

How would the category *Christian* look in fuzzy-relational terms?

First, Christians would be those related to Christ in one way or an-other. For some people he would be their Lord, for some a guru show-ing them the way, for some a great philosopher teaching them some truth, and for some a good man to be emulated.

Second, there would be no sharp dividing line between Christians and non-Christians. Rather, there would be degrees of being *Christian*. Some would be faithful disciples of Christ, others casual followers, oth-ers interested in his teachings, and others indifferent or opposed to him.

Third, two variables in the types of change would be noted. One would be direction of movement. Things can move in any direction, and conversion to Christ would be seen as a series of partial turns toward Christ. People might make Christ the Lord of some areas of their lives and not other areas. There need be no "point of conversion," of turning around and going in a new direction. The other variable would be the degree of closeness to Christ.

Church as an Extrinsic Fuzzy Set

What would the church be like in fuzzy-relational terms?

First, the church would be composed of people who have some com-mitment or relationship to Christ, ranging from general interest to radi-cal commitment The church would seek to strengthen that dedication to Christ.

Second, the church would have no clear boundary. It would be a loose collection of people with varying degrees of commitment to Christ and to one another. All would be welcome to join the church and its activities, with little emphasis on their agreement with the beliefs of the church.

Third, the church would recognize degrees in becoming Christian and in growing in maturity. There would be those who know much about Christ, but become only nominally committed to him and those who know little about him but are totally committed disciples.

Conversion would be seen as a series of decisions, as a process of turning around and moving toward Christ. Many in the church would be seen as partly converted and in need of further conversion. Sanctification or maturation, too, would be seen as a process in which all persons should be involved.

Missions and Extrinsic Fuzzy Sets

Finally, what would the Christian mission look like from this type of perspective?

First, seekers and new converts would immediately be baptized and incorporated into the activities of the church, including the Lord's Supper. There would be a stress on discipling them and entrusting positions of leadership to them.

Second, no sharp distinction would be made between Christianity and other religions. The uniqueness of Christ as the only way to salvation would not be stressed. In the extreme this view would affirm that all religions lead to God.

There would, therefore, be little emphasis on evangelism and conversion. Rather, the emphasis would be on helping each person to find the way that best leads him or her to God and a satisfying faith.

Theological Critique and Application to Missions

An understanding of set theory helps us understand how our cultures shape the way we interpret Scripture, and carry out mission. We need to move beyond this phenomenological analysis, however, to a biblical critique of set formation. What is reality according to divine revelation?

The church has at points in its history contextualized its theology and mission in each of these worldviews. People have been saved and churches built. But these worldviews do not all equally communicate the essential message of the gospel. In the long run, sub-Christian worldviews can distort our theology, skew our lives of faith, and weaken our mission to the lost.

Sets and Conversion

Let us return to our original question. What do we mean when we say Papayya, a nonliterate peasant, has become a Christian?

In answer to this, it is clear that we must first clarify how we create categories such as *Christian*—whether we are thinking in terms of bounded, fuzzy, centered, or fuzzy-relational sets. If we do not do so, we will often talk past each other, and our disagreements will arise out of different subconscious presuppositions rather than different theologies.

The worldview of Scripture, I believe, is based primarily on a centered-set approach to reality. Relationships are at the heart of its message, our relationship to God and our relationships, therefore, to one another. This is the essential message that God so loved the world that he gave his only Son to redeem it. This is the message of Paul in Galatians when he argues that the heart of Christianity is our relationship to God, not the keeping of the law. The Bible is primarily a book about the history of relationships, not a treatise on the intrinsic nature and operations of reality.

Furthermore, Scripture affirms clear boundaries at several key points. Christ is declared to be the only way to God. In the end people will either be saved or lost, and sinners are called to turn radically away from their evil ways to righteousness and love. There is no *both-and* approach to these and other essential matters in the Bible.

A centered-set approach to life, however, raises some important questions. First, how do we know when people are truly Christians? God looks at human hearts, and knows who are his. We, because of our finiteness, can only look at external criteria—what people say and do. Consequently, to us conversion often looks more like a process than a point, and the church more like a fuzzy body made up of people with different degrees of commitment to Christ. The problem here is not the true nature of spiritual realities, but the limits of our human perception. Through revelation we do see reality as God sees it, but only through a glass darkly. We do not yet see fully as he does.

Second, how can we organize a church on centered-set principles? This is a problem particularly for those of us from the West for whom institutional order and planning are so important.[27] It is clear that we need to rearrange our priorities. We must make people more important than programs, give relationships priority over order and cleanliness, and spend more time in prayer than in planning. In this we can learn much from the churches in relationally oriented societies.

Sets and Cross-Cultural Confusion

An understanding of sets can help us understand some of the confusion that arises in intercultural relationships when people with bounded-set thinking meet those with fuzzy- or relational-set thinking.

27. It is interesting to note that the independent church movements in India, such as that of Bhakt Singh, organize themselves in terms of centered sets. They have several levels of loosely defined membership in the church and give leadership to a few elders at the center.

One example of this was the encounter of an American mission executive with the leaders of an Indian church. The executive wanted to know the exact number of members in the churches. When the Indian leaders gave him only an approximate figure, the executive wanted to know why they didn't keep church membership lists. He urged them to introduce church membership roles to make clear who belonged to the churches and who did not. The leaders suggested that this was not appropriate in Indian villages where people range from those casually interested, to seekers, believers, baptized members, and elders and leaders. To draw too sharp a line, they suggested, would drive people away. This upset the North American, who urged them to draw a sharp line between people who are truly Christians, and those who are not.

The differences between the mission executive and the Indian leaders lay, in part, in the ways they created their cognitive categories. The executive, being American, wanted sharply defined categories. The Indians thought more in terms of fuzzy sets.

A similar problem surfaced when I noticed that Hindus often give offerings in the church, or ask Christ to heal their child. The clear lines between Hindu and Christian seemed to be blurred. The same occurs between Hinduism and Islam. Hindu villagers commonly venerate Muslim saints and make offerings to Allah.

Another example has to do with the organization of Indian village churches. In mission-controlled churches, democratic elections were introduced to select the leaders. Theoretically only members vote. In practice, however, Christian candidates for office often recruit their Hindu relatives and friends to come to church to vote for them. Because the church did not want to draw a sharp line between members and nonmembers, the church elections became community affairs with Hindus joining with Christians to elect their candidates.

Churches that have developed their own indigenous church structures do so, not on the basis of democratic voting, but on informal councils of elders. These are not formally elected leaders but wise old Christians who have earned the respect of the others for their impartial and balanced judgments.

When issues arise, several elders are called to pass judgment. Anyone can attend the session, and all are encouraged to voice their opinions. In the end the elders form a judgment that articulates the consensus of the people and seeks the well-being of the community as a whole. The decision is enforced by social pressure. In the extreme, members of the church cease to associate or fellowship with the offender until he or she repents and is reconciled to the body.

For the most part, where democratic procedures have been introduced to the rural churches in India, political infighting and little growth have resulted. Where indigenous forms of church polity have emerged, the churches function more smoothly and grow more rapidly. Clearly, North American bounded-set thinking does not work well in societies that think in terms of other sets.

Clearly, we must study our own hidden worldview to see how it biases our understanding of Scripture. By bringing our biases to light, we are freed from their subtle control over our thoughts. We then can read Scripture with new eyes and let it speak to us in new ways. We can begin to reshape our worldview and make it more biblical.

7

Order, Creativity, and
the Mission Task

Paul Hiebert, Cynthia Strong, and David Strong

"If we understood that it takes us a long time to establish credibility in a new culture, and that this credibility has to be gained in terms of what the people think, not in terms of what we think, the cause of missions would be greatly advanced." On the surface this plaintive cry of a new missionary has to do with personalities. Some missionaries seem to have a greater sensitivity to cultural differences, a greater patience for learning from others, and a greater willingness to subordinate personal goals to mission and national church objectives—traits essential to establishing and maintaining cross-cultural relationships. At a deeper level, however, credibility relates to the worldviews of the missionaries and the people they serve.

As missionaries, we take with us not only our cultural beliefs and practices but also the fundamental assumptions on which these are built. The self-evident truths about the nature of things comprise our worldview. We take them for granted and regard people who question them, not as wrong, but as crazy, primitive, or subversive.

It is hard for us to see our own worldview, because, like glasses, it is what we look *with*, not what we look *at*. We often see best after we live deeply in another culture—after we put on other glasses and then look back on our own cultural presuppositions.

At the core of our worldviews are our values—our definitions of what is true and what is false, what is appropriate and what is not, and what is right and what is wrong. Ultimately our values have to do with our allegiances, with our "gods."

In this essay, we want to examine one of our deepest Western values, that of "order," to see how it affects our credibility in other societies.

Order

All societies establish order to survive. They organize their conceptual worlds by creating cognitive categories, systems of logic, and basic beliefs. They order their social worlds by defining interpersonal relationships, assigning authority, and prescribing proper ways to behave.

Order in Western Cultures

We in the West place a very high value on order, and define it primarily in terms of the inherent structure of things. We lay streets out on grids, mark the edges by curbs, and indicate lanes by lines. We mow, weed, and edge our lawns to keep them neat and uniform. We plant flowers in rows, and use fences and borders to mark boundaries between lots.

Inside our homes we put knives, forks, and spoons into separate bins, place pans on one shelf and dishware on another, and sort our laundry. We use moldings to separate walls from floors, and borders to frame doors and windows. We carefully scrape paint off the window glass. We use trim to cover seams on wall panels, hems to mark the edges of cloth, and ties to cover cracks down the front of dress shirts.

We structure time to create order. We expect meetings to begin and end "on time." We see punctuality, efficiency, and organization as unquestionably good.

We use long-range planning, appointments, calendars, schedules, programs, flow charts, punch clocks, and watches to regulate our lives. We buy tickets in April to fly from Chicago to London on September 29, leaving at 4:33 P.M., and we are angry if the plane is an hour late. We even treat relationships as subordinate to time—we make ten-minute appointments, and plan "quality time" with our families!

Our view of cleanliness is tied as much to our sense of structural order as it is to sanitation. Dirt is anything out of place, anything that upsets our sharp categories. Soil in the house is filth; flowers in the lawn are weeds; books on the floor are clutter; and clothes on the floor are a mess. We abhor rings around collars or tubs, spots on crystal, stains on clothing, specks on windows, blotches on faces, blemishes in china, and streaks in paint.

Our sense of beauty, too, is linked to structural order—to symmetry, balance, and harmony. In our yards we arrange flowers and plants by category to create a sense of beauty. We remove or hide litter, trash, and junk that threaten our sense of order. In our offices we want our desks neat and clean.

Our sense of law is a part of our view of order. We believe that impersonal mechanical laws govern the material world. Only God can breach these laws, and when he does so it is a miracle. We believe that the human societies are based on law, not on love, courtesy, and generosity. As Christians we define sin largely in terms of breaking the rules, and justice as punishing violators. We expect transgressors to feel guilty and want them to pay for their misdeeds.

Finally, we associate order with good and chaos with evil. People who are orderly, clean, organized, and law abiding are good people. Those who are unkempt, disorderly, and late are not only undesirable, but in some fundamental sense bad. For many of us chaos—the breakdown of structural order—is the greatest evil we fear.

Order and the Western Worldview

This view of order is based on our Western concern with the intrinsic structure of things, and with our desire for dominance.[1] We want to know how things are made, how they fit together, and how they function so that we can control them.

We believe that life and events are highly predictable, and if we know how things work, we can rule nature, engineer our societies, make things happen, and be in charge of our lives. We get upset when things go wrong, rather than accepting the unexpected as a normal part of life. We are quick to place blame and correct faults. We assume that if we do things right we will succeed, whether this be running a company, building a high rise, or planting a church. Dominance of nature, and of one another, has been very much a part of our Western view of order.

---

1. This view of order originates in Greek thought. One of its roots is the Greek concern with the intrinsic structure of reality discussed in E. J. Dijksterhuis, *The Mechanization of the World Picture: Pythagoras to Newton*, trans. C. Dikshoorn (Princeton, N.J.: Princeton University Press, 1986). A second root is a mechanistic view of nature. The consequences of this on Western thought are traced by Peter L. Berger, Brigitte Berger, and Hansfried Kellner in *The Homeless Mind: Modernization and Consciousness* (New York: Random House, 1973) and by Jacques Ellul in *The Technological Society* (New York: Random House, 1964). A third root is the Greek hierarchical view of the world order, analyzed by Arthur Lovejoy in *The Great Chain of Being: A Study of the History of an Idea* (Cambridge, Mass.: Harvard University Press, 1936).

With control comes a stress on tasks and performance, rather than on people and relationships. We place a high value on planning, efficiency, productivity, and profit. Our leaders are movers-and-shakers who get things done. As Jacques Ellul points out, our emphasis on tasks leads inevitably to a focus on techniques—on how to do things, rather than on goals.[2]

This concept of structural order is also rooted in our belief in hierarchy.[3] C. S. Lewis notes, "According to this conception, degrees of value are objectively present in the universe. Everything except God has some natural superior; everything except unformed matter has some natural inferior."[4] Scientists classify plants and animals according to their complexity. Business leaders rank workers on organizational charts that delineate lines of authority. Workers are paid different salaries, based on some definition of their worth. The government and the military enforce chains of command. Universities rank professors, and hospitals classify doctors. Class and ethnic hierarchies are accepted as normal elements of social organization. We fear that if no one is in control, order will break down.

Order and the Church

Our emphasis on order has profoundly influenced our Christian lives. In many churches, Sunday worship services are highly ordered. Silence, bulletins, robes, badges, and set times make sure that the worship proceeds smoothly. Sanctuaries are kept clean and beautiful, parking lots are paved and striped, and signs are posted to prevent confusion. We want things to be done decently and in order, and order takes priority over relationships.

As Christians, we frequently equate order and cleanliness with godliness and righteousness, and chaos with evil. We unconsciously think of sinners as disheveled, dirty, and poor, and associate conversion with taking baths, getting a haircut, dressing nicely, and living orderly lives. Noisy children, tardiness, soiled rugs, and dirty kitchens are quickly dealt with in church.

Western churches are also task-oriented. Westerners value activity and success. Planning, constitutions, bylaws, committees, budgets, and minutes comprise as much a part of church life as worship services. To thrive, a church must have programs: Sunday school, seniors' and singles' classes, a youth program, retreats, and a food distribution center. Even outreach is seen as one of the programs of the church.

2. Ellul, *Technological Society*.
3. Lovejoy, *Great Chain of Being*.
4. C. S. Lewis, *A Preface to Paradise Lost* (London: Oxford University Press, 1960), 73.

Relationships

In addition to order, societies need relationships. Parents and children work together in families for their common good. People organize groups to build houses, till fields, and protect themselves from danger. They organize communities and institutions such as businesses and schools to satisfy their corporate needs. Without relationships societies collapse.

Relationships in Traditional Cultures

In most tribal and peasant societies, life revolves around relationships. Friends and relatives gather unannounced to enjoy one another's company, not waiting for holidays or a special invitation. Husbands bring friends home unexpectedly at meal time, and hospitality is freely extended to strangers. Children are considered a great blessing and mingle freely with the adults.

To Westerners enculturated to structural order, such relational living often appears chaotic and unproductive. But true relationships are inherently chaotic. Babies introduce mess and disorder into family life. Friends keep us from work we might do. Eugene H. Peterson notes,

> Lovers quarrel, hurt and get hurt, misunderstand and are misunderstood in their painstaking work of creating a marriage: apologize and explain, listen and wait, rush forward and pull back, desire and sacrifice as love receives its slow incarnation in flesh and spirit.[5]

In traditional societies, relationships take precedence over structural order. Work must wait when relatives and friends arrive unexpectedly. Marriages are more than personal covenants between two persons; they are alliances between kinship groups that take years to negotiate. Caring for children and the aged is accepted as normal family life, and not as intrusions on one's personal plans.

In contrast with the West, relationships in traditional societies are often ends in themselves, and not means to an end. People do work together to complete common tasks, but they often gather informally to gossip, discuss, visit, and enjoy one another's company. In such gatherings there is little hierarchy. Everyone's voice must be heard and his or her dignity preserved.

Even in organized activities, members of the group desire consensus. Maintaining social harmony is the chief value, and breaking the peace

---

5. Eugene H. Peterson, *Under the Unpredictable Plant: An Exploration in Vocational Holiness* (Grand Rapids: Eerdmans, 1992), 164.

is the cardinal sin. Chiefs rarely make a decision without soliciting the opinions of the people, and leadership is the art of consensus formation and persuasion. Punishments are designed to enable repentant culprits to save face and be restored to fellowship in the community, rather than to satisfy the demands of some impersonal law.

Because relationships are unpredictable, planning is always tentative. Decisions must be negotiated with others and are subject to unexpected change. A distant relative may appear just as one leaves for church, or a neighbor may decide at the last minute not to join others on a trip. To change an agreement because the situation changes is not only acceptable, it is wise. Agreements in these societies are not contracts that a person must carry out no matter what, but desires people hope to fulfill.

Relationships and Traditional Worldviews

Just as the value of order profoundly affects Western worldviews, the value of relationships shapes many traditional societies. Members of the society find meaning in life, not in accomplishments, but in social connections. A person with no relatives and friends is a nobody and soon forgotten. A person with many relatives, friends, and descendants will long be remembered and honored. Consequently, the people give priority to cultivating relationships over completing tasks.

Notions of beauty in these societies are linked to relationships, rather than to physical appearances. Beautiful people are generous people. They show hospitality to strangers and share their goods with others.

Wisdom, too, has to do with relationships. Wise people are those who can untangle the knots in human relationships. They are impartial in dealing with problems that threaten the peace of the community and are able to achieve agreement and reconcile adversaries.

Relationships also define good and evil. To live in peace with others is the greatest good. To offend another brings shame. The greatest evil is to be alienated and alone. Chaos, on the other hand, is not necessarily evil. Because true relationships are not predictable, chaos is the unformed potential out of which order can be created.[6]

Relationships and the Church

Churches oriented around relationships are different from those focusing on order. Meeting times are not governed by impersonal clocks

---

6. It changes our perspective, for example, if we walk into our child's disorganized room and say, "Here is a great potential for creating order," rather than, "This room is dirty and bad. Clean it up!"

but by human exigencies. Services begin when the people can gather and end when the activity is over, sometimes the next day. Adults feel free to come and go, and children are welcome as long as they do not disturb the others too much. Time is prioritized according to personal and social relationships rather than by task.

Church polity, too, is different. Many denominational churches have inherited constitutions, voting, and *Robert's Rules of Order* from Western missionaries but find these unsuited to their cultures. The result is often confusion. On the surface, modern organizational principles are practiced; but beneath the surface, old relationally based practices continue to thrive.

Independent churches usually adopt the relational practices of their societies. They often choose elders based on public trust, not elections. Ideal leaders are regarded as those who seek the consensus and unity of their congregations. Much time is spent in fellowship and in building relationships in the church.

Conflicting Worldviews and the Missionary Task

All societies need order. All societies need relationships. How do order and relationships fit together? Which is more fundamental?

Order and Relationships

As we have seen, the West places a higher priority on order. We believe that relationships can be built only after order is established. Walter Wink points out that this obsession with order and fear of chaos is the basic plot for most westerns, mysteries, and detective stories.[7] Good must triumph over evil before it can establish a just order, but it may use evil means in the battle to gain control. The detective can lie and enter a house without a warrant, because he is trying to restore a good order. The sheriff can shoot the villain without a trial if he does so in self-defense. Gangsters threaten the world with chaos until Superman, Superwoman, Spiderman, Super Chicken, Underdog, or Mighty Mouse defeat them and restore order. The message is clear—it is all right to do evil in order to restore order, because order must be established *before* righteousness can be instituted.

This priority on order influences us in the church. We meet long-lost friends at Sunday morning service but don't spontaneously invite them for lunch because we remember that the house is in disarray. So we settle for a restaurant, clearly second best from a relational point of view.

7. Walter Wink, *Engaging the Powers: Discernment and Resistance in a World of Domination* (Minneapolis: Fortress, 1992).

We do not let our immigrant neighbors use our church halls because the facilities will get dirty.[8]

Our fear of chaos has also stifled creativity in the church. Peterson writes,

> Creativity is not neat. It is not orderly. When we are being creative we don't know what is going to happen next. When we are being creative a great deal of what we do is wrong. When we are being creative we are not efficient. . . . [T]he moment tidiness and conduct become the dominant values, creativity is, if not abolished, at least severely inhibited. For then the souls of men and women come to be viewed as energies to manage, objects to control.[9]

Our emphasis on order also shapes our missionary work. We work hard to teach people to be on time; to construct straight walls; to paint without slopping on the windows and floor; to keep buildings clean; to plan for future activities; to keep accurate minutes and straight accounts; to stand in line; to maintain sharp borders on paths and roads; and to keep books, medicines, and other supplies in order on shelves. National leaders have been refused the right to live in missionary homes for fear that they will get the houses dirty or bring chickens inside.

Our fear of chaos has been a great hindrance to indigenization. We are afraid hospitals will become dirty, schools unorganized, churches disorderly, accounts irregular, and the order of the church chaotic if things are controlled by the people. Underlying this is often the hidden fear that we will lose control of the work. Our distrust of the people destroys our credibility among them.

Christians in other lands are often confused by the Western obsession with order and lack of relational skills. Westerners rarely open our homes spontaneously to visitors. We are more interested in keeping our possessions than sharing them. We are more concerned with following *Robert's Rules of Order* than with achieving consensus. We are too busy doing things to take time just to sit and visit.

For Christians in many non-Western societies, the central issue in Christianity is not order but right relationships. The gospel to them is good news because it speaks of *shalom*—of human dignity, equality, justice, love, peace, and concern for the lost and the marginalized.

---

8. One church in California decided to open its dining hall and sanctuary to immigrant communities around it. To solve the problem of order and the wear on facilities caused by chaos, the church included in its mission budget, money to install new rugs throughout the church each year.

9. Peterson, *Under the Unpredictable Plant*, 162–65.

Building Credibility

How can missionaries build credibility in other societies? First, we need to understand both the people we serve and ourselves. *We need to look below the surface-level cultural differences to the deep worldview assumptions we bring with us.* To us, these assumptions are so self-evident that we assume everyone thinks the way we do. We do not recognize that they are a fundamental part of the cultural baggage we bring with us.

Second, we must build credibility in terms of what the people think, not in terms of what we think. In many societies this means Western missionaries must let go of the need for high order and control, and be willing to live with ambiguity and unpredictability. We must learn to be flexible, to change our plans on short notice. We must overcome our phobia for dirt and disorder. *We need to see chaos, not as evil, but as the unformed potential out of which truly human relationships and creative activities can be shaped.*

Giving up control and living with ambiguity is particularly important for the indigenization of the church. So long as we demand high order and want control, we will resist turning responsibilities over to national leaders. *We must overcome the fear that the church is no longer ours—in fact, it never was.*

Third, we need to focus on building people, rather than programs. This means we must learn the personal skills of listening, sharing, encouraging, mediating, and reconciling. We must avoid the temptation to come with our programs and keep control. *We must empower young leaders and permit them the greatest privilege we allow ourselves—the right to make mistakes and to learn from them.*

This shift to relational thinking calls for a radical change in our worldview. We in the West are well trained to do jobs. We are not skilled in building relationships. Yet the fruit of the Spirit are expressed in relationships, and relationships are at the heart of all lasting evangelism.[10]

Finally, we from the West must critique our own modern worldviews and learn from our non-Western churches the central place of relationships in Scripture. We tend to read the Bible through the lens of order.[11] We see salvation primarily as freedom from the punishment of the law, rather than reconciliation with God. We stress the unchanging essence

10. In an insightful article, Mortimer Arias shows us the importance of hospitality as the chief means of evangelism in the Old Testament ("Centripetal Mission or Evangelism by Hospitality," *Missiology: An International Review* 10 [January 1982]: 69–81). The people of Israel were to welcome and incorporate widows, orphans, strangers, and visitors. The Court of the Gentiles in the temple was the court of evangelism, where outsiders could see God's people in worship and decide to join them.

11. This creates problems for us, for example, in interpreting Gen. 1:2. How could God create a world that was formless and chaotic? We equate these with evil, not potential.

of God, rather than his relational characteristics. The gospel is about re-lationships, not programs—about relationship with God, one another as Christians, and a lost world.

We in the West have been shaped to too great an extent by the mech-anistic worldview that places priority on production and success, mea-sured in programmatic terms. Our mission is to win people to Christ and to incorporate them into the community of saints, a community of *shalom*. Spirituality is measured not in achievements, but in relation-ships. Peterson writes, "We cannot nurture the life of Spirit in a parish-ioner [or young church] while holding a stopwatch. We cannot apply time management techniques to the development of souls."[12] Unfortu-nately, our churches in the West often function more like corporations and clubs than like covenant communities.

We do need order to carry out the mission of the church, but order should never take priority over relationships. Only when we learn this lesson will we build credibility in the eyes of the people we serve.

12. Peterson, *Under the Unpredictable Plant,* 164.

8

The Bicultural Bridge

How does the gospel move from one culture to another? In a day of mass media and modern technology we are tempted to think of radio, television, and the printed page as the chief means of communication. Rather, communication of the gospel across the chasms of cultural differences rests upon the quality of interpersonal relationships between human beings—between missionaries and the people they serve. This relationship between people of one culture and those of another culture is the *bicultural bridge*.

The Biculture

Communication across the bicultural bridge takes place within the *biculture:* a new culture that arises in the interaction of people from two different cultural backgrounds (see fig. 8.1). When missionaries leave their own native culture to enter a new society, they take with them their cultural maps. They have ideas of what is food and how to cook it, who should raise the children, and what values should be taught to them, how to worship properly, and a great many other things. No matter how hard they try, they cannot "go native." The culture of their childhood can never be fully erased. But for missionaries to totally import their culture is impossible, even if they try. They are influenced by the culture they enter—their second culture.

Local people who interact with the missionaries also become part of the biculture. They have their own ideas about food, child-rearing, val-

This chapter first appeared in *Mission Focus* 10.1 (March 1982): 106–18 . Used by permission.

Figure 8.1

The Bicultural Bridge

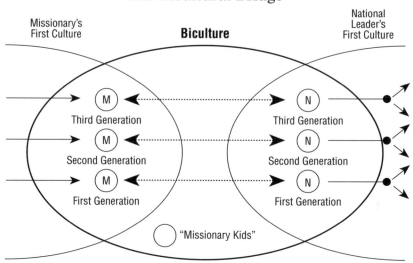

ues, and worship. Even though they may not leave their country, they are exposed to new ideas and beliefs.

In order to relate to each other, missionaries and nationals must create new patterns of living, working, playing, and worshiping—a new culture. Much of the effort of a bicultural community, in fact, is spent in defining what that culture is:

What types of clothes should be worn?

Should missionaries and nationals each wear their own type of dress?

Should they both wear Western clothes or the clothes of the local culture?

What type of food should they eat?

What type of house should they build?

Should missionaries have cars, and, if so, should national leaders also have them?

Where should the children of the two groups go to school and in what medium of instruction?

How should missionaries and nationals relate to each other?

These and a thousand other questions must be answered in order to build a stable biculture that enables foreigners and nationals to communicate and work together.

While the biculture may borrow from the different cultures of its participants, it is more than the sum or synthesis of those cultures. New cultural patterns often emerge out of the interaction. In the end, if communication is to take place between people of different cultures, a satisfactory biculture must be worked out in which both sides find a measure of mutual understanding and satisfaction. Without this, it will be difficult for the gospel to cross the bicultural bridge.

The bicultural bridge is only one stage in the communication of the gospel from one culture to another. The missionary has been trained by parents, pastors, and teachers before going to a new society. Upon arrival, he or she generally works most closely with national Christian leaders who are part of the same biculture. They in turn communicate the gospel to other people throughout the land. The greatest share of village evangelism and church planting has been done by national workers.

Our concern here is with relationships between missionaries and national church members, for it is here that the gospel and church are translated into a new culture. Whether people trust the gospel and whether they see the church as foreign or indigenous to their culture depends to a great extent upon the nature and quality of relationships of this bicultural bridge.

Generationalism in the Biculture

As in other cultures, generational differences emerge within the biculture. There are newcomers—the missionaries and nationals who have recently entered the biculture. And there are old-timers—those who have spent much of their lives in the biculture.

First-Generation Missionaries

First-term missionaries belong to the first generation of the biculture. For the most part they are idealistic. They have taken an assignment because they have a great vision for the work and tremendous zeal. The goals they set for themselves are high—at times unrealistic. They will evangelize all of India in five years, or, if not all of India, at least Andhra Pradesh. Or they will build a large hospital or Bible school. Moreover, they are ready to sacrifice everything in order to complete their mission. They have little time for family or relaxation.

First-termers are often called "plungers" because of their willingness to identify more closely with the national culture than do many of the old-timers. If they are encouraged in this identification they can be bonded to the local culture and people. However, if they are acculturated into the missionary culture they will acquire the belief that it is impossible to fully identify with the national people.

The success or failure of first-termers depends to a considerable extent upon their place within the structure of the biculture. Placed at the top of a new venture, such as opening a new field, starting a new hospital, or building a new Bible school, they can be a tremendous success. They begin with nothing; when they leave, there is a church or an institution. No precedents hinder them, and they have the power to build a program according to their own plans. For example, when the first missionary doctor moves to an area, there is often only an empty field. When he or she leaves, there is usually a hospital, complete with operating rooms, admissions offices, and wards. First-termers placed at the top of new ventures also can be tremendous failures. They have no institutional constraints and often no peers to check their bad decisions. They set a direction for new programs that is difficult to change later.

When first-generation missionaries are placed at the top of old, established programs they have a potential for moderate success. They have the power to institute their own ideas, but they inherit a legacy from the past. When they try to change established procedures, they will be reminded, "That is not the way the founder did it," or "That is the way we have always done it." Later leaders of the program can never measure up to the remembered image of the founder whose picture hangs on the wall in the central hall. What the founder established as an ad hoc procedure, by the second generation becomes law and by the third becomes a sacred tradition. But if first-termers can be only moderately successful in initiating their programs, they can be only moderate failures. They are guarded from making great mistakes by the institution, which has begun to acquire a life of its own. An institution has a way of staying alive and of tempering the failures of its leaders. Too many people have vested interests in the institution to let it die easily.

First-generation missionaries placed at the bottom of old programs have little possibility for success or failure. They have little power to initiate change; this, combined with their vision and zeal, generally leads to frustration. A special type of person is needed to serve in such a position and to do so with a measure of joy.

One of the primary characteristics of missionaries' first terms is culture shock. Often for the first time, the newcomers have to come to terms with another culture—to learn its ways and to respect, even love, its people and their customs. The types of attitudes and relationships worked out during the first term will generally characterize the missionaries' ministries for the rest of their lives.

Second-Generation Missionaries

Second-generation missionaries are those who are experienced in the work they are doing. Often they are on their second, third, or fourth term of service.

Second-generation missionaries share certain characteristics. First, they tend to be more realistic in their assessment of their work. They have come to grips with the fact that they cannot evangelize all of Japan—or even Osaka—in five years. They realize that it is worth their life to build up a Bible school and to train a number of good leaders or to plant four or five strong churches.

They are more realistic, too, about their own lifestyles. They become increasingly aware that they have only one life to live. If they are going to have time with their children they will have to take it now, before the children are grown. If they are to have rest and relaxation, they must do so at the expense of some other activities. They are no less committed to the task. In fact, their commitment has become a long-term one. But they are no longer willing to pay any price to attend meetings, classes, and wards. They begin to realize that their children and they themselves are part of the greater work of God.

The second-generation missionaries, together with their experienced national coworkers, do the greatest share of the mission work. They know the language and the local customs. Consequently, they are able to give themselves to the long, hard labor required to plant the church.

One of the important tasks of experienced missionaries is to help first-termers adjust to the field. Even when this task is turned over to the church, experienced missionaries have an important pastoral role in helping the new missionaries to deal with culture shock.

Third-Generation Missionaries

Third-generation missionaries are sometimes referred to as the old-timers. In the study by John and Ruth Useem and John Donoghue in which the concept of bicultural generationalism was first presented, the old-timers were those who served abroad during the colonial era.[1] Many of them, with some notable exceptions, accepted notions of Western superiority and colonial rule. They assumed that the missionary should be in charge of the work and live like foreigners, with their compounds and bungalows. We are not to judge them, for they, like us, were people of their times. Many of them sacrificed much more than do

1. John Useem, Ruth Useem, and John Donoghue, "Men in the Middle of the Third Culture: The Rites of American and Non-Western People in Cross-Cultural Administration," *Human Organization* 22 (Fall 1963): 169–79.

modern-day missionaries. Missionaries then served seven or more years before going on furlough. Most of them buried spouses and children where they served, and many could not take vacations in the summer hill stations because the journeys by cart or boat were too difficult and long.

But times have changed. No longer do we live in a world in which colonial rule and foreign superiority are accepted. Today we need missionaries who identify with the people and their aspirations. Consequently, we find a generation gap between those who look back with nostalgia to the colonial era when missions played a central role in the life of the church and those who see the task of missions to be one of partnership in service with an autonomous church.

Generationalism among National Leaders

Generationalism is also evident among the national leaders in the biculture. The young often have a great vision and zeal for the work. In our day of increasing nationalism, this is often linked to strong convictions that the national church should take responsibility for its own affairs. Like their missionary counterparts they are usually willing to pay almost any price for the sake of the work. In many cases they have to sacrifice the support of families and kinsfolk who may have planned more traditional careers for them. First-generation leaders given responsibility for important tasks can be great successes—and great failures. Placed in a position of little authority and not allowed to lead, some of the best of them leave to join other (often nativistic) churches or to start movements of their own. Too often we have lost our best young men and women because we have not entrusted them with responsibility.

Second-generation national leaders are those who have committed themselves to long-term work in the church or mission. Paired with experienced missionaries, they carry out the major share of the work.

Third-generation national leaders are those who grew up during the colonial era. For many of them the rapid movement toward nationalism is frightening and unsettling. They look back with nostalgia to the day when the mission was in charge and there was a great deal of security.

Stress Points in the Biculture

The biculture is a culture in the making. It has little time-depth and is created by people from different cultures who have little or no idea of what the new culture should be like. It is not surprising, then, to find points at which stress appears. Furthermore, stress likely will remain part of the biculture for some time because few areas of the world have changed so rapidly as have international relationships. The shift from colonialism to nationalism—and now to internationalism—and the change in world powers as one nation and then another rises and falls in world power and prestige, influence the biculture greatly.

The Creation of the Biculture

One area of stress has to do with the creation of the biculture itself. What shape should it take? What should be borrowed from each of its parent cultures? Should missionaries and nationals relate to one another as parents and children, as contractual partners, as undifferentiated equals, or as something else? If national leaders in developing countries receive the same salaries as do missionaries, will they not be alienated from their people and many be attracted to the ministry by the affluent lifestyle? On the other hand, should there be differences that speak of cultural distance and segregation?

Today there is considerable emphasis on the missionaries' identification with the culture to which they go. To the extent possible, missionaries should live within the cultural frameworks of the people to whom they go, for in doing so they are able to bring the gospel most of the way across the bicultural bridge. The distance between cultures is often great, and someone must bring the gospel from one culture to another. The further missionaries bring the gospel to a new culture, the more effective will be its acceptance and the less distance the national leaders will have to carry it to make it indigenous.

Early attempts at identification often focus on visible cultural practices regarding food, houses, clothes, cars, and lifestyle. Identification on this level is important, although we must recognize the limits of human adaptability. Some people must retain more ties to their cultural past than do others, in order to maintain psychological balance and effective ministry.

But identification on the level of practices can hide inner feelings of distance. On the level of roles, missionaries may feel that they should not work under the direction of nationals. On the level of attitudes they may be convinced of the superiority of their culture or race, and will not try to identify fully with the people.

Search for Identity

One of the big questions facing members of the biculture has to do with their cultural identity. Personal identity is tied to identification with a society and culture. Bicultural people belong to two sociocultural worlds.

Missionaries are often unaware of the profound changes that take place within them. They think of themselves as Americans or Canadians living abroad for a time. When they return to their first cultures, they expect to assimilate back into the culture with a minimum of adjustment. Often, however, they experience severe culture shock. To the extent they adapt successfully to the biculture, they experience a greater reverse culture shock on their return home.

Missionaries are shocked to find their relationships with relatives and friends strained and distant. They expect these folk to be excited to hear about their many experiences, but after an hour or two, conversation drifts off to local affairs—to local politics, church matters, or family issues. The people at home have no frame of reference within which to fit these tales from abroad. Their world is their town and state or province. Missionaries have lost touch with local matters and have little to say.

The gap often is accentuated by the altered worldview of the missionaries. They return with a bicultural and worldview perspective that no longer identifies the home culture and nation as "right," treating all others as less civilized. When missionaries criticize their first cultures, they arouse the suspicions of relatives and friends. Missionaries often find they are no longer close to relatives and friends. Their closest friends are among other bicultural people—people who have lived abroad. It does not matter much which other countries bicultural people have been in; a sense of mutual understanding, a common bicultural worldview, draws these people together.

National leaders, too, face a cultural identity crisis. In their relationships with missionaries they adopt foreign ideas and practices. Some travel abroad and become part of a world community of leaders, but in so doing, they leave their traditional cultures. They may find it hard to live in their native houses, dress in their former dress, or even speak their childhood language. Like the missionaries they belong, not to their first or second cultures, but to the biculture that has emerged. When the leaders return home, they are often treated with suspicion or indifference. In the end they also feel most at home with other bicultural people.

Both nationals and missionaries are people of two cultures. While externally they may resolve the tension between the two by creating the biculture to order their lives and relationships, internally they must still face the question of reconciling two often divergent sets of values and assumptions. This internal tension may be handled in a number of ways. First, some people attempt to build *ghettos* in order to preserve their first cultures. Too often, external withdrawal from the local culture represents a far deeper rejection of it at the psychological level. The result is a biculture far removed from the people, often ineffective in communicating to them the message of the gospel.

A second and opposite response is to attempt to *go native* in the second culture. Missionaries, for example, may try not only to identify fully with the people of their adoption, but also to deny their first culture. Similarly, nationals may reject their childhood culture and adopt fully the foreign culture to which they are exposed. This response is seldom successful. We can suppress, but never kill the culture into which we are enculturated as children. It remains buried, but it will rise someday to haunt us.

A third response is *compartmentalization*: to accept both cultures but to keep them separate. One or another is used, depending upon the occasion. An example of this is the modern African chief who is a member of the national parliament. In the village he dresses in traditional dress, keeps several wives, and speaks his native language. In the city he dresses in Western clothes, has a modern wife, and speaks French or English. In one such case described by Colin Turnbull, the chief had a two-story house. Upstairs was modern, and downstairs was traditional. But the two worlds never met. Missionaries, too, can become cultural schizophrenics. In the long run, however, the tension between the two cultures is not resolved, and the persons live fragmented lives.

A fourth response to the tension of living in two cultures is to seek *integration* of the two. Parts of both are combined in a new synthesis—a synthesis that is generally based on a multicultural perspective that accepts cultural variance. Rarely is synthesis fully achieved, but in seeking to bring the two cultures together, the individual strives for internal wholeness.

Most bicultural people, with the possible exception of those who deny one or the other of their cultures, maintain symbolic identification with both cultures. For example, Western missionaries in India tend to talk about Western politics, greet all Americans and Canadians as old friends, and go to Western restaurants when they are in the cities. During the war years they received food packages with cheese, Spam, and Fizzies. These were put away for special occasions, to be eaten with American friends in a sort of ritual meal of identification with America. Upon return to the West, these same missionaries tend to talk about Indian politics, greet all Indians as old friends, and eat in Indian restaurants whenever possible. Suddenly Spam and Fizzies carry no symbolic value at all. The same identification with two cultures is found in Indians who are part of a biculture. This ritual identification with each culture is important, for it reaffirms the different parts of the lives of bicultural people.

Figure 8.2
Alienation in Third World Countries

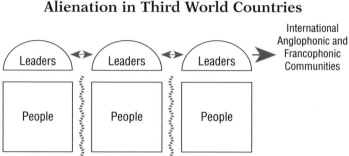

Alienation

A second problem facing bicultural people is that of alienation from their first cultures. In the case of missionaries this is less of a problem so long as they live abroad where their primary task lies. On their return to their first culture they sense the growing distance between them and their people.

The problem is more severe for national leaders. While they participate in the biculture, they continue to be involved in their first culture. For them to separate the two cultures geographically is impossible. Daily they must shift gears as they move from one culture to the other. Moreover, their task is to bring the gospel to their native culture, so they must retain close ties with it. If they identify too closely with the biculture, they become alienated from their people and are mistrusted as foreigners.

The emergence of a cultural gap between leaders and people is a serious problem in much of the developing world (see fig. 8.2). This is true in politics and business as well as in the church. National leaders are given advanced training in English or French, travel around the world, and form friendships with people from other countries. They are often more at home in a plane and hotel than in their hometowns. With the emergence of this international leadership, broad strategies for world evangelization can be planned. But these leaders often find it hard to minister directly to the people in their countries. They can no longer serve as village evangelists and health workers. The danger in missions is to concentrate on advanced training for national leaders who can no longer identify with the people. The training of indigenous leaders is one of the greatest tasks facing the church around the world.

For national leaders, alienation creates another problem, that of dependency upon outside support. Many of the top leadership positions in developing countries are dependent upon foreign funds. When funds are cut off—an increasing possibility in an age of political turmoil—leaders in these positions are vulnerable. Missionaries generally can return to their home countries and find other jobs. The national leaders have lost their support, and because of their training and cultural tastes, they find it hard to take jobs within their traditional society. Moreover, they have become politically identified with the West, and if some anti-American government comes to power they may be marked for punishment or death. Unlike the missionaries, they cannot leave. In planning mission strategies we must be particularly sensitive to the difficult position in which we may place our national colleagues, and appreciate more the tremendous sacrifices they often have to make.

Missionary Children

Some of the most difficult decisions facing missionaries have to do with their children. First, to which culture do these children belong? Unlike earlier mission movements when migration to a new country was common, the modern mission movement has been characterized by missionaries seeing themselves and their children as citizens of the missionaries' home country. In times of crisis and at retirement they expect to return to it. They assume that their children will marry and settle there.

Here is a fundamental misconception. Children raised in the biculture do not belong to their parents' first culture. For the children, the biculture is their first culture. Their home is neither the American nor the Indian nor the Brazilian culture, but the culture of the American-living-abroad or the Indian-living-abroad. Consequently many of these children suffer culture shock and problems of adjustment when they *go* (rather than *return*) to their parents' first culture. To them it is a foreign country. It is also not surprising that many of them try later in life to find vocations abroad that will take them back home. Sadly, that world is gone. However, because of their cross-cultural experience, they are often able to adapt to other bicultural situations. Most missionary kids adapt in varying degrees to their parents' culture, but for them it always will be their second culture. The cultural imprint of their childhood can never be erased.

If migrating to their parents' home culture creates problems for missionary children, so does going native. Foreign children abroad have a special role in the society. They attend different schools, speak a different language, and have bicultural values—all factors that set them apart from the local people. With few exceptions, they suffer serious culture shock if they adopt local citizenship, marry into the society, and compete for local jobs. They are still outsiders.

When the decision is made that the children should eventually identify with their parents' home culture, the problem of education arises. Local schools generally do not correspond either in language or in curriculum with that of the children's country. In the past, missionaries often left their young children in their homeland with relatives for education. Missionary children's schools eventually became common. In some instances missionary mothers tutor their children at home. Each approach has had its difficulties.

Institutionalization

Bicultural relationships are essential if the gospel is to bridge the gulf between cultures. If they are to be enduring and fruitful, these relationships must take place within a bicultural context. But as is true of any culture, institutionalization sets in. What starts as a means to communicate the gospel across cultures becomes an end in itself. Over time, defining and maintaining the biculture occupies more and more time and resources, for both the missionaries and national leaders have vested interests in maintaining it. Effective evangelists and teachers become administrators and builders. The flexibility that allowed early missionaries and national leaders to respond to local opportunities gives way to rules, policies, and hardening of the categories.

To be effective, mission requires a measure of flexibility and mobility. It is the church in action, reaching out to plant the church in worship. The balance between an ad hoc approach and constitutional order—between individual initiative and corporate planning—is difficult to maintain.

Implications for Missions

If the success of missions depends largely upon the quality of the relationships between missionaries and the people to whom they go, the parent/child relationship model is not biblical. The biblical model is that of incarnation. To bridge the cultural gap between heaven and sinful earth, God became human and dwelt among us, eating our food, speaking our language, and suffering our sorrows, yet without giving up his divine nature. Incarnation is identification, but it does not deny who we originally are. It is, in fact, a bicultural or bipersonal state. Just as God became one with us in order to save us, we must become one with the people to whom we go in order to bring them the message of salvation.

9

Missions and the Renewal
of the Church

"O Lord, revive thy work in the midst of the years" (Hab. 3:2b KJV).

Any long-range vision for missions must include not only the planting of new churches but also the renewal of old ones. The former without the latter eventually leads only to lands full of dead and dying churches. The birth of new congregations is no guarantee that they will remain spiritually alive.

Many missionaries and church leaders have tried to establish "steady-state" churches—churches that remain forever strong in faith and ministry. But there is no spiritual "steady state," neither in churches nor in individuals. Spiritual life, like all forms of life, involves the processes of health and illness, of reinvigoration and decay. A church can remain vitally alive only as it periodically experiences times of life renewal. We deal here with one set of processes that affects the life of a church and one type of structure for renewal.

Institutionalization

Christianity is a set of allegiances and beliefs. But it is more. It is a set of relationships. Faith may be an intensely personal matter, but Christianity is also a community of believers, the church, united under the lordship of Christ.

Because the church is a corporate body of human beings, it must take on social forms. Without these forms, there would be no relationships among believers and no visible congregation. There would also be no transmission of the gospel from one people to another or from one

This chapter was first published in, *Exploring Church Growth*, ed. Wilbert Shenk, ©1983 by William B. Eerdmans Publishing Co., Grand Rapids, Mich. Used by permission.

generation to another, for transmission of the gospel also requires social structures. To be sure, the church cannot be understood solely as a social organization. It is the body of Christ, and the Spirit of God is at work within it. But to the extent that the church is made up of people and congregations in relationship with one another, it will be influenced by the social and cultural dynamics of human institutions. Here we will look only at one of those dynamics—the process of institutionalization and its positive and negative effects on local congregations and other church organizations.

Generations in an Institution

Institutions, including churches, mission agencies, and schools, undergo changes from the time of their birth to their maturity. These changes can be analyzed by looking at the successive generations of people within a particular institution.

The first generation is made up of the "founding fathers and mothers," who are drawn together by a vision of something new, for which they have paid a high price. Often they have left some old institutions to join the new movement. Friends and relatives sought to draw them back and, when this failed, cut them off. Moreover, they have faced high risk, for there was no assurance that the new organization they founded would survive. Cut off from their old world, they are bound together by strong ties of fellowship and oneness of purpose. New converts are like first-generation members. They pay a high price to leave the old and join the new.

The second generation is made up of the children of the founders. Here a major structural change takes place. While the founders paid a high price to leave their old institutions to form the new one, their children grow up within the framework of the new institution and its programs. The cost they pay is not so high, but neither is their necessary commitment. Members of the second generation do grow up amid the excitement, sacrifice, and commitment of a new movement, but they acquire secondhand the vision that motivated their parents.

By the third, fourth, and fifth generations, the new movement has become "the establishment." These generations grow up within the institutional structures. In churches the children go to Sunday school and youth meetings with their friends. With those friends they make profession of faith and are baptized. In schools and mission agencies, people work their way through the ranks to positions of leadership. To remain within the institution is the path of least resistance and cost.

The strength of these generations lies in their stability and continuity over time. The life of the church, like any institution, depends upon one generation succeeding another. But the weakness of these successive generations becomes nominalism in commitment. The spiritual vision of the founders is dimmed by the routines of institutional life. What began as a movement has become a bureaucratic organization.

Processes of Institutionalization

Over the generations, an institution normally grows and matures. And with maturation come the problems of middle age—loss of vision and a hardening of the categories. This maturation or institutionalization of human organization is characterized by a number of related processes.

First, informal associations give way to formal social roles. At the beginning of a movement there are few formal roles. There is often no official or salaried custodian, or secretary, or treasurer. Different members volunteer to type correspondence, to handle finances, and to welcome newcomers. As an institution grows, more and more roles are formalized.

Second, ad hoc arrangements are replaced by rationally formulated rules and constitutions in which relationships are standardized and generalized. At the onset, many things are handled by casual arrangements. At the last moment the pastor may ask someone to lead the singing or read the Scriptures. Later such arrangements must be made well in advance so that the names can be put into a bulletin. In time the question arises: Who can appoint the song leader? The decision becomes part of the growing number of rules by which the church is run. Finally, when these rules become unwieldy and confusing, a constitution is drawn up to organize them into a formal whole. What began in the first generation as a casual arrangement, by the second becomes normative, by the third law, and by the fourth sacred. To change it becomes increasingly difficult.

In part, formal rules and constitutions are functions of size. They are necessary for large institutions to function smoothly. They are also functions of culture. Western cultures, with their obsession for uniformity, efficiency, and rationality, tend to organize institutions along the lines of bureaucracies in which tasks and relationships are divided and allocated to different people. The result is a mechanical approach to human organization, in which people become standardized parts within a "factory." The goals are production and gain. In many parts of the world social organizations are based on kinship and are organic in nature. Tribes, clans, lineages, and families tend to be more particularized or tailored to the individual characteristics of the persons involved. Moreover, they must be inclusive, for they cannot reject kinsfolk just because they do not fit into the structure.

Third, charismatic leaders are succeeded by bureaucratic leaders. As Max Weber points out, founders of new movements tend to be dynamic, prophetic leaders who command a following by means of their personal charisma.[1] Such leaders can rarely lead a mature, established institution, for they act too much on personal impulse and outside established procedures. Formalized roles and relationships call for a priest or administrator who is selected by due institutional processes and is identified with the people and the institution. This transition from charismatic founder to bureaucratic leader is crucial for the survival of an institution. If it does not take place, the institution dies. It is for the succeeding leaders to turn the vision of the founder into reality; to do so they must build and administer a complex institution.

The most difficult leadership position to fill is that of successor to the founder, for it is here that the transition must begin. Often it is a position with little honor. Honor goes to the founder, whose picture is generally central on the wall of fame. Only as personal knowledge of the founder dies and memories of him or her fade are leaders measured by their own contributions.

Finally, unity based on implicit trust in one another's faith gives way to unity based on explicit affirmation of common creeds and written confessions of faith. In the intimacy of the early gatherings, everyone knows everyone else personally. In such cases, theological differences are bridged by mutual trust. As churches and other institutions grow and become more impersonal, the bond holding members together must be formally defined. Moreover, outsiders want to know what the organization stands for. Consequently there are pressures to make explicit the beliefs and goals of the institution.

Benefits of Institutionalization

In a number of ways the processes of institutionalization are beneficial for the building of churches. One benefit, *redemption and lift,* is found particularly in churches that spring up in poor non-Christian communities. In many parts of the world Christian converts come from the lower classes of society. First-generation members are generally nonliterate, economically poor, and socially powerless. But many of these early converts send their children to mission or church schools, so that second-generation members are school teachers and government clerks. They in turn send their children to college to become doctors, college teachers, and government officials. This rapid rise of

1. Max Weber, *The Theory of Social and Economic Organization* (New York: Free Press, 1964).

Christian communities means that, in time, even churches planted among the poor become self-supporting and develop their own advanced leadership. The danger, of course, is that in this rapid social rise the church loses contact with the community from which it came and can no longer witness effectively to that community.

A second benefit of institutionalization is *efficiency*. Unformalized social organizations consume a great deal of time and energy to maintain themselves. New decisions must be made for each activity, no matter how small. In a sense, institutionalization is for social organizations what habit formation is for individuals. It reduces the constant effort necessary to operate the institution by clarifying decision-making processes and by creating a routine for making decisions.

A third benefit of institutionalization is the *ability to mobilize large numbers of people and resources* to carry out an otherwise impossible program of missions and ministry.

A fourth benefit is the theological maturation of the church. New converts, particularly in mission churches, are often theologically naïve. Most come from non-Christian backgrounds and have little understanding of the Bible or of a biblical worldview. Their children, raised in the church and often a Christian school, have a much deeper understanding of the Bible and its message. By the third generation there arise Bible scholars, translators, and theologians who can translate the message of the gospel into their own cultural mindset far more effectively than can any missionaries. The long-range survival of the church in a land—and its ability to remain true to the Christian faith through the centuries—depends to a considerable extent upon the emergence of leaders rooted in a deep understanding of the Scriptures.

Dangers of Institutionalization

Institutionalization also has its dangers. What begins as a means to help the congregation can, in the end, strangle it.

The first danger of institutionalization is that *the vision is lost* in the process of carrying it out. For example, in order to evangelize a neighboring community, the church forms a committee. To keep committee minutes, a secretary is hired and an office set up. In the end, the secretary, pressured to type letters and make reports, sees little connection between those tasks and the evangelization of the neighborhood.

A second danger is that the focus on goals gives way to *a concern for self-maintenance*. Churches are started to evangelize and minister to peoples among which no churches exist. But as time passes, more of their resources and effort are spent on simply maintaining the institutional structures. Young churches often make do with the simplest of facilities in order to focus their efforts on their mission to the world. Older churches spend more and more on sanctuaries and parking lots for themselves and schools for their children. Older mission agencies and educational institutions tend to spend an increasing proportion of their efforts and budgets on administration.

This shift of priorities from tasks to self-maintenance is due, in part, to the fact that there is no one in the administrative structures or on the committees where decisions are made who represents the world outside and its needs. Decisions are made by the insiders—by those whose cars get muddy in the unpaved lot. The process of turning inward also occurs as the identity of members gets tied up with the organization and their roles within it.

A third danger is that *flexibility gives way to inflexibility.* In the early stages of an institution's life, decisions are made on an ad hoc basis. Eventually rules and procedures establish order and reduce the number of decisions that must be made, but these also reduce flexibility in decision making. Too many exceptions to administrative rules make them useless, so pressures build to insure conformity.

The fourth danger is the *shift in focus from people to programs.* Young institutions are generally more people oriented. There is a strong emphasis on fellowship, trust, and meeting human needs. As an institution grows, more and more emphasis is placed on building programs and maintaining institutional structures. In a showdown, institutional needs take priority over human needs.

Processes of Renewal

In view of these processes, which seem almost inevitable, is there no hope for institutions? True, there are some benefits, but the evils seem to outweigh them in the long run.

Some say the only hope is to get rid of institutions, to oppose the formation of formal social organizations and return to a relatively unstructured way of life: Get rid of the establishment with its bureaucratic organization, its rules and procedures, and its dehumanizing power. But, as Peter Berger points out, antistructural movements have never been successful.[2] They remain unable to build stable, enduring societies or to organize people into communities of common purpose and mutual support. At best such movements survive because they have a symbiotic relationship to a more institutionalized society. Also, such movements are themselves subject to the subtle forces of institutional-

2. Peter L. Berger, Brigitte Berger, and Hansfried Kellner, *The Homeless Mind: Modernization and Consciousness* (New York: Random House, 1973).

ization. The symbols of their rebellion soon become the emblems of their identity, which they impose with institutional harshness upon their members.

The answer to the hardening of institutional categories is not institutional destruction but institutional renewal. Institutions can be regenerated periodically so that their evils are tempered and their ministries enhanced.

Since we speak here of the renewal of the church as a human organization, we must make it clear that spiritual renewal is first and foremost the work of God. This work cannot be programmed. There is no "formula" for revival. To seek one is itself idolatry, for formulas make human gods capable of forcing God to do their bidding.

But God does work through the spiritual, cultural, social, and psychological processes he created in human beings. In discussing historical awakenings Edwin Orr points out that God responds to sincere prayers.[3] God also uses individuals, human experiences, sermons, songs, books, sacred places, sacred times, and other cultural symbols to move in the lives of people. When we seek renewal, we need to understand the human processes that can make us open to the possibility of renewal, that can help us to listen so that when God speaks we will hear.

Conversion

One pattern of institutional renewal is a renewed emphasis on personal conversion. Stressing personal commitment to Christ and to the church after one has reached the age of accountability recreates the breaking away from an old life and the joining of a new that empowered the founders. Individuals understand the cost of leaving an old way of life and the high commitment to a new one. Ideally, each new generation enters with a fresh vision and new life.

In reality, however, two factors temper this ideal. First, the children are now, in fact, raised as if inside the church. Theologically, during their most formative years they are rarely considered really lost. Institutionally, moreover, they are very much insiders. They attend services and are treated as participants. In the face of widespread acceptance, the meaning of their exclusion from the few technical rights of church membership often escapes them.

The second factor weakening the conversion experience is the institutionalization of conversion itself. Young people are expected to experience conversion at certain times in their lives, at certain occasions,

---

3. J. Edwin Orr, *The Eager Feet: Evangelical Awakenings 1790–1830* (Chicago: Moody, 1975).

and in certain ways. Furthermore, young people often act in imitation of one another. Consequently, conversion can become the path of least resistance rather than a costly new beginning. When all are being converted, those who hold back may have to pay a greater price.

New Beginnings

Another pattern of renewal is through the beginning of a new institution or movement. As bureaucratic inertia and nominalism deaden a church or denomination, those with vital spiritual life are strongly tempted to begin anew. The possibility of reviving the old seems almost hopeless.

In some cases these revival movements must remain under the umbrella of the existing establishment. Their theology does not permit Roman Catholics to split. Consequently their new beginnings take the form of new movements or orders within the church. For example, the Franciscans, Jesuits, Dominicans, and other Roman organizations began as renewal movements that led eventually to fully institutionalized orders. The result, again, was a proliferation of bureaucratic structures, in which each of the movements must face the question of renewal. In Protestant churches, renewal movements sometimes result in new denominations.

Intersecting Renewal Movements

The best modern example of *crosscutting renewal movements* is the East African revival that has continued for over forty years. People interested in spiritual life and the renewal of the church gather in informal meetings for Bible study, prayer, confession and forgiveness of sins, and mutual exhortation. They come from many different churches and denominations. There is little or no formal structure to the movement. The institutionalized churches raise funds, organize schools, hospitals, and church programs, build church buildings, and hire pastors. The revival groups meet informally, carry out no large organized activity, and maintain no offices or paid personnel. The result is an ongoing renewal of the established churches from within.

The pattern closest to this in Western churches is the emergence of such parachurch organizations as the Christian Business Men's Club, Navigators, InterVarsity Christian Fellowship, Youth for Christ, and Campus Crusade for Christ. However, unlike the East African revival, these movements led to formal organizations that, in time, experienced the problems of institutionalization. Moreover, parachurch organizations have drawn personnel and resources from churches and often engaged in rivalries with church organizations. Because parachurch movements can limit their membership to those with talent and high spiritual commitment, they attract some of the best Christian leaders. But the church, which cannot turn away the weak, the poor, the uneducated, and the broken outcasts of society, is left weakened by the loss of talents and resources. There is often less excitement and honor in the care of those on the margins of society.

Rituals

A fourth structure for renewal is rituals. Rituals play an important part in all religions. In them people draw apart from the secular routines of everyday life to focus attention on religious matters. Ever since the Reformation, the Protestant churches in the West have tended to look at rituals with a disapproving eye. The rise of secularism (probably due in part to this antiritualistic stance) has only reinforced this rejection of ritual. The result has often been to stress corporate fellowship rather than worship of God as the central purpose of Sunday services, and to introduce informal, but no less rigid, ritual forms, such as bulletins, special clothes, and implicit spiritual hierarchies.

It may well be that Protestants need to rediscover the importance of multivocal rituals if they wish to counteract the growing secularism of the modern age, for rituals, like sacred symbols, are languages for speaking of spiritual things. As in the case of institutions, the answer to dead rituals is not no rituals, but living rituals. Such rituals are important in bringing renewal, not only to individuals, but to institutions as well.

Rituals of Renewal

Rituals play an important part in all religious life. This is particularly true of nonliterate peoples for whom rituals and myths are the encyclopedias that store religious knowledge. Literate people store such information in books, but nonliterate people must do so in forms that can be easily recalled. Easily remembered stories are the primary means by which most people around the world retain and transmit their religious beliefs.

Religious rituals are also important in the expression of religious feelings. Rudolph Otto demonstrates a close connection between religious experience and a sense of mystery, awe, and fear in the face of the supernatural.[4] Such feelings are important to express and reinforce the beliefs we hold most deeply.

---

4. Rudolph Otto, *The Idea of the Holy: An Inquiry into the Non-Rational Factor in the Idea of the Divine and Its Relation to the Rational,* trans. J. W. Harvey (original German title, *Das Heilige,* 1917; translation, Oxford: Oxford University Press, 1923).

Finally, rituals call for personal response, often in some tangible form. To participate in a ritual is to reaffirm one's commitment to the beliefs it enacts.

Structure in Rituals

All rituals share a basic structure: They stand as sacred events in opposition to ordinary, secular life. Everyday life is semichaotic. Unexpected occurrences and accidents interrupt a sequence of events that in itself often lacks order. In the face of this disorder, secular life, left to itself, becomes increasingly meaningless.

Rituals of Restoration

Rituals can be divided into two types. The first, and by far the most common, is the *ritual of restoration*. In this type, people gather to restore their faith in the beliefs that order their lives, and to rebuild the religious community in which these beliefs find expression.

Rituals of restoration share several basic characteristics. First, they are generally characterized by a high degree of ritual order. For example, the order of Sunday morning worship is often fixed and repeated from week to week. The Lord's Prayer is recited again and again. In ordinary life such repetition appears foolish—one does not tell the same joke again and again to the same audience. The songs are generally printed and their melodies and words highly predictable. Even the congregational responses may be spelled out in detail. Only the sermon allows some originality; even there the content must remain within the normally expected theological framework. This high order restores in the participants a sense of order and meaning in the universe, in their community, and in their own lives.

Second, restorative rituals take place within the state of community. That is, people occupy formal roles and relate in institutionalized ways to one another. In ordinary church services the members act as pastor, deacon, choir leader, and layperson. Many of these distinctions are reinforced by titles, differences in clothing, and special locations in the sanctuary. Role differentiation and hierarchy are evident in the organization of the service. The leader is a priest or head appointed by the institution who represents the people before God. Consequently, restorative rituals reinforce the authority and structures of the establishment.

Third, there is a sharp focus on religious activity and a strong sense of expectation that something will occur. People leave behind the cares of everyday life. Ordinary tasks are forgotten as full attention is given to the service at hand.

Finally, these regenerative rites are generally held in places central to the lives of the people. The church, particularly in villages and towns, is in the middle of the community and carries with it the religious feeling of home—a place where people find security, meaning, and a sense of rest.

Rituals of Transformation

If rituals of restoration are characterized by a high degree of structure, *rituals of transformation* are characterized by a high degree of creativity and antistructure. They often reject the normal structure of an institution and seek to create a new one. They cut through established ways of doing things and restore a measure of flexibility and personal intimacy to the organization.

Transformational rituals are found in all religions of the world, including Christianity. They include such practices as pilgrimages, camps and retreats, special revival services, festivals, mass rallies, and, in many countries, religious fairs. On the level of the individual and family they also include rites of passage associated with birth, marriage, death, and other transitions of life. In the early and medieval church, transitional rituals played an important part in the lives of the people. Only in recent years, in Western Protestant churches in secular urban settings, have these rites lost much of their significance.

In crucial ways transformative rites are the opposite of restorative rites. First, they are characterized by what Victor Turner calls *liminality*. This is the state of being in limbo—of being torn out of the familiar settings and relationships in which we live our lives.[5] For instance, the pilgrim leaves familiar territory to travel to a strange place where everything is new. There is a structure, but it is totally new and characterized by flexibility, creativity, and change rather than the reinforcement of an existing order. The result is an openness to change, for the ties to everyday life that draw us back into existing structures are broken.

Second, transformational rituals are characterized, not by *community*, but by *communitas*. This term, introduced by Turner, connotes a lack of formal roles and relationships.[6] In *communitas* there is no rigid social structure and no hierarchy. Participants are all equals. In the presence of God, human distinctions become meaningless. This sense of *communitas* bonds participants into a single group and opens them up to change.

5. Victor Turner, *The Ritual Process: Structure and Antistructure* (Chicago: Aldine, 1969).
6. Ibid.

There is an exception to this state of *communitas*. For the leaders of the pilgrimage, camp, or festival, the ritual is not a place set apart from their normal lives. It is their place of work. Consequently, for them these rituals are their community. But leaders of such rites are generally prophets. They are often charismatic leaders who in the role of addressing "the voice of God" to religious institutions and their members often pose a threat to the "priests" who run the establishment.

Communitas is a short-lived state of affairs. One cannot live in it for long without beginning to transform it into community, for *communitas* does not provide for all the requirements of ongoing social life. In time people need doctors, merchants, teachers, and a variety of other workers to maintain the society. When Peter suggested on the Mount of Transfiguration they build houses, he had already begun the transformation from an ethereal experience to ordinary life (Matt. 17:4; Mark 9:5).

Third, rituals of transformation, like those of restoration, are associated with a high sense of focus and of expectation. Outside matters are left behind. In transformational rituals this often includes a geographic separation that makes disengagement from the world complete.

Finally, transformative rites allow for a great deal of creativity. This creativity destroys the old order, but it also builds a new one.

The goal of transformative rites is to bring about change. The combination of liminality, *communitas*, high expectations, and antistructural creativity makes deep and lasting changes possible in short periods of time. Changes in fundamental beliefs are often reinforced by strong emotions and a commitment to act upon the new convictions. These transformations are often spoken of as *conversions, rededications*, and *new commitments*.

Transformative Rituals and the Renewal of the Church

Transformative rituals were very much a part of Judeo-Christian life until recent times. In the Old Testament the levitical priests, scattered throughout the land, conducted the normal restorative rituals. However, three times a year all adult males, particularly heads of families who served as family priests, were expected to go to Jerusalem. There they gathered as pilgrims in the great festivals of regeneration. All ordinary social distinctions were broken down as the people assembled before the Lord. Special music, art, and even dance gave expression to the creativity of these events. It is not surprising, therefore, that the most important events in the life of Christ—his initiation into Jewish adulthood, his death, and his resurrection—took place on such occasions.

Festivals, pilgrimages, and even Crusades played important roles in the medieval church. The toil of daily life and the routine of local services were broken by special occasions that made the people aware of a greater Christendom, of the world outside, and of the great historical heritage of their faith. The great cathedrals, the pilgrimage sites, and Palestine itself restored to many a sense of the sacred and of God's presence in human history.

Even in frontier America, transformative services played a key part in the religious life of the people. The evangelistic crusades, revival meetings, and mission conferences were annual events on the calendar of many churches.

Today, in Western urban society, transformative rites are largely secular—sports events, political rallies, and professional conferences. In churches the revivals and crusades have been replaced by summer camps and weekend retreats. They play an important part in personal renewal, but they have less effect upon the structures of the institutionalized church. Denominational conferences, anniversary celebrations, and such festivals as Easter and Christmas involve whole churches, but they are often controlled by the priests of the institution. Citywide crusades break down barriers among denominations and provide Christians with a greater vision of the scope of Christianity as a whole, but they are sporadic.

Restorative rites can renew commitment and vision, but only by reaffirming the institutional structures. It takes transformations and revolutions to break the stranglehold these structures can have in the church. It may well be that churches in the West need to rediscover the importance of such transformative rituals if they want to counter the evils of institutionalization and bring new life back into the church.

Transformative Rituals and Missions

What implications does all this have for missions? It is clear that we must strive, not only to plant new churches, but to constantly renew spiritual life within the old ones. Dead forms of Christianity are little better than non-Christian religions. Consequently, missionaries and church leaders must think and plan for the life of the church for fifty years and longer into the future.

But there is another reason why missions must take renewal rituals into account. Many societies to which missions are directed are nonliterate. These societies encode their beliefs in religious rituals. Missionaries who come from literate societies that store their beliefs in books often do not appreciate this difference and seek to get rid of rituals, dramas, stories, and other folk means of preserving knowledge. The result is that new Christians often have few ways to remember their beliefs. They cannot read the Bible. The preacher may come only on rare occasions. P. Y. Luke and John B. Carman found that theology in such cultures is memorized and sung in the homes at night, sustaining the people's faith.[7]

The contrast between Protestant worship services and the people's traditional ceremonies is probably greatest in the areas of transformative rituals. Festivals, religious fairs, pilgrimages, and such rites of passage as birth, initiation, marriage, and death break the drudgery of everyday life, provide excitement, and make life more meaningful. Here modern Christian missionaries have provided the fewest functional substitutes to replace the old ways. Consequently, Christianity often appears drab and uninteresting.

Several innovative attempts have been made to change this picture. J. T. Seamands began a Christian religious fair in South India that attracts Christians from a wide area for a week of meetings and excitement. Korean churches unite for nationwide rallies that strengthen the believers and witness to the people of the growing church in the land.

Church planting and church renewal are the two central tasks of missions. The first without the second leads to widespread nominal Christianity; the second without the first leads to life without a mission. The two go together. An effective mission to the world often revives the home church, and renewal at home often leads to a new missionary vision.

---

7. P. Y. Luke and John B. Carman, *Village Christians and Hindu Culture*, Commission on World Mission and Evangelism, World Council of Churches (London: Lutterworth, 1968), 127.

10

Banyan Trees
and Banana Trees

"Nothing grows under a banyan tree." This South Indian proverb speaks of leadership styles. The banyan is a great tree. It spreads its branches, drops air-roots, develops secondary trunks, and covers the land. A full-grown banyan may cover over an acre. Birds, animals, and humans find shelter under its shade. But nothing grows under its dense foliage, and when it dies, the ground beneath lies barren and scorched.

The banana tree is the opposite. Six months after it sprouts, small shoots appear around it. At twelve months a second circle of shoots appears beside the first, which are now six months old. At eighteen months the main trunk bears bananas, which nourish birds, animals, and humans, and then it dies. But the offspring are now full gown, and in six months they too bear fruit and die. The cycles continue unbroken as new sprouts emerge every six months, grow, give birth to more sprouts, bear fruit, and die.

Training Followers

Many leaders are like banyan trees. They have great ministries, but when they pass from the scene, there are no leaders to step into their shoes because they have trained followers, not leaders.

It is gratifying to train followers. They are an appreciative audience who make us feel important. They imitate our ways. They do not challenge our thinking or go beyond our teaching.

It is easy to train followers. We decide what they should learn and how they should learn it. We encourage them to raise questions and we

This chapter first appeared in *The Christian Leader* 53.3 (13 February 1990): 24. Used by permission.

give the answers. We teach them to follow our directives and to guess our minds.

There is an immediate success in training followers. We can mobilize many to build our program. This approach is also efficient. It takes time to train leaders, and to allow them to learn by making mistakes. But the success of follower development is short-range—when we depart, we leave sheep but no shepherds.

As husbands or wives, and as parents, it is easy to treat spouses and children as followers—to demand that they obey us, and think and behave as we do. As ministers it is easy to train our parishioners to be followers—to make them dependent upon professional leadership to carry out the ministries of the church. As missionaries it is easy to treat native converts as followers. We need not take the chance of entrusting them with authority as long as we are around, and we can make certain they carry on the work in the same ways we do. Such a leadership style creates dependent people and kills leadership potential. Such spouses, children, parishioners, and natives never grow up. To do so they must rebel against us.

Training Leaders

Training leaders is less rewarding for our egos. We must teach people to think and decide on their own, to challenge our beliefs, and to argue with our decisions. When they take over they will go beyond us, and take credit for their own growth and accomplishments.

Training leaders is more difficult. We must value their input and encourage a critique of what we say. We must grade them, not on how much they agree with us, but on how well they think. We do not ask them to guess our minds, and we avoid putting them down, even when their initial responses are naïve and simplistic. We focus on problems they must solve, rather than on fixed bodies of information.

Training leaders is less efficient in the short run because it takes time and effort that could be spent on completing more immediate tasks. Decisions must be negotiated, plans constantly changed, and schedules and goals adjusted. But it is more efficient in the long run. Our reward comes when we find ourselves surrounded by young leaders who are discovering their own new abilities, assuming new responsibilities, and raring to take over and go beyond where we have reached.

Spouses who encourage their husbands or wives to be leaders develop family styles of mutual submission. Parents who build their children as leaders begin early to teach them to think; they relate to their children as to young adults. Pastors who teach their laity to be leaders encourage Bible studies and lay initiatives in the ministries of the church. Missionaries who train nationals as leaders give them responsibilities early and support their decisions. All must allow budding leaders the greatest privilege they allow themselves, the right to make mistakes.

Training Leaders Who Train Leaders

Training leaders, however, is not enough. Too often we train leaders who, in turn, train followers. We teach them to think ideas, but not to build humans. They learn to use people to build programs, not programs to build people.

It is hardest of all to help young leaders to catch the vision of training leaders and to pass that vision on, but this is essential for a successful family, church, and mission.

Paul writes, "And the things you have heard me say in the presence of many witnesses entrust to reliable men who will also be qualified to teach others" (2 Tim. 2:2).

11

Window-Shopping
the Gospel

The young couple strolled through the shopping mall, looking at the wares displayed in the large plate-glass windows, stopping occasionally to point out a suit or pair of shoes. Slowly they made their way to a photography shop to buy a camera, stopping to look at those on display in the window before entering. There they inspected the wares in the glass cases more closely and then asked the salesman, a stranger, to show them several models. Finally, after eliciting some further information, they bought one of the cameras.

In a sense this is a parable of decision-making in a modern, urban society, repeated a million times each day. Like any analogy, we dare not push it too far, but there are lessons it teaches about the way people in cities make decisions and about the dynamics of urban churches and urban evangelism.

People around the world make decisions in much the same way. In everyday life they act more or less rationally, according to the rules and expectations of their individual culture. Yet in some significant ways, decision-making in large, complex cities is different from that in more intimate, face-to-face societies.

Decision-Making in Small Societies

In tribes with a strong sense of corporate identity, important decisions involve group interaction because a person's identity is closely tied to the group to which he or she belongs. Marriages are arranged by

This chapter first appeared in *Urban Mission* 4.5 (May 1987): 5–12. Used by permission.

parents and kinspeople. Fresh game is divided, with much discussion, by relatives and neighbors according to tradition—the hunter gets only a small portion of the kill.

Similarly, in small peasant villages decisions are based on family tradition and personal trust. A villager goes to shops where she or he has gone for years and where a relationship of trust in the integrity of the merchant has been established. To change shops is a major decision, for it means a realignment of relationships in the village.

Larger villages generally are segmented into smaller communities on the basis of ethnicity and/or class. African towns are made up of different tribal groups, Indian towns of different castes, and American towns of different classes or life-style enclaves.[1] Residents of smaller communities must take into account how their decisions affect their relationships to others in their own communities. They worry about what others will think.

But larger villages also have individuals and families who are not attached to local communities—merchants from outside vend their wares in the market, migrants seek to make a living, government officials are assigned to the district. They may have ties to communities elsewhere, but in the town they tend to make decisions largely on their own.

Many small, tightly-knit American towns retain some of these social patterns, but increasingly they are being shaped by urban values and lifestyles. Shops have big display windows, and shoppers expect to shop around.

It should not surprise us that the decision-making process in strongly group-oriented societies influences the way people come to Christ. Important decisions regarding faith affect the whole community, and people must be given time to talk matters over with their peers before they are called to make a decision. For this reason some evangelistic teams in Thai villages no longer call for individual responses to the gospel after an evening meeting. Rather, they encourage everyone to discuss their decisions with their families and fellow villagers and to let the evangelistic team know the outcome the next morning before it leaves. In another part of the world a village preacher does not call for a decision each night of an evangelistic campaign, but tells the people they must be ready to make a decision on the final night of the campaign. Throughout the week tensions mount in the village as people discuss with one another what they will do when the call to follow the gospel is finally given.

It should also not surprise us that in group-oriented societies people

1. Robert N. Bellah, et al., *Habits of the Heart: Individualism and Commitment in American Life* (Berkeley, Calif.: University of California Press, 1985).

often come to Christ as families and groups. Sometimes a whole community makes a public decision to become Christian, even though some members may object. In such cases it is best to wait with baptism and to instruct the group for some months in order to allow people to reassess their decisions. Having publicly affirmed their oneness with the group by going along with the original decision, those who oppose becoming Christian are now permitted by the group to disagree and withdraw from Christian events. It is best to wait for this to occur before organizing the church.

Decision-Making in the City

But what about the city? How do people make decisions in urban settings?

At the outset it is important that we avoid reducing decision-making in the city to a single stereotype. As in so many areas of city life, we face a bewildering diversity of reasoning styles. In the city can be found pockets of small village-like communities where people live much as they did before they migrated to the city. Within that community they shop at family-owned stores where personal ties are important. They discuss choices with their neighbors. Outside the neighborhood, however, they learn to make decisions as city folk do, and this begins to change their community.

People in ghettos, *bustees, favelas,* and other enclaves of the poor have their own ways of making decisions.[2] As Oscar Lewis shows, economic decisions must be made on the basis of survival, while other decisions are often made on the spur of the moment.[3] It is hard to make lasting commitments and long-range plans when relationships are fragile and the future uncertain.

Even in old, urban, middle-class, American suburbs, people make decisions in different ways. In some matters they ask the advice of knowledgeable friends and neighbors—"opinion leaders" whose advice they trust in the matter at hand. They ask one friend about cameras, another about doctors. In other matters they are influenced by neighborhood fads such as riding mowers or clothing styles.

The tendency in urban life, however, is for people to make individual decisions, and to do so on the basis of a knowledge of the product, not on a personal relationship with the seller. Much of this knowledge is acquired through the media. Billboards, advertisements, television, news-

---

2. *Bustee* is the term used in India for urban slums; *favela* is the term used in Latin America.
3. Oscar Lewis, *The Children of Sanchez* (New York: Random House, 1961).

papers, and radio keep us informed of what is going on. But even with this knowledge in hand, city folk often want to "window-shop" new ideas and products before making a final decision to adopt them.

Neutral Territory

Window-shopping is closely tied to the concept of *territory*. Edward Hall, Robert Ardrey, and others have argued that all people have a sense of territory—a sense that geographic and social space *belongs* to a people or group and is used for different functions.[4] This concept of ownership is far broader than legal possession. People living together may feel that they own their neighborhood, even though the streets and parks belong to the general public.

An example of the social use of space can be seen in American cities where a fundamental distinction is made between public and private life and between public and private land. A home is a family's private castle. There the family may live pretty much as it pleases. Others must get permission to enter the house. A street, on the other hand, is public—anyone can use it.

A shop is semipublic, for strangers may enter, but the space belongs to the owners and sales people who are free to talk to the strangers about buying goods and services. Consequently, to enter a store is a tentative commitment to buy something. People do not expect to go to a shop just to visit or eat a sack lunch.

Similarly, a church is semipublic, and people who enter it are assumed to be seriously interested in Christianity. But what about those only casually interested? Where can they look at Christianity without being pressured to convert?

Neutral territory is public space not owned by any particular-interest group. It includes sidewalks and shopping malls where people can look at commodities displayed in the windows. Other neutral sites are public roads, with their billboards and parades; stadiums and public auditoriums, where one can remain a spectator lost in the crowds; and fair grounds, with their stalls and displays. In all of these, people can examine new ideas and products without the pressure to buy.

Neutral Territory and Evangelism

What implications does all this have for evangelism in the city, particularly Western cities? One thing is clear: many city folk will not come

---

4. Edward T. Hall, *Silent Language* (Greenwich, Conn.: Fawcett, 1961); Robert Ardrey, *The Territorial Imperative: A Personal Inquiry into the Animal Origins of Property and Nations* (New York: Dell, 1968).

to a church, even for evangelistic meetings. They see the church as religious territory. To enter a church is to make the first positive step toward becoming a Christian, a step they are not ready to make. They may be willing to look at it, but they will do so only in some neutral territory where no previous commitment is needed. They just want to window-shop the gospel.

What are some of these neutral territories that the church should explore in its evangelistic outreach?

Parks, Stadiums, and Auditoriums

Streets, parks, stadiums, and auditoriums are public spaces. Although they may be used for specific functions, such as rock concerts or trade fairs, they are generally thought of as neutral territory. The sheer size of the gatherings guarantees one's anonymity, and the fact that different types of functions are held at the same site prevents it from being identified closely with any one of them.

The church in the city has long used parking lots for tent meetings. More recently it has begun to use stadiums, civic auditoriums, and theaters. For example, the Eagles Communications Team in Singapore stages modern musical concerts in public auditoriums in Singapore and Malaysia. Each concert is followed by an evangelistic challenge and appeal. The team regularly fills the auditoriums two or three nights running with young people, many of them non-Christians. Due to a shortage of land, a number of new congregations in Singapore have bought out theaters for use as church buildings.

Another example is Christian sports teams that compete with local clubs in public arenas and share their faith during the intermission.

Restaurants and Banquet Halls

City folk eat out. In American cities, people now eat one-third of their meals away from home, and the figure is slowly climbing towards one-half. It should not surprise us, therefore, that churches are discovering the importance of eating habits in planning evangelism. For years the Christian Business Men's Committee and the Full-Gospel Businessmen's Association have used restaurants to make non-Christian businessmen feel at home. More recently Frank Tillapaugh has pointed out the value of restaurants as meeting places for Sunday school classes for young adults.[5]

In Singapore the Eagles Communications Team ministers to upper-

5. Frank R. Tillapaugh, *The Church Unleashed: Getting God's People Out Where the Needs Are* (Ventura, Calif.: Regal, 1982).

class professionals by organizing banquets in top-rated hotels. They contract for the meal and sell tickets to Christian doctors, lawyers, teachers, and businessmen who invite non-Christian friends as guests. The banquet is followed by a musical concert and a brief evangelistic presentation. Most of these guests would feel uncomfortable in a church, but at the hotel they have an opportunity to enjoy an evening together with friends and to look at Christianity without the pressure to convert.

Shops and Shopping Centers

Early scholars spoke of the secularization of the inner-city. Church buildings can readily be seen in the suburbs, but, with the exception of some old "First Churches" struggling to survive, the inner-city has few conspicuous symbols of the presence of the church.

Recent studies have shown that this conventional wisdom is too simplistic. Religious groups continue to thrive in the inner city, but in forms unfamiliar to most of us. Small shops are turned into storefront churches. Recreation centers and school rooms are rented for religious gatherings. Rescue missions provide whole ministries to a multitude of transients. The multifunctional use of these buildings—and the ministries of these Christian groups to the physical as well as spiritual needs of the people—keep the facilities they use from being identified only as Christian territory.

Private Homes

Probably the most important neutral territory for evangelism is the Christian's home. Here friends and neighbors can gather and window-shop the gospel without feeling pressured to accept it.

Mortimer Arias has pointed out the importance of hospitality as one of the key methods of evangelism in the Old Testament. God instructed the people of Israel to invite strangers and marginals into their homes. In doing so they were proclaiming God's love by their actions. Arias argues convincingly that churches today would be more effective in their urban witness if they showed such hospitality to the strangers, migrants, and neighbors around them.[6]

Hospitality was an important method used by Elmo Warkentine to plant a number of urban churches on the West Coast.[7] He organized church members into small groups of three or four families. Once a

6. Mortimer Arias, "Centripetal Mission or Evangelism by Hospitality," *Missiology: An International Review* 10 (January 1982): 69–81.

7. Elmo Warkentine served as an urban church planter on the West Coast for the Mennonite Brethren Conference until his death in 1992.

month he dismissed the Sunday evening service, and each group met in one of its member's homes. Non-Christian friends and neighbors were to be invited for a time of fun and fellowship. Preferably the number of non-Christians should outnumber the Christians so they would not feel uncomfortable. The evening was to be spent simply in building friendships and showing love. If the discussion turned to Christianity, fine, but there was no compulsion to make the evening a time of witness. Later, after hospitality had built trust, church members were encouraged to share their faith with their friends or to invite them to church. Warkentine pointed out that non-Christians need to see Christians as ordinary people and not only as evangelists. They need to see them in everyday life.

Camps, Retreats, and Pilgrimage Centers

In recent decades, evangelicals have discovered the importance of camps and retreats, but the idea is not new. Throughout history Roman Catholics have extensively used retreats as places for spiritual formation and also as places where people could explore faith.

Evangelicals have made less use of pilgrimage centers and parades. For Catholics, shrines such as those at Lourdes and Guadeloupe are important places where common folk gather in great numbers, many simply to see what is going on. On festival days in particular, the shrines are centers of religious fairs and parades. Religious beliefs and rituals are brought into the streets alongside shops and amusement stalls. This mix of religious and secular activities tends to disturb Western evangelicals. It seems to cheapen the gospel. But the festival also has a powerful appeal and impact on common folk.

J. T. Seamands and his fellow missionaries in India began a Christian fair that has had a significant impact on Christianity in Andhra Pradesh, not only strengthening believers but also making the public aware of the Christian presence among them. In the United States, a few places—such as the shrine for Martin Luther King, the Oral Roberts Medical Center, and the Crystal Cathedral—may be seen as pilgrimage centers, for they regularly attract large numbers of out-of-town visitors.

More could be said of neutral territory and its importance in evangelism, and of Christ's use of neutral territory in his ministry, but let us turn our attention briefly to the role neutral territory can play in other church ministries.

Neutral Territory and the Church

How does neutral territory relate to sacred territory? The analogy of the couple window-shopping to purchase a camera is a commercial model. It assumes that, in order to reach urban people who think largely in terms of buying and selling, we may need to present the gospel in market terms. This may be necessary to reach modern, urban non-Christians, but we dare not stop here or we will end up handling the church as we would a business. In a profound sense we cannot "buy into" the gospel. It is not a commodity we choose because it meets some of our needs better than do other products on the market. In city churches there is a real danger that this market-driven commodity view could distort the gospel. Churches and denominations become franchises, and individuals are free to go to the church that meets their current needs and tastes. As their tastes change they change churches, with little thought to questions of truth, Christian community, and their responsibility to minister rather than be ministered to.

The church is called to evangelize outside itself. Inside it is called to worship and minister to one another. The work outside often can be done best in neutral territory, but work inside calls for "sacred" space and time. Christ ministered on the streets, but periodically he took the disciples and withdrew into the countryside. The church, too, needs a place to be the church and to renew itself. Not that outsiders are excluded—they are welcome. But here the church gathers for its central calling, the worship of God. Without such worship, the church ends up worshiping its corporate self. Here, too, the church gathers to minister to the body.

The form of the sacred place will vary. Some congregations seek to express the greatness, mystery, and providence of God over all creation by building a cathedral. Others emphasize the presence of Christ in the midst of his people by building a church. Still others symbolize the power of the Holy Spirit in the life of each believer by constructing a chapel. Social class and ethnic taste affect people's ideas of what kind of place should be set apart as sacred. But what is common to all Christians is that a sacred place provides a rendezvous where the congregation, as a congregation, gathers regularly to meet God. Without sacred symbols, such as place and time, to express our experiences with God, Christians may be drawn into the secular world of the city and become nothing more than a social club that talks about religion.

The church also needs sacred space as a testimony to the world of the presence of the church in its midst. Non-Christians may not enter a church building, but its very existence reminds them of Christianity. In Seoul, Korea, the rapid proliferation of church buildings is seen by non-Christians and Christians alike. Even the empty churches in England and Europe are mute witnesses to a church that once was vitally alive but now is weak.

The tension between neutral space and sacred space reflects the tension the church faces between being *in the world, yet not of it.* If it lives only in neutral territory it is in danger of losing sight of its Lord, if only in sacred territory it may become ingrown and old. The church needs to be present in both.

Part 3

Reflections on Spiritual Encounters

12

The Flaw of
the Excluded Middle

The disciples of John the Baptist asked Jesus, "Are you he who is to come, or shall we look for another?" (Luke 7:20 RSV). Jesus answered, not with logical proofs, but by a demonstration of power in curing the sick and casting out evil spirits. This much is clear. Yet when I once read the passage from my perspective as a missionary in India and sought to apply it to missions in my day, I felt a sense of uneasiness. As a Westerner, I was used to presenting Christ on the basis of rational arguments, not by evidences of his power in the lives of people who were sick, possessed, and destitute. In particular, the confrontation with spirits that appeared so natural a part of Christ's ministry belonged in my mind to a separate world of the miraculous—far from ordinary everyday experiences.

Another situation, early in my ministry in India, gave me the same uneasiness. One day, while teaching in the Bible school in Shamshabad, I saw Yellayya standing in the door at the back of the class. He looked tired, for he had walked many miles from Muchintala where he was an elder in the church. I assigned the class some reading and went with him to the office. When I asked why he had come, he said that smallpox had come to the village a few weeks earlier and had taken a number of children. Doctors trained in Western medicine had tried to halt the plague, but without success. Finally, in desperation the village elders had sent for a diviner, who told them that Maisamma, goddess of smallpox, was angry with the village.

To satisfy her and stop the plague the village would have to perform the water buffalo sacrifice. The village elders went around to each

This chapter first appeared in *Missiology: An International Review* 10.1 (January 1982): 35–47. Used by permission.

household in the village to raise money to purchase the buffalo. When they came to the Christian homes, the Christians refused to give them anything, saying that it was against their religious beliefs. The leaders were angry, pointing out that the goddess would not be satisfied until every household gave something as a token offering—even one *paisa* would do.[1] When the Christians refused, the elders forbade them to draw water from the village wells, and the merchants refused to sell them food.

In the end some of the Christians had wanted to stop the harassment by giving the *paisa,* telling God they did not mean it, but Yellayya had refused to let them do so. Now, said Yellayya, one of the Christian girls was sick with smallpox. He wanted me to pray with him for God's healing. As I knelt, my mind was in turmoil. I had learned to pray as a child, studied prayer in seminary, and preached it as a pastor. But now I was to pray for a sick child as all the village watched to see if the Christian God was able to heal.

Why my uneasiness both in reading the Scriptures and in the Indian village? Was the problem, at least in part, due to my own worldview—to the assumptions I as a Westerner made about the nature of reality and how I viewed the world? But how does one discover these assumptions since they are so taken for granted that we are rarely even aware of them? One way is to look at the worldview of another culture and to contrast it with the way we view the world.

Ills and Remedies in an Indian Village

There are many illnesses in an Indian village. According to the Indian worldview, people become sick with hot diseases, such as smallpox, and must be treated with cold medicines and foods; or they have cold diseases like malaria and need hot foods and medicines. Some need treatment for boils, cuts, and broken bones, others for mental illnesses. Women may be cursed with barrenness. Individuals or whole families may be plagued by bad luck, by constantly being robbed or by having their houses burn down. Or they may be seized by bad temper, jealousy, or hate. They may be possessed by spirits or be injured by planetary forces or black magic.

Like all people, Indian villagers have traditional ways to deal with such diseases. Serious cases, particularly those that are life-threatening or have to do with relationships, they take to the *sadhu* (saint), a person of god who claims to heal by prayer. Because god knows everything, including the nature and causes of the illness, the saints ask no questions.

1. The *paisa* is the smallest coin in India, now worth about .03 of one penny.

Moreover, because they are spiritual they charge no fees, although those healed are expected to give a generous offering to god by giving it to the saint.

Other cases villagers take to a *mantrakar* or magician, particularly cases in which the villagers suspect some evil human or supernatural cause. The magician cures by knowledge and control of supernatural spirits and forces believed to exist on earth. If, for example, one were to venture out on an inauspicious day when the evil forces of the planets are particularly strong he or she might be bitten by a viper. To cure this the magician would have to say the following *mantra* (magical chant) seven times—once for each stripe across the viper's back: OM NAMO BHAGAVATE. SARVA PEESACHI GRUHAMULU NANU DZUCHI PARADZURU. HREEM, KLEM, SAM PHAT, SVAHA.

This combines a powerful formula to counter the evil forces with a series of powerful sounds *(hreem, klem, sam, phat, svaha)* that further empower the formula. Sometimes the magician uses visual symbols *(yentras;* see fig. 12.1) or amulets to control spirits and forces in this world. Because they can divine both the nature and the cause of the evil plaguing the patient they need ask no questions, and, like the saints, they receive the offerings of those who have been helped.

A third type of medical practitioner are the *vaidyudu* (doctors), who cure people by means of scientific knowledge based on the *ayyurvedic* or *unani* systems of medicine. Because of their skills in diagnosis, these, too, ask no questions. Villagers report that these *vaidyudu* feel their wrists, stomachs, and bodies and are able to determine their illnesses. They charge high fees, for this knowledge is powerful, but they give a guarantee: Medicines and services are paid for only if the patient is healed.

In addition, there are village quacks who heal people with folk remedies. Their knowledge is limited so they must ask questions about the illness: Where does it hurt and for how long has the pain been felt? Have they been with someone sick ? What have they eaten? For the same reason they charge low fees and give no guarantees. People have to pay for the medicines before receiving them. It should not surprise us that Western doctors are often equated at the beginning with the quacks.

What happens to villagers who become Christians? Most of them take problems they formerly took to the saints to the Christian minister or missionary. Christ replaces Krishna or Siva as the healer of spiritual diseases. Many of them in time turn to Western allopathic medicines for many of the illnesses they had taken to the doctor and quack. But what of the plagues that the magician cured? What about spirit possession or curses or witchcraft or black magic? What is the Christian answer to these?

Figure 12.1
Magical Charms in an Indian Village

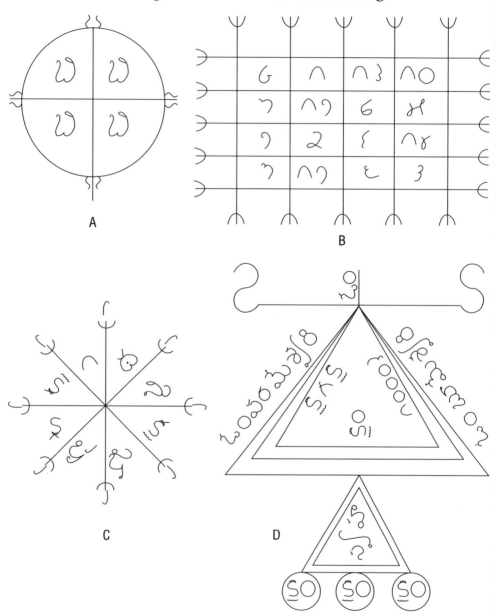

Magical charms, when properly used in a south Indian village, will automatically bring about the desired results. These charms combine powerful figures, sounds, and words. *(A)* Yantra for a headache, involves writing it on a brass plate, lighting a candle in front of it after it is wrapped in string, covering it with red and yellow powders, and tying it to the head. *(B)* Yantra for ensuring conception, involves inscribing it on a piece of paper or copper sheeting and tying it to the arm of the barren woman. *(C)* Used for malaria. *(D)* To the god Narasimha, for power and general protection. (SOURCE: *Konduru* by Paul G. Hiebert: Copyright ©1971 by the University of Minnesota. Used by permission.)

Often the missionary evangelist or doctor has no answer. These do not really exist, they say. But to people for whom these are very real experiences in their lives, there must be another answer. Therefore, many of them return to the magician for cures.

This survival of magic among Christians is not unique to India. In many parts of the world, the picture is the same. In the West, magic and witchcraft persisted well into the seventeenth century, more than a thousand years after the gospel came to these lands.

An Analytical Framework

In order to understand the biblical texts, the Indian scene, and the failure of Western missionaries to meet the needs met by magicians, we need an analytical framework. To create this framework we need two dimensions of analysis (see fig. 12.2).

The Seen-Unseen Dimension

The first dimension is that of *immanence-transcendence*. On one end is the empirical world of our senses. All people are aware of this world and develop folk sciences to explain and control it. They develop theories about the natural world around them—how to build a house, plant a crop, or sail a canoe. They also have theories about human relationships—how to raise a child, treat a spouse, and deal with a relative. When a Naga tribal person attributes the death of the deer to an arrow, or a Karen wife explains the cooking of a meal in terms of the fire under the pot, they are using explanations based upon empirical observations and deductions. Western science, in this sense, is not unique. Western science may be more systematic in the exploration of the empirical world, but all people have folk sciences.

Above this level (more remote from the experience of humans) are beings and forces that cannot be directly perceived but are thought to exist *on this earth*. These include spirits, ghosts, ancestors, demons, and earthly gods and goddesses who live in trees, rivers, hills, and villages. These live, not in some other world or time, but with humans and animals of this world and time. In medieval Europe these beings included trolls, pixies, gnomes, brownies, and fairies, all of which were believed to be real. This level also includes supernatural forces, such a *mana*, planetary influences, evil eyes, and the powers of magic, sorcery, and witchcraft.

Furthest from the immediate world of human experience are transcendent worlds beyond this one—hells and heavens and other times, such as eternity. In this transcendent realm fit African concepts of a

Figure 12.2
Framework for the Analysis
of Religious Systems

Organic Analogy
Based on concepts of living beings relating to other living beings. Stresses life, personality, relationships, functions, health, disease, choice, etc. Relationships are essentially moral in character.

Mechanical Analogy
Based on concepts of impersonal objects controlled by forces. Stresses impersonal, mechanistic, and deterministic nature of events. Forces are essentially amoral in character.

	Organic	Mechanical	
Unseen or Supernatural Beyond immediate sense experience. Above natural explanation. Knowledge of this based on inference or on supernatural experiences.	**High Religion Based on Cosmic Beings:** cosmic gods angels demons spirits of other worlds	**High Religion Based on Cosmic Forces:** kismet fate Brahman and karma impersonal cosmic forces	**Other Worldly** Sees entities and events occurring in other worlds and in other times.
Seen or Empirical Directly observable by the senses. Knowledge based on experimentation and observation.	**Folk or Low Religion** local gods and goddesses ancestors and ghosts spirits demons and evil spirits dead saints	**Magic and Astrology** mana astrological forces charms, amulets and magical rites evil eye, evil tongue	**This Worldly** Sees entities and events as occurring in this world and universe.
	Folk Social Science interaction of living beings such as humans, possibly animals and plants.	**Folk Natural Science** interaction of natural objects based on natural forces.	

high god, and Hindu ideas of Vishnu and Siva. Here is located the Jewish concept of Jehovah, who stands in stark contrast to the baals and ashtaroth of the Canaanites, who were deities of this world, of the middle zone. To be sure, Jehovah entered into the affairs of this earth, but his abode was above it. On this level, too, are the transcendent cosmic forces such as *karma* and *kismet*.

The Organic-Mechanical Continuum

Scholars have widely noted that humans use analogies from everyday experience to provide pictures of the nature and operations of the larger world. Two basic analogies are particularly widespread:

    1. *organic analogy*—sees things as living beings in relationship to each other,

2. *mechanical analogy*—sees things as inanimate objects that act upon one another like parts in a machine.

In the organic analogy the elements being examined are thought to be alive in some sense, to undergo processes similar to human life and to relate to each other in ways that are analogous to interpersonal relationships. For example, in seeking to describe human civilizations, philosopher Oswald Spengler and historian Arnold Toynbee speak of them in terms of an organic analogy: Civilizations are born, they mature, and they die. Similarly, traditional religionists see many diseases as caused by evil spirits that are alive, that may be angered, and that can be placated through supplication or the offering of a sacrifice. Christians see their relationship to God in organic terms. God is a person and humans relate to him in ways analogous to human relationships.

Organic explanations see the world in terms of living beings in relationship to one another. Like humans and animals, objects may initiate actions and respond to the actions of others. They may be thought to have feelings, thoughts, and wills of their own. Often they are seen as social beings who love, marry, beget offspring, quarrel, war, sleep, eat, persuade, and coerce one anther.

In the mechanical analogy all things are thought to be inanimate parts of greater mechanical systems. They are controlled by impersonal forces or by impersonal laws of nature. For example, Western sciences see the world as made up of lifeless matter that interacts on the basis of forces. When gravity pulls a rock down to the earth it is not because the earth and rock wish to meet—neither earth nor rock have any thought in the matter. In Western science even living beings often are seen as being caught up in a world ultimately made up of impersonal forces. Just as we have no choice about what happens to us when we fall out of a tree, so it is often thought that we have no control over the forces in early childhood that are believed to have made us what we are today.

Mechanical analogies are essentially deterministic; living beings in a mechanistic system are subject to its impersonal forces. But if they know how these forces operate, they can manipulate or control them for their own advantage. In a sense they exert god-like control over their own destiny.

Mechanistic analogies are basically amoral. Forces are intrinsically neither good nor evil. They can be used for both. Organic analogies, on the other hand, are characterized by ethical considerations. One being's actions always affect other beings.

Many of the similarities among modern science, magic, and astrology that have been pointed out by anthropologists are due to the fact that all three use mechanistic analogies. Just as scientists know how to

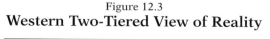

Figure 12.3
Western Two-Tiered View of Reality

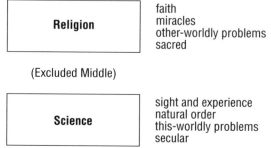

control empirical forces to achieve their goals, the magician and astrologer control supernatural forces of this world by means of chants, charms, and rituals to carry out human purposes.

One of the greatest cultural gaps between Western people and many traditional religionists is found along this dimension. The former have bought deeply into a mechanical view of this universe and of the social order.[2] To them the basis of the world is lifeless matter controlled by impersonal forces. Many tribal religionists see the world as alive. Not only humans, but also animals, plants, and even rocks, sand, and water are thought to have personalities, wills, and life forces. Theirs is a relational, not a deterministic, world.

The Excluded Middle

The reasons for my uneasiness with the biblical and Indian worldviews should be clear: I had excluded the middle level of supernatural this-worldly beings and forces from my own worldview. As a scientist I had been trained to deal with the empirical world in naturalistic terms. As a theologian I was taught to answer ultimate questions in theistic terms. For me the middle zone did not really exist. Unlike Indian villagers, I had given little thought to spirits of this world, to local ancestors and ghosts, or to the souls of animals. For me these belonged to the realm of fairies, trolls, and other mythical beings. Consequently I had no answers to the questions they raised (see fig. 12.3).

How did this two-tiered worldview emerge in the West? Belief in the middle level began to die in the seventeenth and eighteenth centuries with the growing acceptance of a Platonic dualism and of a science

2. Peter L. Berger, Brigitte Berger, and Hansfried Kellner, *The Homeless Mind: Modernization and Consciousness* (New York: Random House, 1973).

based on materialistic naturalism.[3] The result was the secularization of science and the mystification of religion. Science dealt with the empirical world using mechanistic analogies, leaving religion to handle other-worldly matters, often in terms of organic analogies. Science was based on the certitudes of sense experience, experimentation, and proof. Religion was left with faith in visions, dreams, and inner feelings. Science sought order in natural laws. Religion was brought in to deal with miracles and exceptions to the natural order, but these decreased as scientific knowledge expanded.

It should be apparent why many missionaries trained in the West had no answers to the problems of the middle level—they often did not even see it. When tribal people spoke of fear of evil spirits, they denied the existence of the spirits rather than claim the power of Christ over them. The result, Lesslie Newbigin has argued, is that Western Christian missions have been one of the greatest secularizing forces in history.[4]

What are the questions of the middle level that Westerners find so hard to answer, and how do they differ from questions raised by science and religion? Science as a system of explanation, whether folk or modern, answers questions about the nature of the world that is directly experienced. All people have social theories about how to raise children and organize social activities. All have ideas about the natural world and how to control it for their own benefit.

Religion as a system of explanation deals with the ultimate questions of the origin, purpose, and destiny of an individual, a society, and the universe. In the West the focus is on the individual; in the Old Testament it was on Israel as a society.

What are the questions of the middle level? Here one finds the questions of the uncertainty of the future, the crises of present life, and the unknowns of the past. Despite knowledge of facts such as that seeds once planted will grow and bear fruit, or that travel down this river on a boat will bring one to the neighboring village, the future is not totally predictable. Accidents, misfortunes, the intervention of other persons, and other unknown events can frustrate human planning.

How can one prevent accidents or guarantee success in the future? How can one make sure that a marriage will be fruitful and happy and will endure? How can one avoid getting on a plane that will crash? In the West these questions are left unanswered. They are accidents, luck,

3. Roger K. Bufford, *The Human Reflex: Behavioral Psychology in Biblical Perspective* (San Francisco: Harper and Row, 1981), 30.
4. Lesslie Newbigin, *Honest Religion for Secular Man* (Philadelphia: Westminster, 1966).

or unforeseeable events, and hence unexplainable. But many people are not content to leave so important a set of questions unanswered, and the answers they give are often stated in terms of ancestors, demons, witches, and local gods, or in terms of magic and astrology.

Similarly, the cries and misfortunes of present life must be handled: sudden disease and plagues, extended droughts, earthquakes, failures in business, and the empirically unexplainable loss of health. What does one do when the doctors have done all they can and a child grows sicker, or when one is gambling and the stakes are high? Again, many seek answers in the middle level.

And there are questions one must answer about the past: Why did *my* child die in the prime of life? Who stole the gold hidden in the house? Here again transempirical explanations often provide an answer when empirical ones fail.

Because the Western world no longer provides explanations for questions on the middle level, many Western missionaries have no answers within their Christian worldview. What is a Christian theology of ancestors; of animals and plants; of local spirits and spirit possession; and of principalities, powers, and rulers of the darkness of this world (Eph. 6:12)? What does one say when new tribal converts want to know how the Christian God tells them where and when to hunt, whether they should marry this daughter to that young man, or where they can find the lost money? Given no answer, they return to the diviner who gives definite answers, for these are the problems that loom large in their everyday life.

Implications for Missions

What implications does all of this have for missions? First, it points out the need for missionaries to develop holistic theologies that deal with all areas of life (see fig. 12.4), that avoid the Platonic dualism of the West, and that take seriously both body and soul.

On the highest level, this includes a theology of God in cosmic history—in the creation, redemption, purpose, and destiny of all things. Only as human history is placed within a cosmic framework does it take on meaning, and only when history has meaning does human biography become meaningful.

On the middle level, a holistic theology includes a theology of God in human history—in the affairs of nations, of peoples, and of individuals. This must include a theology of divine guidance, provision, and healing; a theology of ancestors, spirits, and invisible powers of this world; and a theology of suffering, misfortune, and death.

Figure 12.4
A Holistic Theology

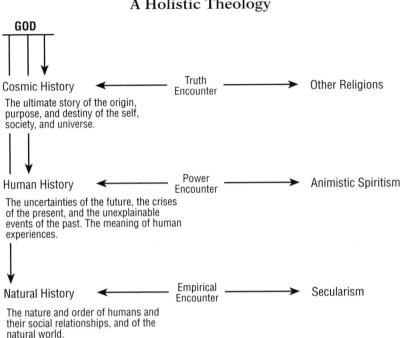

On this level some sections of the church have turned to doctrines featuring saints as intermediaries between God and humans. Others have turned to doctrines of the Holy Spirit to show God's active involvement in the events of human history. It is no coincidence that many of the most successful missions have provided some form of Christian answer to middle-level questions.

On the bottom level, a holistic theology includes an awareness of God in natural history—in sustaining the natural order of things. So long as the missionary comes with a two-tiered worldview, with God confined to the supernatural and the natural world operating for all practical purposes according to autonomous scientific laws, Christianity will continue to be a secularizing force in the world. Only as God is brought back into the middle of our scientific understanding of nature will we stem the tide of Western secularism.

There are two dangers against which we must guard when we formulate a theology that deals with the questions raised at the middle level. These middle-level questions include the meaning of life and death for the living; well-being and the threats of illness, drought, flood, and failure; and guidance in a world of unknowns. *The first danger is secularism.* This is to deny the reality of the spiritual realm in the events of human life, and to reduce the reality of this world to purely materialistic explanations. This is the answer offered by modern scientism.

The second danger is a return to a Christianized form of animism in which spirits and magic are used to explain everything. In spiritism, the spirits dominate reality, and humans must constantly battle or appease them to survive. In magic, humans seek to control supernatural powers through rituals and formulas to achieve their own personal desires. Both spiritism and magic are human and ego-centered; a person can gain what he or she wants by manipulating the spirits and controlling the forces. Both reject a God-centered view of reality, and both reject worship, obedience, and submission as the human response to God's will. The early church struggled against the animistic worldviews around it. Today there is a danger of returning to a Christianized animism in reaction to the secularism of the modern worldview.

Scripture offers us a third worldview that is neither secular nor animistic. It takes spiritual realities very seriously. In contrast to secular writings, it is full of references to God, angels, Satan, and demons. However, it takes the natural world and humans very seriously. In contrast to the Greek and Roman mythologies, and other great religious texts such as the *Avesta* and *Mahabharata*, the Bible does not focus its primary attention on the activities of the spirit world.[5] Rather, it is the history of God and of humans, and their relationship to each other. Humans are held responsible for their actions. They are tempted, but they choose to sin. God calls them to salvation, and they must respond to his call. The Bible also presents creation as an orderly world, operating according to divinely ordained principles.

In saying this, I do not want to deny the need to deal with the spirit world and related subjects. Yet we need to center our theology on God and his acts and not, as modern secularism and animism do, on human beings and their desires. We need to focus on worship and our relationship to God, and not on ways to control God for our own purposes through chants and formulas.

The line between worship and control is subtle, as I learned in the case of Muchintala. A week after our prayer meeting, Yellayya returned to say that the child had died. I felt thoroughly defeated. Who was I to

---

5. This is reflected in a simple word count in the Bible. In the KJV the word *God* is used 3,594 times, *Jehovah* 4 times, *Christ* 522 times, *Jesus* 942 times, and *Spirit of God* 26 times. Many other references to *lord* and *spirit* also refer to God. There are 362 references to angels and cherubim, and 158 to Satan, Lucifer, the evil one, and demons. There are 4,324 references to humans.

be a missionary if I could not pray for healing and receive a positive answer? A few weeks later Yellayya returned with a sense of triumph. "How can you be so happy after the child died?" I asked.

"The village would have acknowledged the power of our God had he healed the child," Yellayya said, "but they knew in the end she would have to die. When they saw in the funeral our hope of resurrection and reunion in heaven, they saw an even greater victory—over death itself— and they have begun to ask about the Christian way."

In a new way I began to realize that true answers to prayer are those that bring the greatest glory to God, not those that satisfy my immediate desires. It is all too easy to make Christianity a new magic in which we as gods can make God do our bidding.

Having formulated a theological response to the problems of the middle zone, it is important that we test the beliefs of the people we serve. Some of the things they may attribute to nature spirits, such as lightning, small pox, and failure in business, can better be explained through the order of creation under the superintendence of God. Other things are indeed manifestations of Satan and the other fallen angels. But much of Satan's work lies hidden to the people, and we must discern and oppose it.

In confronting animistic worldviews, our central message should always focus on the greatness, holiness, and power of God and his work in human lives. It is he who delivers us from the power of the evil one and gives us the power to live free, victorious Christian lives.

13

Biblical Perspectives on Spiritual Warfare

Ancient myths die hard.[1] They continue in disguise in popular culture long after they are rejected in orthodox religious thought. It is important, therefore, that we carefully examine our understanding of cosmic history.

One such story receiving considerable attention in North American Protestant churches today is "spiritual warfare."[2] This coincides with the decline of the modern era with its faith in secular materialism and the emergence of the postmodern era with its emphasis on various types of "spirituality."[3] It also coincides with a loss of confidence in human efforts to solve the world's problems and a widespread fear concerning the future.

Interest in spiritual matters must be both welcomed and tested. It must be welcomed because the church too often has bought into the worldview of a secular science that denies the reality of sin and spiritual realities. It must be tested because we are in danger of returning to the views of our pagan past.

This chapter first appeared in *Mission Focus* 20.3 (September 1992): 41–50. Used by permission.

1. The term *myth* is used in its technical, not popular, sense. In popular parlance, *myth* means fiction. In the social sciences, it means the big true story by which all other stories can be understood. In this sense, the Exodus in the Old Testament is both true history and the story by which Israel was to interpret their tribulations. Whenever they were in trouble, they reminded themselves that just as God had delivered them from Egypt, so he would deliver them from their present troubles.

2. Frank E. Peretti, *This Present Darkness* (Westchester, Ill.: Crossway, 1986); idem, *Piercing the Darkness* (Westchester, Ill.: Crossway, 1989); C. Peter Wagner and F. Douglas Pennoyer, *Wrestling with Dark Angels: Toward a Deeper Understanding of the Supernatural Forces in Spiritual Warfare* (Ventura, Calif.: Regal, 1990); Timothy Warner, *Spiritual Warfare: Victory over the Powers of This Dark World* (Wheaton, Ill.: Crossway, 1991).

3. Russell Chandler, *Understanding the New Age* (Waco, Tex.: Word, 1988).

As we will see, the pagan Indo-European myth of our ancestors is still alive in our North American fables, sports, movies, politics, and business. To what extent has our renewed interest in spiritual warfare been drawn from Indo-European mythology, and to what extent is it from the Bible?

The Indo-European Myth

Central to the Indo-European worldview is the myth of a cosmic spiritual war between good and evil.[4] With the spread of the Indo-Europeans from inner-Asia to Europe, Mesopotamia, and South Asia, this myth in its various forms became the basis for the religions of Babylon, Sumer, Canaan, Greece, India, and Germany, to name a few.[5] What worldview sustained this myth? Unfortunately, worldviews are largely implicit and difficult to examine. They are made up of the categories, values, and assumptions we use to examine our world, the cultural lenses that shape the way we see the world. Worldviews assure us that this is the way things really are.

A careful study of root myths and metaphors of Indo-European religions suggests the following worldview themes.

The Eternal Coexistence of Good and Evil

Fundamental to the Indo-European myth is the belief that good and evil are two independent entities in coexistence from eternity. In this dualism good and evil come from two different and opposing superhuman agencies. The classic example is found in ancient Persia in the battle between Ahura Mazda, the good divine being, and Ahriman, the equally eternal and powerful personification of evil. Human beings are nothing but puppets or pawns in their hands. As David Bosch points out, it is hardly coincidence that the game of chess was developed in Persia, and reflects the fundamental Indo-European view of reality.[6] Omar Khayyam aptly expresses,

> 'Tis all a chequer-board of nights and days
> Where destiny with men for pieces plays;

4. Gerald J. Larson, et al., eds., *Myth and Indo-European Antiquity* (Berkeley, Calif.: University of California Press, 1974); Jean Puhvel, ed., *Myth and Law among the Indo-Europeans: Studies in Indo-European Comparative Mythology* (Berkeley, Calif.: University of California Press, 1970).

5. Mary K. Wakeman, *God's Battle with the Monster: A Study in Biblical Imagery* (Leiden: E. J. Brill, 1973).

6. David J. Bosch, "The Problem of Evil in Africa: A Survey of African Views of Witchcraft and of the Response of the Christian Church," in Pieter G. R. deVilliers, ed., *Like a Roaring Lion: Essays on the Bible, the Church, and Demonic Powers* (Pretoria, South Africa: C. B. Powell Bible Centre, 1987), 38.

Figure 13.1

Indo-European View of Good and Evil

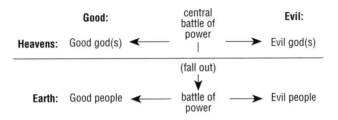

Hither and thither moves and mates and slays,
And one by one back in the closet lays.[7]

In this battle, the ultimate good is order and freedom, and to achieve this one side or the other must gain control. The ultimate evil is chaos and enslavement (see fig. 13.1).

The evil gods (Asag, Vritra, Tiamat, Ravana, and others) are autonomous beings in constant battle with the good gods (Ninurta, Indra, Marduk, Rama, and others) for the control of the world. Applied to the biblical narrative, this view sees Satan and the demons as autonomous beings. They may have been created by God in the beginning, but now they no longer depend on God for their continued existence. Creation was an act completed in the distant past.

Given this dualism, all reality is divided into two camps: God and Satan, angels and demons, good nations and evil ones, good humans and wicked ones. The good may be deceived or forced into doing bad things but, at heart, they are good. The evil have no redeeming qualities. They must by destroyed so that good may reign.

The line between the two camps is sharp. There are no shades between them. The result is a bounded-set view of reality (see chapter 6). Our dualism is seen in our American tendency to categorize in opposites: good-bad, big-small, sweet-sour, success-failure, and truth-falsehood.[8] This duality colors our political views. Other nations are either developed or undeveloped.

Order and Control

In dualism the central issue is order. Two competing parties create a fundamental danger of chaos. Only when order is established can we

---

7. Ibid.
8. Conrad M. Arensberg and Arthur H. Niehoff, *Introducing Social Change: A Manual for Community Development* (Chicago: Aldine, 1971), 207–31.

speak of building a just society. Peace, love, righteousness, and harmonious relationships are secondary values.

To establish order, someone must be in control. Hierarchy, therefore, is essential to prevent the rise of chaos. In Indo-European mythology, the gods and demons live on one plane and rule over humans who live on another plane (fig. 13.1). The latter are hapless victims of cosmic affairs. The old adage says, "When the elephants fight, the mice are trampled." Humans, therefore, live in fear of the spirits, both good and evil, for these control their destiny. Humans, for their part, seek to manipulate the gods to do their bidding. Magic and manipulation become the means.

The perennial question is: who is lord in the heavens? *Lord* here means one who controls the others and establishes order, by force if need be. It is the king who rules by might and commands the obedience of his vassals. Such a king should be strong, aloof, and proud.

The Battle in the Cosmos

The question of cosmic control is determined in Indo-European mythology by a battle between a good party and an evil one, in which power determines the outcome. The highest value is success. If good wins, righteousness, peace, and love can rule. If evil wins, then evil reigns. To win, therefore, is everything.

Morality in these power encounters is based on the notion of fairness and equal opportunity. To be "fair" the conflict must be between those thought to be more or less equal in might. In other words, the outcome of the battle must be uncertain. It is "unfair" to pit a seasoned gunman against a youngster, or the Los Angeles Rams against a high school football team. "Equal opportunity" means that both sides must be able to use the same means to gain victory. The good side cannot use evil means first, but if the evil side does, the good side can, too. In westerns, the sheriff cannot draw first, but when the outlaw does, the sheriff can gun him down without a trial. In Indo-European battles the good become like their enemies: they end up using violence, entering without warrants, lying, committing adultery, and killing without due process. All of this is justified in the name of victory. Righteousness and love reign only after victory is won.

In Indo-European mythology, land is important. Gods and humans battle for and rule different territories. Lesser spirits control the mountains, the rivers, the plains, and the seas. Earthly kings turn to their gods to give them victory in wars against their enemies and their enemies' gods. If they lose, it is because their god is defeated. In this worldview, it is unthinkable that a god would let enemies win to bring judgment on the people because they have sinned. Loyalty in battle is more important than righteousness.

Underlying the Indo-European worldview is the deep belief that relationships in the cosmos are based on competition, that competition is good, and that good will ultimately win. Success is proof that one is right. Consequently, warriors are the second class of society. They are considered noble and rank only below the priests.[9]

Victory as the Goal

After victory the gods can inaugurate a kingdom of justice and peace. Righteousness and relationships are secondary to order. Two dilemmas remain. First, if the gods use wicked means to win the battle, have they not become a party to evil? One answer, found in Hinduism and the New Age, is that good and evil are ultimately one, two sides of the same coin. Dualism is reduced to monism. A second answer, found in Zoroastrianism, is that both coexist in an eternal, cosmic struggle. In both views no victory is final. Evil is never fully defeated; it rises again to challenge the good. Good must constantly be on guard against future attacks.

In the Indo-European worldview, the battle is the center of the story. When it is over, the story is done. The final words are "and they won (or were married) and lived happily ever after." But there is no story worth telling about the "happily ever after." The adventure and thrill is in the battle, and it is to this that we return again and again.

This fascination with battle is evident in our modern sports. People pay to see a football game. When the battle is over, everyone goes home and waits for the next battle. We see it in the reactions to the end of the Cold War. Francis Fukuyama, a policy planner in the U.S. State Department, perceives the end of the Cold War as "the end of history," leaving the world with no master plot, only "centuries of boredom" stretching ahead like a superhighway to nowhere.[10] We need an enemy to give meaning to our lives.

The Indo-European religions have died in the West, but as Walter Wink relates, the Indo-European cosmic myth dominates modern American thought.[11] It is the basis for our westerns, detective stories, murder mysteries, and science fiction. It is told in Superman, Spiderman, Super Chicken, Underdog, and most of our cartoons. It is reen-

9. Bruce Lincoln, *Myth, Cosmos, and Society: Indo-European Themes of Creation and Destruction* (Cambridge, Mass.: Harvard University Press, 1986).

10. Melvin Maddocks, "Lenin on the Golf Links," *World Monitor* (January 1990): 16.

11. Conference plenary address, Seminary Consortium for Urban Pastoral Education (SCUPE), Chicago, 1989.

acted in "Star Wars" movies, dramatized in video games, and taught in the New Age movement. It is played out in football, basketball, and tennis. It is affirmed in theories of evolution and capitalism.

An Evaluation

The Scriptures speak of spiritual warfare (see Eph. 6:10–20; Rev. 19:19–20), but that warfare does not fit the Indo-European myth. First, *the central issue in biblical warfare is not power but faithfulness.* In the Old Testament both Israel's victories and defeats are attributed to God. Their victories are due to their faithfulness to God and his laws; their defeats to God's punishment when they forsake him (Judg. 4:1–2; 6:1; 10:7; 1 Sam. 28:17–19; 1 Kings 16:2–3; 20:28; 2 Kings 17:7–23). In no instance is their loss blamed on Yahweh's defeat at the hands of other gods. In fact, the prophets declare that no other gods exist even to challenge him (Isa. 37:19; Jer. 2:11; 5:7). To put any other on the same level with God is itself idolatry (Exod. 20:4–5). The central issue is not power, but shalom. It is the relationship between people and God. This view of Israel's defeat stands in sharp contrast to the views of the peoples around Israel (1 Kings 20:23). They attributed their defeat to the power of Yahweh, and their victories to the power of their gods.

Second, in contrast to the Indo-European myths in which humans are hapless victims of the cosmic battles of the gods, *the Bible places the blame for suffering on humans themselves.* They are sinners, co-conspirators with Satan and his host in rebellion against God. They turn from God. In contrast to Indo-European myths full of the activities of angels and demons, the Scriptures speak surprisingly little about them. The central story is the story of humans and their acts, and of God's acts.

Third, *the Scriptures are clear that the cross is the ultimate victory.* This makes no sense in Indo-European terms. Christ should have taken up the challenge of his tormentors and come down from the cross with his angelic hosts. He should have defeated Satan when he met him in the desert. Scripture makes it clear that the cross itself was Satan's defeat (1 Cor. 1:18–25). It was not an apparent loss saved at the last moment by the resurrection.

Fourth, *righteousness and love are the ultimate end.* It is in the *fallen* world that the lion eats the lamb (Isa. 11:6), and competition, not cooperation, works as a way of organizing society. This, however, is not God's way, which is the way of caring for one another, loving one's enemy, and seeking reconciliation and peace.

If this is not the biblical image of spiritual warfare, what is?

Figure 13.2
Biblical View of Good and Evil

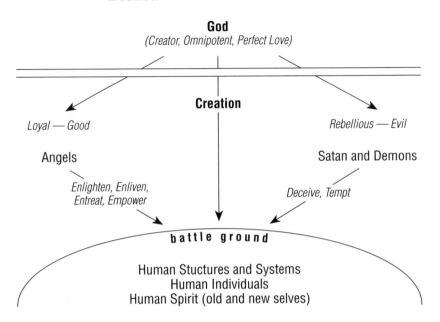

Biblical Images of Spiritual Warfare

The biblical images of spiritual realities differ radically from Indo-European mythology at several key points and give us a very different view of the cosmic spiritual warfare in which we are engaged.

Eternal Good, Contingent Evil

Good is eternal and evil is contingent. The Bible is clear: God and Satan, good and evil, are not eternal and coexistent. In the beginning was God, and God was good. Satan, sinners, and sin appear in creation. Moreover, God's creation depends upon him for continued existence. God did not, at some point in the past, create a universe that exists independent of him. Satan and sinners, like all creation, are contingent on God's sustaining power. Their very existence in their rebellion is testimony to God's mercy and love (see fig. 13.2).

The central issue, therefore, is not one of brute power. God's omnipotence is never questioned in Scripture. Even Satan and his hosts acknowledge this. The issue is holiness and evil, righteousness and sin. God is holy, light, love, life, and truth. Evil does not exist independently. It is the perversion of good. It is darkness, and deceitfulness, and the source of death. It is broken relationships, idolatry and rebellion against God, alienation, and the worship of the self.

Shalom and Holiness

At the heart of the gospel is shalom. This begins with a right relationship with God involving worship, holiness, and obedience. Prayer in Indo-European thought is a means to control the gods; in biblical thought it is submission to God. In prayer we give God permission to use us and our resources to answer our prayer. It can, therefore, be costly.

Shalom also involves right relationships with humans. These are not characterized by hierarchy and exploitation, as in the Indo-European world, in which the strong lord it over the weak. Right relationships are expressed in love and care for one another as people fully created in the image of God, no matter how broken or flawed. Shalom means to be for the other, rather than for one's self and to commit one's self to the other, regardless of the other's response.

Shalom gives priority to building community over completing tasks. This demands that we give up our Western need to control people and situations around us. It means we accept corporate decision-making and accountability to the community.

How do love and shalom fit with such images as king, reign, and kingdom? In the Indo-European worldview these are antithetical. A king cannot show love to his enemy and destroy him. He cannot show intimacy with his subjects and rule them. In contrast, Scripture indicates that the ruler is to be a servant of the people, not to lord it over them (Luke 22:25–27; John 13:1–16), and all are to love, not hate, their enemies.

In the biblical worldview, not all chaos is evil. Evil chaos results in destruction and death. Creative chaos is the unformed potential from which spring creation and life. It is the unformed material out of which God created the universe (Gen. 1:2). It is the infant not yet grown to adulthood.

Creative chaos is inherent in genuine relationships. The birth of a child introduces turmoil into the routine of the home. Friendships and intimate marriages mean letting go of power and sharing decisions. Our Western need for order and control works against true communication and fellowship, because it is the passage through chaos that forms the basis for real communication and community.

The image of God as King is free of the Indo-European connotations of territorialism. Unlike the gods of the Canaanites, who are identified with a particular people, their lands, and their successes in battle, Jehovah is the God of the whole world and of all peoples. More-over, he is responsible for the defeats of Israel as well as their victories. Israel's losses are not due to the triumphs of the gods of their enemies. The prophets make it clear that there is no real battle between the gods. Israel's defeats are due to the anger and discipline of their own God! He not only heals (Luke 4:40); he punishes (Acts 5:1–10; Rev. 19:11–21).

Where does power fit into this picture? Clearly, godly might in the Scriptures refers to the power of authority (Matt. 28:18) and rule (Rev. 19:11–16). Might does not make right, nor does battle make the victor legitimate. Rather, with legitimacy comes authority, and with authority comes power.

The Battle in Human Hearts

If the central message of the Bible is not that a cosmic struggle be-tween God and Satan will determine who will rule, what is it about? The battle rages within the human heart, which God and Satan seek to win. Here two metaphors emerge. The first is the wayward son. The father lavishes his love on his son, but the son rebels and turns on his father. The father is not interested in defeating his son but in winning him back, so he reaches out in unconditional love. The son wants to provoke the father into hating him, and twists logic to justify his rebellion. But the father takes all the evil his son heaps on him and continues to love. Similarly, God is love, and loves no matter what his rebellious creations do (Matt. 5:44–45; Luke 6:35–36). If he does less, if he can be provoked to hate, he is less than the perfect God that he is.

It is clear that God continues to love sinful humans, but does that apply to Satan himself? Hard as this may seem, it is even harder to be-lieve that God would hate his own creation. He hates Satan's rebellion and the destruction it has brought, but can he hate Satan, who is his own creation? If he does, he is no longer the perfect God of love. And if he defeats Satan by brute force apart from righteousness, he himself be-comes evil.

What then is the nature of spiritual warfare in the Bible? Compared to Indo-European myths, there are few references to cosmic battles. The central story is about the battle for the spirits of human beings. In this, humans are not passive victims of battles fought on a cosmic plane. They are the central actors and the locus of the action. They are the rebels, and ever since the temptation of Adam, self-worship has been the basis of their idolatry.

Satan, too, is seeking their allegiance, but his methods are deceit and temptation. He and his demons possess those who yield themselves fully to him. For these, salvation must include deliverance from demonic dominance. Jesus cast out the demons of those who came to him, but this was not his central ministry. He did this in passing as he went about preaching the kingdom. In the end it was not the demons that killed Jesus, but humans and their institutions—the Sanhedrin and the Roman government. Today, opposition on earth to God still centers in humans.

Our rebellion is both individual and corporate. As individuals we have turned against God. As groups we develop social and cultural systems that often keep people from coming to Christ. There is good in the cultures and societies humans create, but there is also evil. Individuals may want to follow God, but they become caught in the webs of family ties, religious structures, and sociocultural systems that prevent them from doing so on pain of persecution and death.

What about the battle in the heavens between God and Satan? Here a second metaphor found in Scripture is helpful, that of king and rebellious vassals or stewards (Matt. 21:33–43).[12] At first the stewards are faithful, and their appointment gives them legitimate authority over part of the kingdom. Later they rebel and persecute the righteous. In Indo-European mythology the king must defeat the rebels by might and destroy them. In biblical cosmology the king must first seek reconciliation and demonstrate that the stewards are unrepentant or he can be accused of being selfish and arbitrary. He sends servants, who are mistreated. He sends his son, who is tried by the vassals' court, found guilty, and punished by death. The case is appealed to the supreme court in heaven. There the judgment of the lower court is found to be unjust, so the verdict is overturned. Moreover, the court itself is found to be evil, so it is removed from power and sentenced to punishment. The central issue, then, is not one of power, but of legitimacy.

Given this imagery it is clear why the cross, not the resurrection, is the supreme victory, for there Satan and his supporters are shown to be evil. In the resurrection God overturns the judgment of the Jewish and Roman courts and frees the innocent victim. When the case was overturned, Satan had no more legitimate authority in heaven or on earth. He was therefore cast out.

The focus of the gospel is not battle but reconciliation. God judges those who reject him but reaches out to his enemies in love. He rejoices, not in their defeat, but in their return. His justice and love cannot be separated as they are in Indo-European lore.

---

12. Robert Guelich, "Images in Luke" (inaugural address given at Fuller Theological Seminary, Pasadena, Calif., 1990).

Shalom as the Goal

Shalom, not victory, is the ultimate goal. In Indo-European lore the thrill is in the battle and the chase. The standard ending of the romance is "and they were married and lived happily ever after." In stories of battle it is "and the victor ruled righteously forever." The fact is, however, that there is no story worth telling after the marriage or the victory. In variant endings, the boredom of a peaceful marriage is shattered by the excitement of extramarital affairs, or a victory is temporary and we look forward to another battle. The outcome must at least appear to be in doubt. The victory itself is often anticlimactic.

In Scripture the focus is on an eternity of fellowship with God and one another, characterized by love, joy, and peace—not an eternity of battles and displays of power.

Implications

What implications does the renewed emphasis on spiritual warfare have for us as Western Christians in the twentieth century? It is an important reminder that we are involved in a spiritual battle against evil. The secularism of our surrounding culture too often blinds us to the realities of wickedness or leads us to reduce evil to an illness that requires therapy.[13] We need to recover a sense of the awfulness of evil and oppression in our world, both spiritual and human.

A wrong view of the nature of the warfare in which we are involved, however, can lead us to set our watch on the wrong hill or fight the wrong battles. Satan would like us either to ignore him so that he can carry out his work undetected, or to fear him unduly so that we take our eyes off Christ, our strength.

Several principles must guide our understanding of spiritual warfare:

First, *there is a spiritual battle for the hearts and souls of humans.* The focus in Scripture is not on the battle between God and Satan. That has already been won (Heb. 2:14). Central now is God's willingness to win back humans who joined Satan in his rebellion. He seeks these rebels by love, truth, and the assurance of forgiveness and reconciliation. Satan is trying to keep them by deceit (Rev. 12:9), intimidation, temptation (1 Thess. 3:5), and accusation (Rev. 12:10). He appears, not as a dark angel, but as an angel of light, counterfeiting all that God does.

Second, *Satan has no power over God's people other than what God permits him for the testing of their faith.* Moreover, in every temptation

---

13. Robert N. Bellah, et al., *Habits of the Heart: Individualism and Commitment in American Life* (Berkeley, Calif.: University of California Press, 1985).

God gives us the power to resist (1 Cor. 10:13). This does not mean that new converts may not be oppressed by Satan. The oppressed need to be freed by ministries of deliverance.

Third, *Satan and his hosts can and do demonize people, but those with a demonic presence are to be pitied more than feared.* The church needs teams of pastors, doctors, psychologists, and those with the gift of exorcism to minister to them. The real danger is found in people who coolly and rationally reject Christ and his rule in their lives, lead others astray (Eph. 4:14; 5:6; 2 Thess. 2:3), and build human societies and cultures that oppress people and keep them from coming to Christ. Idolatry and self-absorption, not spirit possession, is still at the heart of human rebellion.

Fourth, *our focus as Christians should be on love, reconciliation, peace, and justice.* If we focus too strongly on a war metaphor we are in danger of applying it in our relationship to the world and to our brothers and sisters in the faith. Satan likes nothing better than to have us fight among ourselves or to feel superior to non-Christians.

Fifth, *the supreme event in spiritual warfare is the cross.* There Christ died, even though he had but to utter one command and ten thousands of angels would have come to his rescue (Matt. 26:53). If our understanding of spiritual warfare does not make sense of the cross, it is wrong.

Sixth, we must avoid two extremes: *a denial of the reality of Satan and the spiritual battle within and around us in which we are engaged and an undue fascination with, and fear of, Satan and his hosts.* Our central focus is on Christ, not on Satan. We should see God's angels at work more than we see demons. Our message is one of victory, hope, joy, and freedom, for we have the power of the Holy Spirit to overcome evil. The cosmic battle is over. We are messengers to declare to the world that Christ is indeed the Lord of everything in the heavens and on earth. All authority has already been given to him (Matt. 28:18).

Our hidden myths profoundly affect the way we live our everyday lives: how we treat our spouses, organize our society, and fight our wars. We underestimate the extent to which enemies, battles, competition, self-interest, and greed are essential to our North American understanding of reality. We ignore the fact that these values have their roots in ancient Indo-European beliefs and form the dominant religion of our society.

Our conversion from our pagan past is not yet complete. We need to read the gospel again, this time with an awareness of our own worldview and how it shapes our interpretation of the Scriptures. In particular, we need to test current teachings about cosmic spiritual warfare to see whether they fit biblical teachings or reinforce a pagan religious worldview. Too often they seem to reflect the fascination with battle that dominates our society and not the love of holiness and shalom that fills the gospel. If we are not careful, we may become more involved in spiritual warfare and live less holy lives.

14

Healing and the Kingdom

In recent years there has been a renewed interest in miraculous experiences in the church. The Pentecostals emphasize tongues and prophecies as proofs of God's presence among his people. The charismatics look for such evidences in ecstatic experiences. Now, in many churches, on television, and in conferences, the focus has shifted to healing, exorcisms, and "words of knowledge."

What should our response be to this renewed interest in miracles? Norman Cohn observes that the issues involved are not new.[1] Periodically in the life of the church leaders have called for miraculous demonstrations of God's power as signs of his presence among his people. St. Gregory, living in the sixth century, described in detail a preacher from Bourges who healed the sick and gathered a large following. A century and a half later, St. Boniface described another itinerant preacher, Aldebert, who claimed to perform miraculous cures and attracted large audiences. Other miracle-workers who followed claimed that the kingdom of God had come in its fullness for those who believed. The results of their ministries were mixed: sometimes the church experienced renewal, but often it was led astray and left in disarray and division. The same is true of revival movements that focused on current problems and miraculous solutions.

Today we hear many prophets claim new revelations and special relationships with God. We need to understand the times and to heed John's exhortation to test the messages against Scripture as it is interpreted within the community of believers.

This chapter first appeared in slightly different form in Jim Coggins and Paul G. Hiebert, eds., *Wonders and the Word* (Winnipeg, Manitoba: Kindred Press, 1989). Used by permission.
1. Norman R. C. Cohn, *The Pursuit of the Millennium* (Oxford: Oxford University Press, 1957).

Understanding the Times:
The Rise of the Modern Worldview

The renewed interest in miracles in the Western church is due in large measure to changes taking place in the foundations of our ways of thinking, our Western worldview. Underlying every culture are basic assumptions about the nature of things. Someone who questions worldview assumptions is seen, not as wrong, but as foolish. For example, in the West if we were to argue that freedom is not inherently good for a society, people would not take us seriously. These assumptions are the lenses through which we view the world.

Currently the Western world is undergoing a radical change in its worldview. The old foundations that provided the basis for Western thought for centuries are crumbling, and no one set of new foundations has replaced them. In such times of uncertainty and fear, prophets often emerge, proclaiming new worldviews that they promise will guide people to a better life. There are a number of such prophets today, both in science and religion. Within this flux we must understand the movements of our day.

The modern worldview that has served the West for the past two centuries was deeply influenced by both the Reformation and the Renaissance. During the Middle Ages, the church regarded the physical world as essentially evil, a place in which Christians suffered on their way to heaven. Consequently, little emphasis was placed on the study of this world or on improving the conditions of life. The truly religious were expected to spend their time in worship, meditation, and prayer. Most common folk, however, were not primarily interested in salvation. They were concerned with the problems of their everyday lives: sickness, plagues, famine, wars, and uncertainty. To deal with these, many turned to Mary and the saints as intermediaries in the church, and to diviners, witch doctors, medicine men, and other practitioners from their pre-Christian past. Others, particularly those without social roots in stable communities, flocked to faith healers who promised them health and success.[2]

The Reformers rejected this wedding of animism and Christianity and stressed the active presence of God in the lives of people here and now.[3] They preached a strong theology of providence—of God as Lord not only of cosmic history but also of human history and of personal biography.

2. Ibid., 281–86.
3. Max Weber, *The Protestant Ethic and the Spirit of Capitalism*, trans. T. Parsons (New York: Scribner's Sons, 1958).

Figure 14.1
Biblical and Western Worldviews Compared

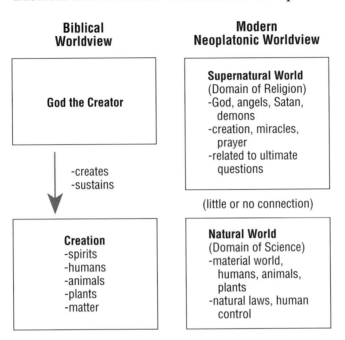

Biblical Worldview

God the Creator

-creates
-sustains

Creation
-spirits
-humans
-animals
-plants
-matter

Modern Neoplatonic Worldview

Supernatural World
(Domain of Religion)
-God, angels, Satan, demons
-creation, miracles, prayer
-related to ultimate questions

(little or no connection)

Natural World
(Domain of Science)
-material world, humans, animals, plants
-natural laws, human control

However, the Renaissance distorted the Reformation worldview by reintroducing a Neoplatonic dualism into Western thought. Instead of the biblical worldview, in which the central distinction is between God the Creator and his creation, the Neoplatonic worldview drew a sharp line between spirit and matter (see fig. 14.1). God, angels, and demons were put together in the world of spiritual beings. Humans, animals, plants, and matter were seen as nature.

Modern Dualism

This shift at the worldview level led to a sharp line of distinction between the *supernatural* and the *natural*. The former has to do with otherworldly concerns, such as God, Satan, heaven, hell, sin, salvation, prayer, and miracles. Nature—the world of matter, space, and time—was increasingly seen as an autonomous realm operating according to natural laws that could be understood by scientists and used to solve human problems on this earth.

Scientists, working within a Christian worldview, at first saw God as the ultimate source and sustainer of the universe, but as science explained more and more in terms of *natural law,* many scientists believed they had no need for God to account for what they observed. The two worlds became divorced from each other and met only at creation, when God made matter and set the laws of nature in motion; and in miracles, when God intervened in nature and overrode natural laws. This had a powerful secularizing effect on Western thought.

By the twentieth century, there was little room for God in the Western worldview. The origins of the universe had been pushed back to a remote time, and scientists had other explanations for much that had been thought to be miraculous. God was needed only to account for what was unknown, and there was a widespread belief that, given time, science would be able to explain what was temporarily inexplicable.

Modern Dualism and Christianity

The modern Neoplatonic dualism left many Western Christians with a spiritual schizophrenia. They believed in God and the cosmic history of creation-fall-redemption-final judgment. This provided them with ultimate meaning and purpose in life. Yet they lived in an ordinary world explained in naturalistic terms, in which there was little room for God. They drove cars, used electricity, and ingested medicines—all products of scientific understandings that reinforced a scientific way of thinking.

This internal tension was increased when Christians read the Bible. There they found God at work in human history with no sharp distinction made between natural and supernatural phenomena. The biblical worldview did not fit with modern secular explanations that denied spiritual realities, particularly in everyday experiences.

The consequences of this modern dualism were destructive in the church. Liberal theologians sought to reduce the tension by explaining the miracles of the Bible totally in naturalistic terms. Conservative theologians affirmed the reality of miracles but often accepted a naturalistic view of the world. Many of them drew a line between evangelism and the "social gospel," thereby reinforcing the dualism that had led to the secularization of the West. For them, evangelism had to do with the supernatural salvation of the soul. The social gospel involved ministry to human bodily needs, such as food, medicine, and education. This they dismissed as of secondary importance.

The Deification of the Self

A second consequence of the modern worldview was the placing of humans at the top of nature. With God out of the picture, humans became the gods of the earth. During the Renaissance, Machiavelli took the next logical step and called people to forget about salvation, which by his day had lost much of its clarity and urgency. Rather, he said, they should focus on enjoying life here on earth, which is real and immediate. Personal health, comfort, and prosperity became the central goals of Western culture, and science was seen as the means to achieve them.

Left alone, however, modern humans faced a crisis of meaning. Now they were gods, but what kind of gods were they? Mechanistic science enabled humans to control nature, but it also gave them the power to destroy nature through violence, nuclear holocausts, chemical pollution, and deforestation. The same science, applied to humans themselves, saw them as animals ruled by needs and irrational drives (Freudian psychology), as stimulus-response machines (behavioral psychology), or as robots programmed by their societies and cultures (sociology and anthropology). God was gone, but so was the human soul. There was no real meaning left in human life.

To recover a sense of meaning, Western philosophers coined the term *self* to replace the concept of *soul.* It was assumed that people are autonomous selves and that, because they are now the gods, their individual well-being is the highest good.[4] This view of humans as independent, self-reliant selves was a radical shift from the biblical and medieval view of them as created in the image of God and dependent upon God at every moment for their existence and meaning.

Replacing *soul* with *self*, however, did not solve the problem. The question now arose, what is this *self?* Some, such as Locke and Descartes, believed it to be reason. Humans are different from animals because they think. Using reason they can create a happy, peaceful, and meaningful world. Others, such as Rousseau and Nietzsche, disagreed. They believed that what makes humans different from animals, and their lives meaningful, is the ability to feel—to envision better worlds and to create them. Humans are culture builders. They are mortal beings who find meaning in realizing their dreams about themselves. Both groups, however, agreed on one thing: Meaning is to be found in self-fulfillment, in the good life here and now. The existential present, not eternity, is of primary importance.

The focus on the self here and now became the dominant theme in Western society during the last decade of the nineteenth century. The traditional Protestant values of salvation, morality, hard work, saving and sacrifice, civic responsibility, and self-denial for the good of others were replaced by a new set of values: personal realization, health, material comfort, immediate gratification, and periodic leisure.[5] These, it

---

4. Allan Bloom, *The Closing of the American Mind: Education and the Crisis of Reason* (New York: Simon and Schuster, 1987), 173.

5. Richard W. Fox and Jackson Lears, *The Culture of Consumption: Critical Essays in American History, 1860–1960* (New York: Pantheon, 1983), 4.

was believed, could be achieved through buying material goods (largely on credit) and accumulating wealth. The gospel of self-indulgence was preached by a host of advertisers. Marlboro cigarettes freed us from the drudgery of city life and put us out in Wyoming, with its clean air, stars, and the thrill of the range. Coke, we were told, was "the real thing."

This focus on the self was reinforced by Abraham Maslow, Fritz Perls, Carl Rogers, and other key figures in the fledgling field of humanistic psychology. They sought to restore human dignity by offering a psychology that glorified the self.

The result of this shift in the modern worldview was an almost obsessive concern with psychic and physical health. Life owed us comfort, health, happiness, success, prosperity, and intense, ecstatic experiences. Failure, loss of self-worth, and boredom, rather than sin, became the implacable enemies. Therapy, consumption, and miraculous cures were the means of salvation. A new Western religion emerged to offer us meaning based on self-realization, not forgiveness of personal sins and reconciliation with God and others.[6] Self had become god and self-fulfillment our salvation. Personal biography replaced cosmic history as the framework on which human significance was to be found. The only story most North Americans felt a part of was their own.[7]

The new gospel had a strong influence on Protestant Christianity, particularly the liberal wing. G. Stanley Hall asserted that the kingdom of God exalted "man here and now."[8] Harry Emerson Fosdick and Norman Vincent Peale provided religious sanctions for the emerging value system.[9] The starting point of Christianity, Fosdick claimed, was not an otherworldly faith, but a faith in human personality: "Not an outward temple, but the inward shrine of man's personality, with all its possibilities and powers, is . . . infinitely sacred."[10]

Bruce Barton reinterpreted Jesus in the ideals of abundant vitality and intense experience. Barton's Jesus personified personal magnetism, vibrant health, and outdoor living. He was no weak Lamb of God. Women adored him, and he was the most popular dinner guest in Jeru-

6. J. A. Walter, *Need: The New Religion* (Downers Grove, Ill.: InterVarsity, 1986).

7. Bloom, *Closing*.

8. Granville Stanley Hall, *Jesus, the Christ, in the Light of Psychology* (Garden City, N.Y.: Doubleday, 1917).

9. Norman Vincent Peale, *The Positive Power of Jesus Christ,* Special FCL ed. (Pawling, N.Y.: Foundation for Christian Living, 1980); idem, *The Positive Principle Today: How to Renew and Sustain the Power of Positive Thinking* (Englewood Cliffs, N.J.: Prentice Hall, 1976).

10. Harry Emerson Fosdick, *Twelve Tests of Character* (New York: Association, 1923), 47.

salem. "He did not come to establish a theology but to lead a life," Barton wrote. "Living more healthfully than any of his contemporaries, he spread health wherever he went. . . . He offered righteousness as the path to a happier, more satisfying way of living."[11] Health was no longer seen, along with sickness and suffering, as part of the human condition within God's greater plan of salvation or as a means by which God works out his purposes. It had become an end in itself, cloaked with religious value, something humans could and should strive to achieve.

This emphasis on self and the present has led to a North American individualism and pragmatism that emphasizes short-term, personal problem-solving, rather than ultimate meaning and truth. Self-realization, in one form or another, has become the dominant religion of the West.

Individualism and the Church

The effects of self-centeredness on the Western church have been profound. Salvation increasingly has become a personal matter between the self and God that has little to do with the formation of a new community in Christ. Many churches have become little more than religious clubs, organized on the basis of voluntary association and common interests. The relationship between members is no longer seen as a sacrament (ordained of God) or covenant (commitment to a group) but as a contract (based on personal need for self-fulfillment). It should not surprise us, therefore, that Christians often do not find a congregation to be a true community and drift from church to church.

This deification of self has made inroads into the church. We hear the good news that we can have health, wealth, and prosperity here and salvation in the life to come—without suffering, persecution, a cross, or a sense of sin. An example of this comes from Gene Ewing, in the introduction to his book *If You Want Money, a Home in Heaven, Health and Happiness, Based on the Holy Bible, Do These Things.* Ewing writes, "This book is designed to *teach you* about the power that you have within you which can lift you up *from the midst of sickness, feeling down, failure, poverty* and *frustration,* and set you on the exciting road to *health, happiness, abundance* and *security.* I have seen miraculous transformations take place in men and women from all walks of life when they begin releasing the power of faith that is within them and

---

11. Bruce Barton, *The Man Nobody Knows: A Discovery of the Real Jesus* (Indianapolis: Bobbs-Merrill, 1925), 143, 149, 151.

sowing faith seeds."[12] Titles of the first four chapters are: "You Can Have the Desires of Your Heart"; "God Wants You to Have Plenty of Money"; "God Wants to Heal You Everywhere You Hurt"; and "God Will Get You That Good Job You Desire."

This is an extreme statement of the health and prosperity gospel, but it illustrates the fundamental assumptions of this theology, which is increasingly heard in the media and in churches.

The Collapse of the Modern Worldview

Despite the physical well-being made possible by science, there is a growing doubt that this alone makes sense out of life or that science is the savior people once believed it would be. Even in the scientific world, many are beginning to reject the Neoplatonic dualism that divorces spiritual from material realities and ultimate concerns from those of this life.[13] There are calls for a postmodern worldview characterized by some type of holism that integrates humans and the world and takes spiritual needs seriously. But what shape should it take? A number of worldviews compete for the postmodern mind.

The Return of Animism

Some leaders promote a return to the animistic beliefs that characterized much of the world before the rise of science—a world in which most things that happen are brought about, whimsically and arbitrarily, by spirits, ancestors, ghosts, magic, witchcraft, and the stars. It is a world in which God is distant and in which humans are at the mercy of good and evil powers and must defend themselves by prayers and chants, charms, medicines, and incantations. Power, not truth, is the central human concern in this worldview.

Such beliefs, suppressed during the reign of science, had never fully left the Western mind. Below the level of orthodox Christianity, an assortment of folk religious beliefs persisted, handed down by word of mouth, despite the opposition of church leaders and the ridicule of scientists. Samples of this folk religion can be seen in the tabloid publications sold in supermarkets and in the stories of ghosts, witchcraft, evil-eye curses, and fulfilled prophecies. Such printed or oral stories titillate the imagination when passed along as gossip.

This resurgence of interest in the animistic worldview extends into

12. Gene Ewing, *If You Want Money, a Home in Heaven, Health and Happiness, Based on the Holy Bible, Do These Things* (Atlanta: Rev. Gene Ewing, 1981), 5 (emphasis in original).

13. Huston Smith, *Beyond the Post-Modern Mind* (New York: Crossroad, 1982).

mainstream North America. The Saturday morning children's cartoons are full of super men, witches, little people of various sorts, magic, curses, and transformations. From movies to TV "sitcoms," plot lines commonly work in exorcisms, black magic, spirits, and resurrections. Similar themes appear in such games as "Dungeons and Dragons" and in rock music. These ideas may be presented as fiction, satire, humor, or horror, but to those without a clear conceptual framework by which to test reality, the very presence of these ideas opens the door to the acceptance of their reality.

Most disturbing is the resurgence of serious pagan and occult practices in the West. As the Christian belief that humans are created in the image of God fades from Western thought, there has been a revival of pre-Christian paganism that puts humans in the same category with other natural phenomena. All beings exist at the mercy of capricious, invisible spirits and forces. The only human defense is to gain power over these spirits and forces by rituals and magic. Fertility rites, white witchcraft, divination, palmistry, fortune-telling, and astrology are gaining credibility and acceptance in cities. Many bookshops now have sections set aside for the occult.

At the center of animism is the shaman, the religious practitioner who is a master of ecstasy, healing, prophecy, and dealing with the spirit world.[14] The shaman seeks power through a personal encounter with a spirit. Through trances, in which the shaman visualizes hidden realities and uses guided imagery, he or she transforms these realities with invisible personalized energy. The shaman performs miraculous cures and predicts future events.[15]

This resurgence of animistic thinking also has influenced some in the church. The earlier denial of Satan and demons by some Christians has been replaced by teachings that evil spirits and spirit possessions account for much of what happens to Christians and non-Christians alike. The indirect source of many of these teachings is Kabala, the syncretistic Jewish folk religion that arose during the exile in Babylonia.

There is a two-fold danger in this return to an animistic worldview. First, *it assigns too much power and authority to unseen spirits and forces in this world and implicitly denies the power and presence of God in everyday affairs, particularly in the lives of Christians.* Humans must live in constant fear of capricious beings. However, when compared to

14. Mircea Eliade, *Shamanism: Archaic Techniques of Ecstasy* (Princeton, N.J.: Princeton University Press, 1964).
15. Cf. Johanna Michaelsen, *The Beautiful Side of Evil* (Eugene, Oreg.: Harvest House, 1982).

pagan mythologies, such as the Babylonian creation myths, the Scriptures are remarkably secular. They speak of a divinely ordained and maintained natural order. They affirm the reality of angels and demons but deny that humans are puppets of capricious supernatural whims. The real focus of the Bible is the story of humans and their response to God. Moreover, in the end, it was normal human beings and their religious systems that crucified Christ, not the demon-possessed.[16] The universal testimony of animists who have responded to the gospel is that Christ has delivered them from their fear of demons.

Second, *the animistic worldview rejects the insights of science.* While modern scientists often reject God, science itself emerged within the context of a Christian worldview.[17] Many early scientists were Christians seeking to understand the order God placed in his creation (Gen. 1:1–2:4). To deny this order is to deny that the world and its history have meaning.

Birth of the New Age Movement

A second response to the collapse of Greek dualism in Western thought is the rise of the new age movement. This is a collection of cults and teachings such as extra-sensory perception (ESP), transcendental meditation, Church of Religious Science, Hari Krishna and other neo-Hindu religions, the new physics, New Age politics, and New Age versions of Christianity.[18] Among its prophets are Shirley MacLaine, John Denver, Teilhard de Chardin, Maharishi Mahesh Yogi, Fritjof Capra, and Carlos Castaneda.

As diverse as these people and movements are, underlying them all is a convergence of teachings rooted in Eastern mysticism. First, *they affirm that "all is one."* Ultimately there is no difference between spirit and matter, God and creation, good and evil, and one person and another. All belong to one interrelated, interdependent, and interpenetrating reality that has no boundaries and no ultimate divisions. This is radically at odds with a Christian view of reality that affirms the difference

---

16. The term *demon possession* is used in its popular sense. Some argue that we should use the term *demonized* to avoid the idea that Christians can be inhabited by evil spirits. We must then also get rid of the term *exorcism*, which carries the same idea. There is a danger in limiting *demon possession* or *demonized* to people who show aberrant behavior, speak in strange voices, and manifest extraordinary power. They are less dangerous to the church than normal, rational persons who are vehemently set against Christ. They, too, are "demonized," just as Christians in everyday life can be "Christ-possessed," and "filled with the Holy Spirit," even though they manifest no extraordinary behavior.

17. Charles A. Coulson, *Science and Christian Belief* (London: Fontana, 1955).

18. Douglas R. Groothuis, *Unmasking the New Age* (Downers Grove, Ill.: InterVarsity, 1986); Karen Hoyt, ed., *The New Age Rage* (Old Tappan, N.J.: Revell, 1987).

between God and his creation, between sin and righteousness, and between facts and figments of human imagination.

Second, *New Age teachers affirm that all is God.* This is a short step from declaring that all is one. If all is God, then God is no longer a person in relationship to other beings and things. God is an impersonal energy, force, or consciousness—an "it." This, of course, denies the personal nature of God as Creator and Lord

A third unified New Age teaching is that *we are gods.* If God is all and all is God, then we too are part of divinity. We are not sinners in need of salvation; we are ignorant of our true selves and need enlightenment. We must discover that we ourselves are God by experiencing a new consciousness of cosmic reality. Self and self-realization become the measure and goal of religious experience. Self-realization can be achieved by exercising the hidden powers within us, the same powers that underlie the universe. Gone are the biblical teachings of sin and salvation; of love, reconciliation, fellowship, and self-sacrifice; and of worship and submission to God.

A fourth belief shared by New Age movements is that *reality is governed by spiritual forces we can control once we are enlightened.* Reality, therefore, is not governed by God, nor by natural forces he has created. We control our own destiny. By imaging, mind control, and faith we can make things happen. But we must experience the consciousness that enables us to see things as they really are. This altered state of consciousness can be reached through transcendental meditation, chanting, dancing, yoga, self-hypnotism, internal visualization, biofeedback, or even sexual intercourse. Only then will we be freed from the tyranny of Western rationalism and materialism.

A fifth New Age affirmation is that *all religions are one and all lead to the truth.* Jesus, Buddha, Lao-Tse, Krishna, Maharishi Mahesh Yogi, and others are enlightened gurus who can lead us to experience our oneness with each other and with the universe. Christ is not the only way, and there is no place for evangelism. Salvation lies within each of us.

Central to New Age teaching is the promise of holistic health. If the mind can control reality, there is no need for anyone to be sick, poor, or unsuccessful. The solution to our problems lies within us, in our mindset, in our faith. New Age practitioners claim to move beyond the sickness to treat the whole person—body, mind, and spirit—by meditation, visualization, biofeedback, psychic healing, transpersonal psychology, guidance from a "spirit guide," and often folk healers.[19] Death itself is viewed as a transition to another state of consciousness.

19. Groothuis, *Unmasking,* 57–70.

This new view of the world, with its roots in Hinduism, is spreading rapidly in Europe and North America because it promises to fulfill the Western search for personal well-being and success. It promises a new age of hope and human fulfillment. Its approach to Christianity is one of subversion. Its promise of spiritual power and ecstasy attracts many Christians who remain unaware of its theological foundations.[20]

A Theology of God's Work in Our Everyday Lives

What alternative do we as Christians have to the worldviews offered by consumerism, animism, and New Age theology, all of which deify the self? What criteria do we use to test the current emphasis on healing and exorcisms and similar movements, so as not to become captive to the spirit of our times? Such captivity has happened to Christians so often in the past. It is important that Christianity stand in prophetic critique of the times in which we live, that we not allow our faith to become just another version of the West's preoccupation with success, health, and the present. To guard against this we must formulate clear theological guidelines rooted in Scripture. To chart a course through the turbulent seas of our times we need a theology of healing, exorcism, provision, and guidance. Such a theology, dealing with God's work in our daily lives, must be part of our broader theological understandings of God, creation, sin, the cross, judgment, and redemption. Furthermore, in such a theology we must reject the old dualism that confines God's work to otherworldly concerns and leaves him a place for only an occasional miracle in our everyday lives. What theological guidelines can help us discover again how God wants to work in our personal lives?

A Trinitarian Theology

A theology of God's work in human affairs must begin with an understanding of God himself—as Father, Son, and Holy Spirit (see fig. 14.2). Often new movements in the church focus their attention on one person in the Godhead and lose sight of the work of the others.

A trinitarian theology takes into account the providence of the Father. Throughout the Scriptures it is clear that God is sovereign over the ebb and flow of history. From creation to final judgment, God is in control. This does not deny humans their freedom to make choices. It does, however, mean that God directs the overall course of history according to his purposes. Moreover, the Scriptures show a God who is concerned about the life of each person, including life's smallest details.

20. David Hunt and T. A. McMahon, *The Seduction of Christianity: Spiritual Discernment in the Last Days* (Eugene, Oreg.: Harvest House, 1985).

For the early Christians, the ongoing involvement of God in world history and in personal biography was a living reality. This awareness guided their lives and sustained them in times of persecution and martyrdom. In fact, more often than not, following Christ meant suffering, sickness, and death, rather than health, prosperity, and long life. This awareness gave answers to the problems of daily living.

Following Constantine, Christianity became identified with government, and God was seen as a distant ruler associated with the religious and political elite. By the Middle Ages, the common folk no longer saw God

Figure 14.2

Trinitarian View of God's Work in the World Today

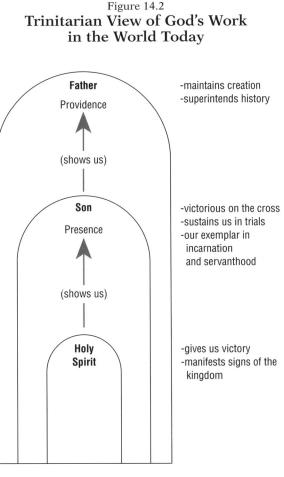

as involved in their daily lives, so they took their troubles to the saints: to St. Anthony when something was lost, to St. Peregrinus Laziosi for cancer, and to St. Luke for other diseases. They also used magical chants, charms, and potions to guard against sickness and danger.

The Reformation not only recovered the biblical understanding of salvation, it also restored the doctrine of providence. Calvin, Luther, Zwingli, and the other Reformers declared that God is indeed the God of individual and collective history. He does not leave his people to fend for themselves in a world of chance and happenstance, nor does he delegate ordinary human affairs to angels and saints. As Father, he himself cares for people in their everyday lives. It was this profound faith that God is the God of human and personal, as well as cosmic, history that gave the Reformation much of its power. Over time, however, this living awareness of God's superintending presence faded, and the doctrine of providence became largely a theological postulate.

The most significant weakness in many of the movements now stressing health and wealth for all Christians is their failure to appreciate the sovereignty of God and its implications. There is little recognition that it may be God's will for a Christian to be sick or suffer or that God can use these for their good. They do not recognize that illnesses are often the body's warning to stop living an unhealthy lifestyle. There is little acknowledgment that Christians and non-Christians share in the common lot of fallen humanity, which includes earthquakes, famines, plagues, and ordinary human sickness. This does not mean that God is uninterested in the lot of Christians. It does mean that he loves both the saved and the lost and that he is working out his purposes within a fallen world and will one day deliver his people from it.

Today we need to recover the doctrine of providence as a living reality, for it is the encompassing frame within which we must understand all human experiences. God is the God of history—of Russia, China, and India as well as of North America and Europe. And God is the God of our lives: of sickness, pain, failure, oppression, and death, as well as of healing, joy, and success. He uses all these for our ultimate good (Rom. 8:28). In times of difficulty we may doubt God's providence. We do not always feel his hand in ours. But later, in retrospect, we realize that God was closest to us during times of trial.

A trinitarian theology takes into account the presence of the Son. Within this bigger frame we need to experience the presence of the living Christ with us. As noted above, we live in a world that suffers the consequences of the fall. Plagues, famines, wars, suffering, and death are part of human experience (Rom. 8:19–23). As Christians in a fallen world, we expect hardships, poverty, and persecution (1 Cor. 4:10–13; 2 Tim. 3:12; 1 Peter 4:12–18). Moreover, we are called to take up our cross and follow Christ (Matt. 10:38–39; 16:24–26). The good news is that in all of these experiences Christ is with us (Matt. 28:20).

This presence first manifests itself in our salvation. It was Christ whose death and resurrection made salvation possible. That salvation is at work in us today; Christ has saved us (2 Tim. 1:9), and is saving us from the power and judgment of sin (Heb. 13:21).

This presence invisibly at work among us is the Master who once walked the lanes of Galilee. Nothing can separate us from his love and care (Rom. 8:35–39). The Father answers our prayers because Christ pleads for us (Heb. 7:25). And Christ provides us with the grace and strength to live with "weaknesses, insults, hardships, persecutions and calamities" (2 Cor. 12:10).

This presence is seen in the reality of the church, which is Christ's body. As John Bright points out, "It is a pitiful and helpless minority composed, for the most part, of people of no account (cf. 1 Cor. 1:26–28), the offscouring and disinherited."[21] Nevertheless, it has turned the world upside-down.

Finally, this presence empowers the hope of our future resurrection—a hope founded on the resurrection of Christ and promised to us who believe (1 Corinthians 15).

This was the message of the sixteenth-century Anabaptists, with their emphasis on living moment by moment in fellowship and obedience to Christ. Later, when the Reformation doctrine of providence was reduced to scholastic debates, it became the message of the Pietists. Today it is the message of the East African revival, whose emphasis on "living in the light" has sustained the church in Uganda through some of the most terrible persecutions in history. It is a message we must recover.

A trinitarian theology takes into account the power of the Spirit. The Pentecostals and charismatics remind us that, within the care of the Father and the presence of Christ, we need to experience the power of the Holy Spirit. This power was demonstrated in the life of Christ and in the early church through signs and wonders. But, as Paul, Peter, John, and the other writers of the New Testament point out in their theological reflections, such demonstrations are secondary to the power of the Holy Spirit within humans as the Spirit leads them to salvation and to a victorious life in Christ.

First, the power of the Holy Spirit is at work to convict people of their sins and woo them to faith in Christ. Without the Spirit there can be no faith.[22] Yet we receive the Spirit when we respond in faith to the gospel. To be more specific than this only leads to endless quibbling about the order of Christian experience. J. Denney notes,

> The faith which abandons itself to Christ is at the same time a receiving of the Spirit of Christ. . . . There are not two things here but one, though it can be represented in the two relations which the words *faith* and *Spirit* suggest. Where human responsibility is to be emphasized, it is naturally faith which is put to the front (Gal. 3:2); where the gracious help of God is the main point, prominence is given to the Spirit.[23]

Not only does the Holy Spirit play an important role in bringing us to

21. John Bright, *The Kingdom of God: The Biblical Concept and Its Meaning for the Church* (Nashville: Abingdon-Cokesbury, 1953), 235.

22. David Ewert, *The Holy Spirit in the New Testament* (Scottdale, Penn.: Herald, 1983), 185.

23. James Denney, "The Theology of the Epistle to the Romans," *The Expositor* 4:426.

salvation, but he also gives us the assurance of that salvation (Rom. 8:16; 1 John 3:24).

Second, the Holy Spirit leads us into the truth (John 16:13). Without his ongoing work in us, we cannot comprehend the mysteries of the gospel. Before his departure, Jesus promised to send to his followers the Spirit of Truth (John 14:16–19; 16:13–15). He also referred to the Spirit as the Counselor who would convince the world concerning sin and righteousness and judgment (John 15:26; 16:7–8).

Third, the Spirit transforms our lives (2 Cor. 3:18). He enables us to have victory over sin (Eph. 6:17). He helps us in our weaknesses (Rom. 8:26). He sensitizes our consciences (Rom. 9:1). He sanctifies us and makes us holy (1 Cor. 6:11; 1 Peter 1:2). He strengthens us and comes to our aid in moments of crisis (Eph. 3:16; Mark 13:11; Luke 12:12). And the Spirit will resurrect our mortal bodies from death just as he raised Christ from the dead (Rom. 8:11).

Fourth, the power of the Holy Spirit is manifest in the preaching and persuasive power of the gospel. Christ himself was anointed by the Spirit to preach the Good News (Luke 4:18–19). Paul repeatedly connects *pneuma* (Spirit) and *dynamis* (power) in contexts dealing with the missionary preaching of the apostles. He writes, "For our gospel came to you not only in word, but also in power and in the Holy Spirit and with full conviction. . . . For you received the word in much affliction, with joy inspired by the Holy Spirit" (1 Thess. 1:5–6 RSV).

There is a danger here of equating "power" with "miracles." The power of the Holy Spirit is manifest in the gospel itself, which is the power of God unto salvation (Rom. 1:16), and in the cross, which is foolishness to the world (1 Cor. 1:18). Paul reminds us that "faith comes from what is heard, and what is heard comes by the preaching of Christ" (Rom. 10:17 RSV).

A trinitarian theology takes into account the whole work of God. The activities of the Father, Son, and Holy Spirit are not three separate works. They are the work of one God. We are often most aware of the Holy Spirit in our lives here and now, for it is his task to lead us day by day. The task of the Holy Spirit (who is also called the Spirit of Christ in Rom. 8:9) is to point us to Jesus Christ and not to himself (John 14:26; 16:13–15). He is God at work within us, leading us to glorify and obey Christ as Lord.

Christ's work is to reveal to us the Father and to glorify him on earth (John 17:1–8). It is in Christ that we humans see the definitive revelation of the nature and being of God the Father (John 14:9–11). The Father's work is to send the Spirit and to exalt Christ, so that at his name every knee shall one day bow, in heaven, on earth and under the earth (Phil. 2:10–11).

Figure 14.3
God's Work in This World

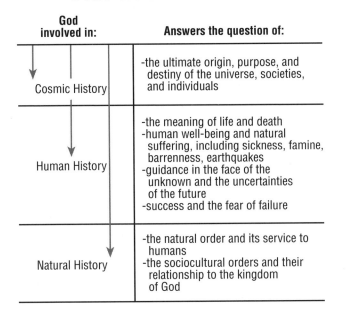

God involved in:	Answers the question of:
Cosmic History	-the ultimate origin, purpose, and destiny of the universe, societies, and individuals
Human History	-the meaning of life and death -human well-being and natural suffering, including sickness, famine, barrenness, earthquakes -guidance in the face of the unknown and the uncertainties of the future -success and the fear of failure
Natural History	-the natural order and its service to humans -the sociocultural orders and their relationship to the kingdom of God

If we overlook the whole work of God on earth and focus on only a part, or if we ignore the central thrust of God's purposes, we are in danger of distorting the truth.

A Theology of Creation and Redemption

In developing a theology of God's work in our everyday lives we must reject the modern dualism that restricts God to otherworldly matters and leaves the natural world to science. We must begin with a theology of creation, God's first act, in order to understand God's original and ultimate purposes. It is within that framework that we must locate our theology of redemption, in which God restores his creation, ruined by sin. In eternity God's perfect creation, redeemed through Christ, will continue, but God's redemptive acts will then be in the past.

A theology of creation and redemption must focus on God at work in cosmic history (in creation, the fall, redemption, and eternity), in human history (in the affairs of nations and individuals to bring about his cosmic purposes), and in natural history through the material order he created, which also awaits redemption (Rom. 8:22; 2 Peter 3:11–13; see fig. 14.3). We are taught the first of these in our churches, but often we explain human and natural history in secular terms and thereby reinforce the Neoplatonic dualism that underlies modern thought. Only as we bring God back into the very center of history and science will we root out the secularism that has plagued our age.

It is not easy for us, however, to return to such a holistic theology. Many of our words in English contain an implicit Neoplatonic dualistic worldview. For example, we speak of *supernatural*, in contrast to *natural*, and *miracle*, in contrast to *ordinary* or *normal*, but these reflect a nonbiblical worldview. The term *nature*, which implies an autonomous, self-sustained universe, is not found in Hebrew thought. Rather, the word used for his world and its order is *bārā'* (created). The term, in fact, is a verb and implies an origin in, and continued dependence upon, God. To us, some events may seem ordinary and others extraordinary, but all are due to the active, sustaining hand of God. In the biblical sense, no birth of a child is "natural," nor any divine healing "unnatural" in the sense of being contrary to the divinely created order.

We first need to see all healing as God's work. If we place too much emphasis on "miraculous" healing, we are in danger of reinforcing secularism. To overstress the miraculous implies that what is not miraculous is natural and can be explained without God. It puts what the church does through prayer in opposition to what humans do by modern scientific medicine in hospitals. To non-Christians the latter far outweighs what the church can show. Christians often turn to medicine when their prayers fail. The dichotomy is false to begin with. God works through both ordinary and extraordinary means.

Second, a focus on miracles as the key evidence of God at work in our lives leaves us essentially with a "God-of-the-gaps." We use him to account for what science cannot. But as science makes new discoveries, it often explains in ordinary terms what we once reserved for the miraculous. For instance, Christians once prayed for protection from lightning; now they put up lightning rods and no longer pray. The error is to see God chiefly at work in the miraculous. We must see his hand as involved in what we think we understand as it is in what we do not.

Third, as we will see below, miracles are reported in all religions. Scripture itself warns us that Satan will perform them (2 Thess. 2:9). In other words, miracles are not self-authenticating; they themselves must be tested in order to determine their source.

When we are new to the faith, it is natural for us to look for visible evidences of God's existence, such as healings and material blessings. As we grow in faith, we root our faith in God's revelation of himself through the Scriptures and in our personal walk with him. We begin to see his hand in the miracle of a child or a tree as well as in a vision, in the ordinary recovery of the body tended by a doctor as well as in a dramatic "extraordinary" healing.

A Theology of the Kingdom of God

Within a theology of creation, we need a theology of the kingdom of God, particularly as this has to do with God's work in the world after the fall. Sickness, suffering, starvation, and death—these are the consequences of sin. Christ's response was to come as a human in order to establish and proclaim his kingdom as the new work of God on earth. This is what he preached (Matt. 4:23; Mark 1:14). The message of salvation includes good news to the poor, release to the captives, sight to the blind, and liberty to the oppressed (Luke 4:18–19). But how does the kingdom of God relate to our experiences as we continue to live in the kingdoms of this world with famine, oppression, poverty, suffering, disease, and death?

Down through history prophets claimed that the kingdom of God had already come in its fullness for God's people.[24] Christians, they said, need not be sick or poor or failures or sinners—or even die. This, in fact, was a heresy in Paul's day, when some claimed that the resurrection had already taken place (2 Tim. 2:18). In recent years we have seen a resurgence of this message, which fits well with our Western cultural emphasis on the self and our health, wealth, success, and denial of death.[25] Despite such preaching, sincere, devout, praying Christians remain poor and broken. They become sick and die.

The kingdom of God *has come to us* in the person of Christ. It is found wherever God's people are obedient to the King. But the kingdom will come *in its fullness* only with Christ's return (Rev. 12:10). Until then, we live, as it were, between two worlds. We are people of this sinful world: we are tempted and we sin, we are weak and we fail, the processes of degeneration and death are at work in us from the moment of our birth. But we are also people of the kingdom: though we sin, in God's sight we are sinless; though we face death, we have eternal life; though we see a decaying world around us, we also see the signs of a heavenly kingdom in the transformed lives of God's people.

"Signs and wonders" is the phrase used in Scripture for self-authenticating demonstrations of supernatural power. The phrase, however, is ambiguous. At times it points to the acts of God (Acts 2:22, 43). At other times it refers to the works of false prophets. Bright notes,

> In the language of the Synoptic Gospels, at least, the miracles of Christ are never spoken of as "signs and wonders" *(se-meia kai terata),* i.e., self-

24. Cohn, *Pursuit.*
25. Robert N. Bellah, et al., *Habits of the Heart: Individualism and Commitment in American Life* (Berkeley, Calif.: University of California Press, 1985); Bloom, *Closing,* 173–84.

authenticating exhibitions of divine power designed to prove the claims of Jesus in the eyes of the people. Indeed, such "signs" (i.e., marvels) were precisely the sort of thing Christ refused to perform (e.g., Mark 8:11–12; Matt. 12:38–40). False messiahs are the ones who show off with "signs and wonders" (Mark 13:22; Matt. 24:24), and for Jesus to have done likewise would have been, from that point of view at least, the flat disproof of his claim to be the true Messiah. On the contrary, his miracles are "mighty works" ("powers," *dunameis*) of the kingdom of God.[26]

There are a number of misunderstandings about these terms against which we must guard. First, *signs* and *wonders* should not be simply equated with miracles. The terms refer to anything that reminds us that God is with us, miraculous or not. The rainbow is the sign of God's covenant with Noah (Gen. 9:12), circumcision the sign of his covenant with Israel (Gen. 17:11), Moses' mighty works signs of God's deliverance of his oppressed people (Exod. 4:17), and the Sabbath a sign of God's covenant with his people (Exod. 31:13, 17). Isaiah walked barefoot as a sign of God's judgment on Egypt and Ethiopia (Isa. 20:3), and the sun went back ten "steps" as a sign of God's healing of Hezekiah (2 Kings 20:9–11). Similarly, in the New Testament, the fact that Christ was wrapped in swaddling clothes and lying in a manger was a sign to the shepherds that this was the Messiah (Luke 2:12), and Judas's kiss a sign that this man was Jesus (Matt. 26:48).

Nor should signs and wonders be associated only with God. Pharaoh's magicians did signs (Exod. 7:10–22), and so do Satan (2 Thess. 2:9) and false prophets (Matt. 24:24). They are not proofs of God's presence—they themselves need to be tested for their source. A sign is anything that reminds us of something else, an event that points beyond itself.

Also, signs and wonders that come from God should not be equated with the coming of the kingdom *in its fullness*. Rather, they are promises, reassuring us that the kingdom will indeed come (Rom. 8:22–25; 2 Cor. 5:1–5). They themselves are not that kingdom—they point to it and show us something of its nature. From time to time God does heal our physical diseases to enable us to do his work and to show us the nature of the kingdom, but the fullness of health will come only with our new bodies beyond death. To claim that Christians should never be ill or that when they are sick God will always heal them is to declare that the kingdom of God has come to them in its fullness. But this denies that death is still at work within them and settles for much too little. In the kingdom yet to come we will not just have our present bodies,

26. Bright, *Kingdom of God*, 218.

healthy and strong—we will have new bodies that transcend anything we can imagine.

Finally, signs and wonders are not ends in themselves. They convey God's message to us. As David Hubbard notes, "The primary motive for divine miracle is not compassion but revelation"—or, one might say, God's mighty works are a revelation of divine compassion (see Psalm 107). Throughout Scripture God performs miracles at critical junctures in history and in the lives of his people. He delivered Israel from Egypt, he defeated their enemies when they were outnumbered, and he spoke to them by messages and miracles through Elijah and Elisha when they had forgotten him. He announced by signs that Jesus was indeed the Messiah, the Christ. Today some turn to God because of a special work he has performed in their lives at their moment of decision. Others experience his presence in particular ways in moments of crisis and despair.

One common temptation is to focus on the signs themselves rather than on the message they bear (see John 6:26; Luke 23:8–9). Many people want healing, but they are not willing to give up all to follow Christ. Like the rich young ruler, they want the blessings of living with Christ, but they do not want to hear him say, "Sell what you have, and give to the poor, and . . . follow me" (Mark 10:21 RSV) or "Whoever loses his life for my sake will find it" (Matt. 16:25 RSV). Nor are they happy when Paul reminds them that Christians often are called to bear persecution, including beatings, mutilations, and other physical wounds and that this suffering is an honor (Phil. 1:29). These are not words they want to hear in an age of self-fulfillment. The kingdom of God comes in signs, but one of these signs is suffering for the sake of Christ.

Another temptation is to confuse the sign with the reality. Those who do this are like the man on his way to San Francisco who saw a sign pointing the way and camped under it, thinking he had arrived.

A Theology of Power

Today in the church we hear calls for demonstrations of power. This should not surprise us, for power is the central concern of our day. Nor should it surprise us that some see divine power as the key to prosperity, to health, to overcoming opposition, and, above all, to controlling their own lives.

The Scriptures have much to say about power. God is the God Almighty (*El Shaddai*, Gen. 17:1), who created and sustains all things by his power (Genesis 1), who defeated Satan and his hosts (John 16:33), and who will bring all things into subjection to himself (Eph. 1:22). Moreover, by his might he saved us and gave us the power to become like him in our lives and bear witness of his greatness. All this we must affirm.

Scripture also has much to say about the ways in which power is to be used. Unfortunately, many Christians think of power as the world around them thinks of it—as demonstrations of might that overcome the resistance of the opposition. Consequently, Christians seek to show the world God's superiority in power encounters that demonstrate his ability to heal and cast out demons, confident that when non-Christians see these, they will believe.

This, however, is not the picture we find in Scripture, nor in history. There are demonstrations of God's power in preliminary confrontations with evil. Elijah called down fire from heaven, Jesus healed the sick and cast out demons, Peter and John healed the lame man at the temple gate, and Stephen, full of grace and power, did many signs and wonders among the people. These demonstrations, however, were not followed by mass conversions. Some believed, but then the opposition arose. Elijah fled to the desert and wrestled with depression as Jezebel appointed new prophets for Baal. Jesus and Stephen were arrested and killed. Peter and John were thrown into jail.

The history of such "power encounters" is that, after the preliminary confrontation, "the powers" mobilize in opposition. These powers are Satan and his hosts. They are also human organizations—institutions, governments, and societies—such as those that crucified Christ and persecuted the early church. Ever since Babel, the center of the opposition to the kingdom of God has been the organized systems of sane people in corporate rebellion with Satan against God. Our first sin as humans was self-deification. We wanted neither God nor Satan to rule over us; we wanted to be our own gods. And the same is still true today.

God's supreme victory over Satan took place at the cross and the resurrection. Satan used his full might, seeking to destroy Christ or to provoke him to use his divine might in response. Either would have meant defeat for Christ, the first because Satan would have overcome him and the second because it would have destroyed God's plan of salvation. Godly power is always rooted in love, not pride; it is rooted in redemption, not conquest; and it is rooted in concern for the other, not the self. It is humble, not proud, and inviting, not rejecting. Its symbol is the cross, not the sword. This is why it is seen as weakness by the world (1 Cor. 1:23–27).

As Christians, and as churches, we must affirm the power of God to heal, deliver, guide, and bless in the everyday lives of people. These are very real experiences in the lives of God's people, and in the evangelistic outreach of the church.

Even more, we are in desperate need of showing God's power in transformed lives and in a Christlike confrontation of evil wherever we find it, whether demonic or systemic. We need also to guard against distortions of a biblical view of power. We must not look at power in worldly terms. Furthermore, we must not divorce power from truth. What we need, some say, is demonstrations of power, not theological reflection. But power is not self-authenticating—it must be tested to unveil its source. Moreover, demonstrations of power seldom lead people to truth and salvation. Jesus healed many, but few of them became his disciples. Of the ten lepers he healed, one returned and then only to give thanks.

Finally, we must guard against temptations to control power ourselves and so to make ourselves gods. The power God gives is never our own. We are simply stewards called to be faithful in using that power to the glory of God, not for our own honor or advancement.

A Theology of Discernment

In dealing with divine healing and provision, we need a theology of discernment. Signs and wonders are not confined to Christianity. Miraculous healings, speaking in tongues, prophecies, resurrections, and other extraordinary experiences are reported in all major religions. For example, Baba Farid, a Pakistani Muslim saint, is said to have cured incurable diseases, raised a dying man to life, converted dried dates into gold nuggets, and covered vast distances in a moment.[27] Hundreds of thousands flock each year to the Hindu temple of Venkateswara at Tirupathi, south India, many of them fulfilling vows because they claim the god healed them when they prayed to him during their illnesses. Similar reports come from Buddhist temples in Southeast Asia and spiritist shrines in Latin America. Yogis claim that they can rise from the dead and shamans report trips into heaven. Upwards of fifteen thousand people claim healing each year at Lourdes, and many more at the Virgin of Guadeloupe near Mexico City. Healing is also central to Christian Science, and testimonies of miraculous healings are reported in every issue of the *Christian Science Sentinel*. One man wrote that he was healed of astigmatism after applying the principles taught by Mary Baker Eddy in *Science and Health with Key to the Scriptures*. Another wrote,

> I had two healings after I had attended the Sunday school for some time. One was a large birthmark on my forehead. The other was a severe skin condition. . . . Some later healings came quickly; others took longer and

27. E. Gilchrist, "Baba Farid," *Outreach to Islam* 3 (1987): 32.

involved more study on my part, sometimes with help from a Christian Science practitioner. But I was always healed.[28]

No *phenomenon* in itself proves God's presence.

How are we to respond to all this? Scripture itself is clear that Satan performs signs and wonders, counterfeiting God's work. It warns us to guard against being led astray (Matt. 7:15–16; 2 Thess. 2:9–10; 1 Tim. 4:1, 7; 2 Tim. 3:1–4:5). Nowhere are we encouraged to let our minds go blank in order to let the Holy Spirit come in. That is a technique commonly found in cults. Rather, we are to seek the wisdom that enables us to test the spirits to see whether or not they come from God (1 Cor. 12:3; 1 Thess. 5:20–21; 1 John 4:1–6). In this our attitude should not be one of skepticism but of openness to hearing the voice of God when he truly speaks to us.

What are the signs that enable us to discern the work of God and differentiate it from the work of self or Satan? It is too simple to say that what God's people do is of God (see Matt. 7:21–23) or that what non-Christians do is of Satan (see Numbers 22–24).

Nor are physical phenomena the test of the work of the Holy Spirit. Many today appeal to warm sensations, fluttering eyelids, involuntary muscle movements, and feelings of "energy" coming into the body as proof that God is at work. D. Martyn Lloyd-Jones warns us that such experiences are common in other religions. He writes,

> You will find in the case of spiritist healing that there is always emphasis on the physical element. People will testify to a feeling of heat as the hand of the healer came upon them, or of a sensation like an electric shock, or something like that—the physical is always very prominent. . . . There is nothing corresponding to that in the New Testament. . . . They do not talk much about their physical sensations but about the Lord and his love for them, and their love for him.[29]

Our experiences must themselves be tested, for they are not self-authenticating. We need to avoid reading our experiences into Scripture and focusing on them rather than on the Scripture itself.

Similarly, the "words of knowledge" widely used in healing services need to be tested. God warned Israel not to take prophesying lightly, for those who speak claim to speak for God (Deuteronomy 13). Those whose prophecies did not come true were to be stoned. Those whose prophecies did come true but who led the people away from God were

---

28. Zella M. Williams, "Testimony of Christian Science Healing," *Christian Science Sentinel* 88.34 (1952).

29. David Martyn Lloyd-Jones, *Prove All Things* (London: Kingsway, 1986), 97.

also condemned. Paul issues the same warning (1 Cor. 12:3; 1 Thess. 5:20–21). Luke commends the church in Berea for testing Paul's teachings (Acts 17:11).

The Bible provides us with other tests:

First, *does the teaching, practice, or movement give glory to God rather than to humans* (John 7:18; 8:50; 12:27–28; 17:4)? Unfortunately, in extremely individualistic, culturally diverse societies, such as we have in North America, people tend to follow strong personalities. Little other social cohesion brings them together into groups. We must be aware, therefore, of the particular temptation in our society to deify strong leaders.

Second, *does it recognize the lordship of Christ* (1 John 2:3–5; 5:3; James 2:14–19)? The test here is primarily not one of orthodoxy, but of obedience. The question is not whether the leader and movement affirm the truth that Jesus is Lord or even that they feel a great love for him. The question is one of submission to Christ. In other words, there must be an attitude of humility, learning, and willingness to obey.

Third, *does a teaching, practice, or movement conform to scriptural teaching?* Are those involved willing to submit their lives and teachings to the instruction of the Scriptures and to the leading of the Holy Spirit? This must be an ongoing process, for the Scriptures provide the norm against which we must examine all doctrine.

Fourth, *are the leaders of a movement accountable to others in the church?* The interpretation of Scripture is, ultimately, not a personal matter but a concern of the church as a hermeneutical community.[30] We must test our understandings with others who are in leadership (Gal. 2:1–2) and with the teachings of the saints down through history. In an age of extreme individualism and a focus on great personalities, this test has particular importance.

Fifth, *do those involved manifest the fruit of the Spirit* (Gal. 5:22–25)? Is there love or self-centeredness? Joy or only excitement? Peace or frenzy and tension? Patience or short tempers? Gentleness or arrogance? Goodness or intrigue? Faith in God, or dependence on human planning? Meekness or arrogance? Moderation or excesses? Luther pointed out that the difference between Christians and pagan miracle workers is not the kinds of miracles they do, but in transformations that take place in their lives. The power of God transforms us into the likeness of Christ; the powers of self and the world do not.

Sixth, *does the teaching and practice lead us toward spiritual maturity* (Eph. 4:11–15)? Some things are characteristic of spiritual immaturity,

---

30. C. Norman Kraus, *The Authentic Witness: Credibility and Authority* (Grand Rapids: Eerdmans, 1979).

such as a dependence on miracles to reassure us that God indeed exists and is with us. As we grow spiritually mature, we leave these things behind and root our faith in God himself (1 Cor. 13:11; Col. 2:6–7), in his self-revelation to us through Scripture and in a personal walk with him.

Seventh, *is the truth kept in balance with other truths* (Matt. 23:23–24)? There are many teachings that are true, but to over- or underemphasize them is error. It is wrong to make secondary truth primary. For example, we can so emphasize peace or justice or healing or exorcisms or even salvation that in practice they become the whole of our gospel. It is Christ who is the center of the gospel, and when he is at the center, the many facets of kingdom teaching find their proper place.

Eighth, *does the teaching lead us to seek the unity of the body of Christ, or is it divisive* (John 17:11; 1 John 2:9–11; 5:1–2)? Love for one another is the hallmark of the church (John 13:35). This does not mean that divisions will not occur. It does mean that teachings that lead us to a sense of spiritual superiority have led us astray. We must work for fellowship and continued relationships with Christians who disagree with us and weep when they reject us or go astray.

A Theology of Suffering and Death

Finally, we need a theology of sickness, injury, suffering, and death. These consequences of sin cannot be divorced from each other. The processes of aging and death are at work in humans from the moment of their conception. The side effects of these processes are sickness and bodily suffering. While God often does heal us by natural and occasionally by extraordinary means, our full deliverance occurs only after death, when we receive our new body. For Christians, death is the final release, for we would not want to live forever in our present world, even in perfect health.

Some today argue that it is God's nature to heal, not to teach us through sickness. To reconcile their position with scriptural teaching regarding suffering, they divorce sickness from bodily injuries suffered in persecution and from death, for the Bible makes clear that the latter are the lot of those who follow Christ (Gal. 5:11; 2 Tim. 3:12; Heb. 11:35–38).

The denial that God can and does use sickness to teach us is hard to maintain on biblical grounds. Paul speaks of his "thorn in the flesh" (2 Cor. 12:7). Most Bible scholars agree that this was some normal bodily affliction or disease. Moreover, Paul refers to colleagues who were not healed (Phil. 2:26–27; 2 Tim. 4:20). Job too was sick, but God used everything that befell him to bring him to a deeper and more mature faith (Job 42:5–6).

That God does not use sickness is also hard to maintain from Christian experience. Many Christians testify to the fact that it was in times of sickness and suffering that they were drawn closest to Christ and learned important lessons of faith. They are times when people realize their own vulnerability and their dependence on God. Furthermore, it is hard to believe that God is more concerned about the illness of Christians in ordinary life than in the wounds and injuries of those who are suffering for the sake of Christ. Why should he heal the former and ignore the latter? Unfortunately, a theology that rejects sickness and suffering fits well into our age, with its denial of death[31] and emphasis on positive thinking.

Dangers

Like most movements in the church, the current emphasis on healing, prophecy, and exorcism has both positive and negative sides. It reminds us of the need to take seriously the work of the Holy Spirit in meeting daily human needs. It is in danger, however, of placing primary emphasis on what is of secondary importance in Scripture. It also presents a danger of bending the gospel to fit the spirit of our times. Satan often tempts us at the point of our greatest strengths. His method is not to sell us rank heresy, but to take the good we have and distort it by appealing to our self-interests (see Genesis 3). What are some of the dangers in the current emphasis on healing and exorcism against which we must guard?

Basing Theology on Experience

Living as we do in a culture based on pragmatism, it is easy for us to base our theology on experience. The test of truth is success. The sign of spiritual life and vital worship is feelings of excitement. The measure of our methods is growth and size. In his evaluation of the great revivals in the 1700s of which he was a part, Jonathan Edwards cautioned against using experience to validate theology. Specifically, he listed twelve results that should *not* be viewed as signs (for or against) that a religious excitement was a work of God. Among them are:

- Great religious experiences in themselves are no sign of their validity or that necessarily they are from God.
- Religious experiences which have great effect upon the body are not necessarily valid.

31. Ernest Becker, *Denial of Death* (New York: Free Press, 1973).

- Multiplied religious experiences, accompanying one another, are not evidence that the experience is necessarily saving or divine.
- Spiritual experiences which stimulate the spending of much time in religious activity and zealous participation in the externals of worship are not necessarily saving experiences.
- Religious experiences which cause men and women to praise and glorify God with their mouths are not necessarily saving and divine.[32]

In worship and in ministry we must test our human experiences against a theology based on biblical revelation and beware lest we use those experiences to determine our theology.

Self-Centeredness

We live in a modern society that places the self at the center of life. In such a setting, we need to guard against a theology that mirrors our times by focusing on ourselves and not on God and his agenda. The danger here is two-fold,

First, *it is dangerously easy to institutionalize immaturity.* New believers do indeed generally come to Christ with their own interests in mind—their salvation, their health, their well-being. God begins with them where they are. The church must do the same. But God calls us to spiritual growth, in which our obsession with ourselves gives way to a love for God and others. Christian maturity imitates Christ who lived for others. While ministering to seekers at their points of need, the primary focus should be on more mature expressions of worship and ministry.

Unfortunately, many Christians have bought into the Western cultural emphasis on personal health and prosperity as ultimate ends. As a result, we focus on ourselves while millions around the world are dying of poverty, oppression, and violence. Health in Scripture is defined, not in terms of personal well-being, but as *shalom* in loving relationships. It begins when we are reconciled to God and our enemies. It manifests itself in our mutual submission to one another in the church and our self-sacrificing service to others in need. Its fruit is physical and psychological health. To focus on personal well-being and prosperity, rather than on *shalom,* is to preach a gospel that treats the symptoms but does not cure the illness.

Second, *it is a small but dangerous step from self-centeredness to self-deification.* Ever since the Garden of Eden, this has been the first and

32. Jonathan Edwards, *Religious Affections,* ed. John E. Smith (New Haven, Conn.: Yale University Press, 1959), 127–81. Edwards's *A Treatise Concerning Religious Affections* was first published in 1746.

most fundamental of human sins. Satan did not tempt Adam and Eve to worship him but to worship themselves—their own freedom, their rights, their potential for becoming gods. Self-absorption, not demon possession, is the greatest danger in Western societies.

The results of this self-centeredness in the church can be devastating. It leads to spiritual pride, the feeling among those involved in a movement that they are spiritually superior to those who are not and a judgmental attitude towards those who disagree with them. It also leads to competition for power, and divisions in the church. Christ-centeredness leads to humility, a desire for the unity of the church, and a willingness to hear as well as to speak (Rom. 15:1–2; 1 Cor. 10:12).

Confusion between Reports and Reality

Those who emphasize miraculous healings often base their claims on personal testimonies of those who have experienced healings. Because such testimonies, and the experiences on which they are based, are powerful and immediate, many people take them to be self-validating. But feelings of well-being, important as they are, are not by themselves accurate, objective measures of health. Mansell Pattison and his associates found that most of those who claimed miraculous healing returned to medical doctors within a week or two of the experience.[33]

Feelings of well-being are influenced by a great many factors. People naturally feel better when others gather around them and make them the focus of attention. Moreover, God has created processes in the body that work toward health. Christian honesty requires that claims of miraculous healing be delayed until careful examinations are made over periods of time by impartial investigators. The lack of such testing for objective reality is one of my strong concerns about the current emphasis on healing in the church.

In contrast to many of the healings claimed today, those performed by Christ were instant, dramatic, and durable. Those crippled for life walked. Those blind from birth saw and recognized what they saw. Lazarus, who was dead for three days, was brought back to life.

Christian honesty also requires that we report our failures as loudly as we proclaim our successes. Lewis B. Smedes notes,

> To the extent that we are eager to sustain people's interests, hopes and expectations, we are tempted to exaggerate successes and disguise failures. . . . Honesty in a crooked world is not as spectacular as healing in a hurting world, but in the long run it is a stronger sign of God's power.

33. E. M. Pattison, N. A. Lapius, and H. O. Doerr, "Faith Healing: A Study of Personality and Function," *Journal of Nervous Mental Disorders* 157 (1973): 397–409.

One requirement of honesty in a public ministry of healing is full and accurate reporting, both to the faithful and to the world-at-large. The minister who engages in healing should publicize his or her failures as loudly as the successes.[34]

Finally, we need to test the source of those healings that do occur. Scripture warns us that not all miracles come from God (Acts 8:9–24; 2 Thess. 2:3–12), and the voice we hear within us may be our own desires (James 4:1–3; 2 Peter 2:15).

Influenced by the spirit of the times, many today take success as a test of what is good and of God. Success in human terms, however, does not necessarily correspond with success in the kingdom of God. Many movements are successful, even though they do not proclaim the truth. We must test all ideas and movements in the light of Scripture. Unfortunately, such tests are often seen as evidence of unbelief, rather than as attempts to obey the biblical mandate to "test the spirits" (1 John 4:1).

A New Christian Magic

One danger is that healings, miracles, success, and prosperity may become a new Christian magic. This is one of the fundamental tendencies we have as sinful humans, for magic makes us feel like gods. We feel we are supreme, for we can carry out our will by controlling nature, supernatural powers, or even God himself.

Magic is the opposite of religion. In magic we are in control, in religion we are in submission to God and his will. The difference between the two is not one of practice—it shows itself in our attitudes. We can pray seeking God's help, or we can pray thinking (often without even admitting it to ourselves) that we can make God do our bidding. We can read the Scriptures to learn and grow, or we can carry them in our pocket, confident that they are an amulet that will protect us from harm. We pray when our child is seriously ill, asking that God's will be done, but soon find ourselves trying to coerce God to do our bidding. We may not even be fully aware when we shift from one attitude to the other.

One sign of magic is a formulaic approach. We believe our prayers will be answered if we say the right things and act in certain ways. Scripture instructs us to pray "in the name of Jesus," but if we think that our prayers have power only when we utter these words, worship has become magic. To pray in Jesus' name is to pray for what he wills in a given situation (James 4:3; 1 John 5:14–15).

---

34. Lewis B. Smedes, ed., *Ministry and the Miraculous: A Case Study at Fuller Theological Seminary* (Pasadena, Calif.: Fuller Theological Seminary, 1987), 76.

Similarly, some argue that, despite the example of Jesus (Luke 22:42), to add "nevertheless, not my will but thine be done" at the end of a prayer shows lack of faith and weakens the prayer. The fundamental attitude of worship is subordination. In worship, it is important that God's will be done, not that our desires be answered. Faith is not some kind of "power" that controls God. It is entrusting ourselves completely to God's care. In magic, on the other hand, our will is supreme.

Unfortunately, Christian magic is very much a part of our times. One recent tabloid advertisement promises health, money, a job, happiness, success, and good fortune to those who pray using the golden cross that will be sent to all inquirers. Other advertisements in the same paper promise health and prosperity to those who write in for the "miraculous Lourdes cross," the "cross of Antron," water from the river Jordan, or the special prayers of Rev. Dr. John. One preacher promises that those who use the paper "prayer rug" he encloses (on which are written special Bible verses) will receive "salvation, joy, love, peace, extra money! new and better homes! new car! putting home back together!—and the desires of their heart!" (exclamation marks in the original). To reassure readers, the letter has the testimony of a man who started with nothing but now has two restaurants, two motels, a Dairy Cream store, a service station, thirty employees, four cars, and three trucks because he used the prayer rug. With the prayer rug comes a book that describes which Bible verses should be "claimed" to gain particular ends.

These blatant cases of Christian magic are easy to detect. Of greater danger are the subtler forms of magic that creep into our thinking unawares. For example, one media preacher asks people to "sow money seeds in God's fields" by giving to his ministry. He promises that God will repay them a thousandfold. In so doing, he reduces biblical principles to mechanical formulas. Another leader advocates the saying of certain phrases in prayers of healing to assure positive results. The appeal of magic is great, for it makes us gods.

Reinforcing Secularism

Contradictory as it may seem, by overemphasizing miracles we reinforce secularism. To the extent that we focus our attention on the "miraculous" nature of some events and differentiate them from other events viewed as "natural," we reinforce our old Western dualism that consigns God to otherworldly matters and explains natural phenomena purely in scientific terms. If we take this approach, claims of miracles do initially remind us of God's work in this world. As these miracles become routine, however, they lose their impact. They are no longer seen as extraordinary—as *real* miracles. Consequently, we must look for new and ever more spectacular miracles to reassure us that God is with us. The net effect of this escalation is the secularization of our thought. We do not see God at work in ordinary, natural processes. As miracles become commonplace they no longer remind us of God. The quest for ever newer demonstrations of God's presence breaks down in the end, and we are left in a totally secularized world in which there are few ways for God to speak to us.

The answer lies neither in seeking miracles, nor in denying them. The answer is to reject this dichotomy altogether, to see the *naturalness* of God's extraordinary healings and the *miraculous* nature of his ordinary ones. We must avoid treating the former, whether explicitly or implicitly, as greater signs of God's presence and making them the center of our church's attention and ministry.

Imbalance

Christian maturity calls for a balanced concern for provision, health, peace, justice, and righteousness—a balance that can be maintained only as Christ, rather than a particular cause, is at the center. When we rediscover a forgotten truth, we frequently overaccentuate it. The problem is not new. As James Aiken points out, "The church in Corinth overemphasized the miraculous, specifically the gift of tongues. Paul wrote not to frown on gifts, but to pursue balance in exercising them."[35] The same caution against overemphasis needs to be made regarding the current focus on healing.

We must avoid focusing more attention on immediate needs than on ultimate realities. When we become obsessed with needs, the result is a new, subtle form of the social gospel. With a renewed emphasis on God's special work in everyday life, we must be on guard lest we lose sight of the greater importance of dealing with sin and proclaiming divine judgment.

This focus on the now is accentuated by our modern Western emphasis on personal needs fulfillment and on theories of psychology that arrange these needs along a continuum from the physical to the psychological, social, and ultimately spiritual. According to these theories, we can deal with higher-level problems only after we have solved more pressing needs. We can spend so much time on human needs that we have little time left for dealing with sin and righteousness, or for focusing our attention on God. The amount of time we spend on something reflects its importance in our thinking, no matter what we say to the contrary.

35. James Aiken, "Charismatic Mennonites, Heresy or Hope?" *The Christian Leader* 50.16 (29 September 1987): 6.

The call of the Scriptures is clear: *We are called to be disciples of Jesus Christ.* Discipleship, not present well-being, is our central message.

A second danger is to emphasize healing, particularly physical healing, and to forget provision, justice, peace, and equality. All of these belong to the kingdom of God (Luke 4:18–19). Feeding the hungry and healing the sick were among Jesus' first acts. In a sense, they were easy to carry out and raised little opposition. Far more costly was his condemnation of oppression, injustice, and violence, for this, in the end, led political and religious leaders of his day to seek his death.

We too need to emphasize the whole gospel, including those parts that demand suffering and sacrifice on our part. The temptation is to emphasize those parts that benefit us personally, or to focus our attention on only one aspect—whether this be healing, peace, or justice. When we do so, however, we are in danger of shifting the center from Christ to ourselves or to a cause. Christ then is on the periphery, and we use him mainly to justify the gospel we preach.

Increasing the Burden

We rejoice when God heals in answer to prayer, and we should do so publicly, but what about those whom God, in his will and foreknowledge, chooses not to heal? What do we say to them, for they are in the greatest need of ministry? If we teach healing but have no answer for those who remain sick or face death, we generate a false sense of guilt and despair in those who are not healed.

To attribute sickness and death to a lack of faith or to spiritual defeat is too simple an answer (see Job; John 9:2; 2 Cor. 12:7–9). Even more than a theology of healing, we need a theology of suffering and death—one that does not see these as failures but as part of God's greater redemptive work. We also need the grace of godly dying, in which our passing is marked by a God-given serenity, anticipation, and hope.

Exalting the Leader

We have already noted that in highly individualistic, culturally pluralistic societies, such as in North America, there is a strong tendency to focus on personalities and to exalt leaders. Few strong social groups hold people together; no dominant set of shared ideas and values unites people in thought. People are left to fend for themselves, and often they are attracted to a "big leader" who claims to know the way.[36] This is true

36. Mary Douglas, *Natural Symbols: Explorations in Cosmology* (New York: Random House, 1970).

in our modern world of business, politics, entertainment, and even the church.

This model of leadership creates a number of problems within the church. It encourages most Christians to be followers, prone to uncritically trust what their leaders say. It gives rise to leaders who are not themselves in submission and accountable to others. Throughout church history, this exaltation of leaders has been most common in movements centered around healing, exorcism, and the meeting of everyday human concerns.[37] Few are tempted to say that the preacher saves the sinner. Many, however, attribute healings to the faith of a particular leader. When others fail, it is to him or her that they take the sick for special prayer.

Healing in the church belongs to the congregation. Some may have the particular gift of praying for the sick, but they do so as members of the body rather than as leaders. Moreover, this is a secondary gift that must be subordinate to worship and the ministry of the Word (1 Cor. 12:27–31).

Healing Ministries in the Church

What significance does all this have for healing ministries in the church? Certainly Scripture commands us to pray for the sick and to take those prayers seriously (James 5:14–15). This should be part of ordinary church life along with prayer for the destitute, the jobless, the homeless, the oppressed, and, above all, the lost. Moreover, prayer for the sick should be a part of the evangelistic outreach of the church. What we need is discernment on how to be faithful to Scripture and to guard against fads. Principles regarding pastoral, teaching, and prophetic ministries are found in Scripture.

A Pastoral Ministry

At the heart of the ministry of the church is a pastoral heart—a love for people and a willingness to share in their struggles and to help bear their burdens. A church must be concerned with the everyday needs of human life and should minister to these needs in both personal and corporate ways.

There needs to be a ministry to the sick. This is particularly true in urban settings, where people have lost the normal support groups of relatives, neighbors, and friends. Pattison, Lapius, and Doerr found that for many who sought prayer for healing, the important thing was

37. Cohn, *Pursuit.*

not that they were physically healed (many were not), but that they felt the support of others in their times of difficulty.[38] As humans we need the spiritual healing that comes from being loved, even more than we need physical well-being.

There also needs to be a ministry to the oppressed—those who are poor, battered, or jobless. They are all around us. They are in our churches, often unseen. And there needs to be a ministry to those whom society tends to consider marginal—those who are lonely, single, older, have mental or physical disabilities, or work as migrants. One key measure of the godliness of a society or a church is the way it treats the oppressed and the marginalized. For its own advantage the world takes care of the successful, the powerful, and the wealthy. The church, however, is entrusted with the care of the poor, the widows, the orphans, the sick, the oppressed, the wayward, the spiritually immature, and the lost. It exists for others. It is not a gathering of the spiritually strong but a community of broken sinners who have experienced the grace of God and who now minister to others who are broken and lost.

These ministries can take many forms. Special times of prayer can be set aside for those in need—the sick, the jobless, the sinner seeking forgiveness, the lonely and sad. In the City Terrace Mennonite Brethren Church these are invited to come to the front for special prayer during worship once or twice a month. In other churches, this ministry is given to Sunday school classes or to evening services.

Care must be taken, however, not to promise that all will be healed. The expectations of the average Christian are frequently too low with regard to what God will do, but to raise them too high can be destructive to those God chooses not to heal at that moment. Moreover, particular care must be given to those who continue to suffer, for they are in the greatest need of ministry. We need to pay special attention to those whom God chooses not to heal, those who face death, those caught in difficult marriages, and others with ongoing problems. For them the church needs a ministry of hope, assurance, and hospitality.[39] It is hard, however, to develop a true ministry of hospitality in our modern churches, for this demands time—often our most precious commodity—as well as other resources.

A Teaching Ministry

Teaching is vital ministry in the church, particularly as it has to do with other ministries, such as healing. The older, more mature Chris-

---

38. See "Faith Healing," 397–409.
39. Mortimer Arias, "Centripetal Mission or Evangelism by Hospitality," *Missiology: An International Review* 10 (January 1982): 69–81.

tians should be examples and teachers at heart. They must begin where young believers are in their faith, but they must not be content with leaving the immature at this level. They should instruct, encourage, rebuke, and model a godly life and do so with a firm but gentle spirit. They should seek to settle disputes and strive for unity and harmony in the congregation, balancing the needs of the members as individuals with the needs of the congregation as a whole. They are to avoid empty disputes over words and senseless controversies that breed quarrels (2 Tim. 2:14, 23), teach with kindness and forbearance, correct opponents with gentleness (2 Tim. 2:24–25), and endure criticisms and slander patiently (1 Peter 2:20).

Paul himself was an example of this. When a movement of ecstasy swept through the church in Corinth, causing some members to exalt speaking in tongues, healing, and other visible manifestations of God's Spirit, Paul took a strong stand for order and unity in the church.[40] He did not reject the spiritually young for their excesses and their pursuit of the spectacular. Rather, he instructed them in love and firmness to work as one body and to guard lest their behavior bring offense to the gospel in the world around them. And he showed them the higher way of Christian maturity—love and mutual submission.

Applying these principles to the current emphasis on healing, we should pray freely for the illnesses and other needs of seekers and new believers, knowing that God often works in special ways in the lives of those at the point of deciding for or against Christ. Then, however, we must lead them from the elementary to the deeper things of faith—discipleship, holiness, witnessing, and suffering for the sake of the gospel. We must help young believers move from a focus on themselves and their immediate needs to a concern for the lost and suffering world.

We should also seek a balance in our church services. There are times when prayer for healing is appropriate. At the same time, prayers should also minister to those who remain sick. In both, we must pray in faith and submit ourselves to the sovereignty of God. The central expectation, however, must be that in prayer we are addressing an omnipotent God. Confession of sin, worship, and response to God's call to ministry and mission are important parts of a full-orbed relationship with God.

A Prophetic Ministry

Finally, the church has a prophetic calling. It must discern the setting in which God has placed it and speak out against evil. It must also

---

40. Ralph P. Martin, *The Spirit and the Congregation: Studies in I Corinthians 12–15* (Grand Rapids: Eerdmans, 1984).

beware lest the church itself become a servant to the spirit of the culture and time in which it lives.

The criteria for making these judgments are not the values of the world, nor even the majority votes of all who call themselves Christian. The standard must be the Word of God, understood and applied by communities of committed believers. Particular responsibility is placed on the leaders (1 Tim. 3:2–7; Titus 1:6–9), who help their congregations discern what God is saying to them. They guard the church lest it be deceived (1 Tim. 4:1–7; 2 Tim. 3:1–4:5).

With regard to the current emphasis on healing, the church must test against Scripture the teachings or manner of spirit at work in the body. The church must also challenge the values of our day: the obsession with the self, with the present, and with health, success, and personal fulfillment. It must guard against popular and pragmatic methods that provide immediate solutions but in the end subvert the gospel. Satan did not challenge God's goal for humans. He simply offered them an instant, easy means to get there.

We who live in the end-times face great opportunities and great dangers. In the last days the gospel will be preached to the ends of the earth. There will also be a great falling away, as many—including Christians—are deceived. It is important, therefore, that we listen to God as he speaks to us through his Spirit and that we test the voices we hear to make certain that they are, indeed, from God. God has given us his Word to keep and proclaim. May we be found faithful to that trust.

Bibliography

Aiken, James. "Charismatic Mennonites, Heresy or Hope?" *The Christian Leader* 50.16 (29 September 1987).

Arac, Jonathan, ed. *Postmodernism and Politics*. Minneapolis: University of Minnesota Press, 1986.

Ardrey, Robert. *The Territorial Imperative: A Personal Inquiry into the Animal Origins of Property and Nations*. New York: Dell, 1968.

Arensberg, Conrad M., and Arthur H. Niehoff. *Introducing Social Change: A Manual for Community Development*. Chicago: Aldine, 1971.

Ariaraja, S. Wesley. *The Bible and People of Other Faiths*. Maryknoll, N.Y.: Orbis, 1989.

Arias, Mortimer. "Centripetal Mission or Evangelism by Hospitality." *Missiology: An International Review* 10 (January 1982): 69–81.

Austin, William. "Complementarity and Theological Paradox." *Zygon* 2 (December 1967): 365–81.

Barbour, Ian G. *Myths, Models, and Paradigms: A Comparative Study in Science and Religion*. New York: Harper and Row, 1974.

Barnes, Barry. *T. S. Kuhn and Social Science*. New York: Columbia University Press, 1982.

Barton, Bruce. *The Man Nobody Knows: A Discovery of the Real Jesus*. Indianapolis: Bobbs-Merrill, 1925.

Becker, Ernest. *Denial of Death*. New York: Free Press, 1973.

Bellah, Robert N., et al. *Habits of the Heart: Individualism and Commitment in American Life*. Berkeley, Calif.: University of California Press, 1985.

Berger, Peter L. *Pyramids of Sacrifice: Political Ethics and Social Change*. New York: Doubleday, 1976.

———. *The Sacred Canopy: Elements of a Sociological Theory of Religion*. Garden City, N.Y.: Doubleday, 1969.

Berger, Peter L., Brigitte Berger, and Hansfried Kellner. *The Homeless Mind: Modernization and Consciousness*. New York: Random House, 1973.

Berger, Peter L., and Thomas Luckmann. *The Social Construction of Reality: A Treatise in the Sociology of Knowledge*. Garden City, N.Y.: Doubleday, 1966.

Berry, John W. "Imposed Etics, Emics, and Derived Etics: Their Conceptual and Operational Status in Cross-Cultural Psychology." In *Emics and Etics: The Insider/Outsider Debate*, ed. Thomas N. Headland, Kenneth L. Pike, and Marvin Harris. Newbury Park, Calif.: Sage, 1990.

Bevans, Stephen. "Models of Contextual Theology." *Missiology* 13 (1985): 185–202.

Bibby, Reginald. *Fragmented Gods*. Toronto: Irwin, 1987.

Bidney, David. *Theoretical Anthropology*. 2d ed. New York: Schocken, 1967.

Bloom, Allan. *The Closing of the American Mind: Education and the Crisis of Reason.* New York: Simon and Schuster, 1987.

Bosch, David J. "The Problem of Evil in Africa: A Survey of African Views of Witchcraft and of the Response of the Christian Church." In *Like a Roaring Lion: Essays on the Bible, the Church, and Demonic Powers,* ed. Pieter G. R. deVilliers. Pretoria, South Africa: C. B. Powell Bible Centre, 1987.

———. *Transforming Mission: Paradigm Shifts in Theology of Mission.* Maryknoll, N.Y.: Orbis, 1991.

Bracht, Tieleman Janszoon van. *The Bloody Theater: Or Martyr's Mirror.* Trans. J. F. Sohm. 1837. Reprint, Scottdale, Penn.: Herald, 1979.

Bright, John. *The Kingdom of God: The Biblical Concept and Its Meaning for the Church.* Nashville: Abingdon-Cokesbury, 1953.

Brown, Colin. *Miracles and the Critical Mind.* Grand Rapids: Eerdmans, 1984.

Buber, Martin. *I and Thou.* 2d ed. Trans. R. G. Smith. New York: Scribners, 1957.

Bufford, Roger K. *The Human Reflex: Behavioral Psychology in Biblical Perspective.* San Francisco: Harper and Row, 1981.

Burtt, Edwin A. *The Metaphysical Foundations of Modern Science.* Rev. ed. Garden City, N.Y.: Doubleday, Anchor, 1954.

Butterfield, Herbert. *The Origins of Modern Science.* London: Bell and Sons, 1949.

Chafer, Lewis Sperry. *Systematic Theology.* 8 vols. Dallas: Dallas Seminary Press, 1947–48.

Chandler, Russell. *Understanding the New Age.* Waco, Tex.: Word, 1988.

Chao, Jonathan. "Indigenization of the Christian Movement in China IV: Deculturalization of the Chinese Church." *Missionary Monthly* 94 (August/September 1987).

Clooney, Francis. "Christianity and World Religions: Religion, Reason, and Pluralism." *Religious Studies Review* 15.3 (1989): 197–204.

Cohn, Norman R. C. *The Pursuit of the Millennium.* Oxford: Oxford University Press, 1957.

Conant, James B. *Modern Science and Modern Man.* New York: Columbia University Press, 1952.

Conn, Harvie. *Eternal Word and Changing Worlds: Theology, Anthropology, and Mission in Trialogue.* Grand Rapids: Zondervan, 1984.

Coulson, Charles A. *Science and Christian Belief.* London: Fontana, 1955.

Denney, James. "The Theology of the Epistle to the Romans." *The Expositor* 4.

Dijksterhuis, E. J. *The Mechanization of the World Picture: Pythagoras to Newton.* Trans. C. D. Dikshoorn. Princeton, N.J.: Princeton University Press, 1986.

Douglas, Mary. *Natural Symbols: Explorations in Cosmology.* New York: Random House, 1970.

Durkheim, Émile. *The Elementary Forms of the Religious Life.* Trans. J. W. Swain. New York: Macmillan, 1915.

Dyrness, William. *How Does America Hear the Gospel?* Grand Rapids: Eerdmans, 1990.

Edwards, Jonathan. *Religious Affections.* Ed. John E. Smith. New Haven, Conn.: Yale University Press, 1959.

Eichrodt, Walter. *Theology of the Old Testament*. 2 vols. Trans. J. A. Baker. Philadelphia: Westminster, 1961–67.

Eliade, Mircea. *Shamanism: Archaic Techniques of Ecstasy*. Princeton, N.J.: Princeton University Press, 1964.

Ellul, Jacques. *The Technological Society*. New York: Random House, 1964.

Ewert, David. *The Holy Spirit in the New Testament*. Scottdale, Penn.: Herald, 1983.

Ewing, Gene. *If You Want Money, a Home in Heaven, Health and Happiness, Based on the Holy Bible, Do These Things*. Atlanta: Rev. Gene Ewing, 1981.

Fosdick, Harry Emerson. *Twelve Tests of Character*. New York: Association, 1923.

Fox, Richard W. and Jackson Lears. *The Culture of Consumption: Critical Essays in American History, 1860–1960*. New York: Pantheon, 1983.

Geertz, Clifford. "Anti-Relativism." *American Anthropologist* 86.2 (1984): 263–78.

————. "Religion as a Cultural System." In *Reader in Comparative Religion: An Anthropological Approach*, ed. William A. Lessa and Evon Z. Vogt. 3d ed. New York: Harper and Row, 1972.

Gilchrist, E. "Baba Farid." *Outreach to Islam* 3 (1987).

Gill, Jerry H. *On Knowing God: New Directions for the Future of Theology*. Philadelphia: Westminster, 1981.

Gitari, David. "The Claims of Jesus in the African Context." *International Review of Mission* 71 (1982):12–19.

Griffiths, R. B. "Is Theology a Science?" *Journal of the American Scientific Affiliation* (September 1980): 169–73.

Groothuis, Douglas R. *Unmasking the New Age*. Downers Grove, Ill.: InterVarsity, 1986.

Grunbaum, A. "Complementarity in Quantum Physics and Its Philosophical Generalizations." *Journal of Philosophy* 54 (November 1957): 23–32.

Guelich, Robert. "Images in Luke." Inaugural address given at Fuller Theological Seminary, Pasadena, Calif., 1990.

Habermas, Jurgen. *Knowledge and Human Interests*. Trans. J. J. Shapiro. Boston: Beacon Press, 1971.

Haleblian, Krikor. "The Problem of Contextualization." *Missiology* 11 (1983): 95–111.

Hall, Edward T. *Silent Language*. Greenwich, Conn.: Fawcett, 1961.

Hall, Granville Stanley. *Jesus, the Christ, in the Light of Psychology*. Garden City, N.Y.: Doubleday, 1917.

Hammel, Eugene A., and William S. Simmons, eds. *Man Makes Sense: A Reader in Modern Cultural Anthropology*. Boston: Little, Brown, 1970.

Harris, Marvin. *Cultural Materialism: The Struggle for a Science of Culture*. New York: Random House, 1980.

Harvey, David. *The Condition of Post-modernity: An Enquiry into the Origins of Culture Change*. Cambridge: Basil Blackwell, 1984.

Hick, John, and Paul Knitter, eds. *The Myth of Christian Uniqueness: Toward a Pluralistic Theology of Religions*. Maryknoll, N.Y.: Orbis, 1988.

Hiebert, Paul G. "Traffic Patterns in Seattle and Hyderabad: Immediate and Mediate Transactions." *Journal of Anthropological Research* 32.4 (Winter 1976): 326–36.

————. *Konduru: Structure and Integration in a South Indian Village*. Minneapolis: University of Minnesota Press, 1971.

Hodge, Archibald Alexander. *Outlines of Theology*. New York: Armstrong and Sons, 1891.

Hofstadter, Douglas R. *Godel, Escher, Bach: An Eternal Golden Braid*. New York: Random House, 1980.

Holton, Gerald. "The Roots of Complementarity." *Daedalus* 99 (1970).

Hoyt, Karen, ed. *The New Age Rage*. Old Tappan, N.J.: Revell, 1987.

Hunt, David, and T. A. McMahon. *The Seduction of Christianity: Spiritual Discernment in the Last Days*. Eugene, Oreg.: Harvest House, 1985.

Hutcheon, Linda. *A Poetics of Postmodernity*. New York: Routledge, 1980.

Hymes, Dell, ed. *Language in Culture and Society*. New York: Harper and Row, 1964.

Jones, E. Stanley. *Christ at the Round Table*. Cincinnati: Abingdon, 1933.

————. *The Christ of the Indian Road*. New York: Abingdon, 1925.

————. *Christian Maturity*. Nashville: Abingdon, 1957.

Juhnke, James C. *A People of Mission: A History of the General Conference Mennonite Overseas Missions*. Newton, Kans.: Faith and Life, 1979.

Kaiser, Christopher. "Christology and Complementarity." *Religious Studies* 12 (1973): 37–48.

Knitter, Paul. "Making Sense of the Many." *Religious Studies Review* 15.3 (1989): 204–9.

Kraemer, C. Hendrik. *The Christian Message in a Non-Christian World*. London: James Clarke, 1938.

Kraft, Charles H. *Christianity in Culture: A Study in Dynamic Biblical Theologizing in Cross-Cultural Perspective*. Maryknoll, N.Y.: Orbis, 1979.

Kraus, C. Norman. *The Authentic Witness: Credibility and Authority*. Grand Rapids: Eerdmans, 1979.

Krumrei, Phil. "An Analysis of Set Theory and Its Application to Christian Faith." Unpubl. ms., Harding Graduate School of Religion, n.d.

Kuhn, Thomas S. *The Structure of Scientific Revolutions*. 2d ed. Chicago: University of Chicago Press, 1970.

Larson, Gerald J., et al., eds. *Myth and Indo-European Antiquity*. Berkeley, Calif.: University of California Press, 1974.

Laudan, Larry. *Progress and Its Problems: Towards a Theory of Scientific Growth*. Berkeley, Calif.: University of California Press, 1977.

Lewis, C. S. *God in the Dock: Essays on Theology and Ethics*. Ed. W. Hooper. Grand Rapids: Eerdmans, 1970.

————. *A Preface to Paradise Lost*. London: Oxford University Press, 1960.

Lewis, Oscar. *The Children of Sanchez*. New York: Random House, 1961.

Lincoln, Bruce. *Myth, Cosmos, and Society: Indo-European Themes of Creation and Destruction*. Cambridge, Mass.: Harvard University Press, 1986.

Lind, Millard C. "Refocusing Theological Education to Mission: The Old Testament and Contextualization." *Missiology* 10 (1982): 141–60.

Linder, Robert D., and Richard V. Pierard. *Twilight of the Saints: Biblical Christianity and Civil Religion in America*. Downers Grove, Ill.: InterVarsity, 1977.

Lloyd-Jones, David Martyn. *Prove All Things*. London: Kingsway, 1986.

Loewen, Jacob A. *Culture and Human Values: Christian Intervention in Anthropological Perspective*. Pasadena, Calif.: William Carey Library, 1975.

Lovejoy, Arthur. *The Great Chain of Being: A Study of the History of an Idea.* Cambridge, Mass.: Harvard University Press, 1936.

Luke, P. Y., and John B. Carman. *Village Christians and Hindu Culture.* Commission on World Mission and Evangelism, World Council of Churches. London: Lutterworth, 1968.

Luria, Aleksandr R. *Cognitive Development: Its Cultural and Social Foundations.* Trans. M. Lopez-Morillas and L. Solotaroff. Cambridge, Mass.: Harvard University Press, 1976.

Lyotard, Jean-Francois. *The Postmodern Condition: A Report on Knowledge.* Minneapolis: University of Minnesota Press, 1984.

MacKay, D. M. "Complementarity." *Aristotelian Society Supplement* (1958).

———. "Complementarity in Scientific and Theological Thinking." *Zygon* 9 (September 1974): 225–44.

Maddocks, Melvin. "Lenin on the Golf Links." *World Monitor* (January 1990).

Mannheim, Karl. *Ideology and Utopia: An Introduction to the Sociology of Knowledge.* London: K. Paul, Trench and Trubner, 1936.

Martin, Ralph P. *The Spirit and the Congregation: Studies in I Corinthians 12–15.* Grand Rapids: Eerdmans, 1984.

McGrane, Bernard. *Beyond Anthropology: Society and the Other.* New York: Columbia Unversity Press, 1989.

Michaelsen, Johanna. *The Beautiful Side of Evil.* Eugene, Oreg.: Harvest House, 1982.

Morgan, Lewis Henry. *Ancient Society.* New York: Henry Holt, 1877.

Newbigin, Lesslie. *Foolishness to the Greeks: The Gospel and Western Culture.* Grand Rapids: Eerdmans, 1986.

———. *The Gospel in a Pluralist Society.* Grand Rapids: Eerdmans, 1990.

———. *Honest Religion for Secular Man.* Philadelphia: Westminster, 1966.

Nida, Eugene, and William Reyburn. *Meaning across Cultures: A Study on Bible Translating.* Maryknoll, N.Y.: Orbis, 1981.

Northrop, F. S. C. *The Taming of the Nations.* New York: Macmillan, 1952.

Orr, J. Edwin. *The Eager Feet: Evangelical Awakenings 1790–1830.* Chicago: Moody, 1975.

Otto, Rudolph. *The Idea of the Holy: An Inquiry into the Non-Rational Factor in the Idea of the Divine and Its Relation to the Rational.* Trans. J. W. Harvey. Original German title, *Das Heilige,* 1917. Translation, Oxford: Oxford University Press, 1923.

Pattison, E. M., N. A. Lapius, and H. O. Doerr. "Faith Healing: A Study of Personality and Function." *Journal of Nervous Mental Disorders* 157 (1973): 397–409.

Peale, Norman Vincent. *The Positive Power of Jesus Christ.* Speical FCL ed. Pawling, N.Y.: Foundation for Christian Living, 1980.

———. *The Positive Principle Today: How to Renew and Sustain the Power of Positive Thinking.* Englewood Cliffs, N.J.: Prentice Hall, 1976.

Peirce, Charles S. *Philosophical Writings of Peirce,* ed. J. Buchler. 1940. Reprint, New York: Dover, 1955.

Peretti, Frank E. *Piercing the Darkness.* Westchester, Ill.: Crossway, 1989.

———. *This Present Darkness.* Westchester, Ill.: Crossway, 1986.

Peterson, Eugene H. *Under the Unpredictable Plant: An Exploration in Vocational Holiness.* Grand Rapids: Eerdmans, 1992.

Piaget, Jean. *The Psychology of Intelligence.* Totowa, N.J.: Littlefield, Adams, 1960.

Pike, Kenneth L. "Here We Stand Creative Observers of Language." In *Approches du Langage,* Colloque Interdisciplinaire, Publications de la Sorbonne, Serie Etudes, ed. E. Reuchlin and Francois, vol. 16. 1980.

———. *Linguistic Concepts: An Introduction to Tagmemics.* Lincoln: University of Nebraska Press, 1982.

———. "The Relation of Language to the World." *International Journal of Dravidian Linguistics* 16.1 (1987): 77–98.

Pobee, John. "Political Theology in the African Context." *Africa Theological Journal* 11 (1982): 168–72.

Polanyi, Michael. *Personal Knowledge: Towards a Post-Critical Philosophy.* Chicago: University of Chicago Press, 1958.

Puhvel, Jean, ed. *Myth and Law among the Indo-Europeans: Studies in Indo-European Comparative Mythology.* Berkeley, Calif.: University of California Press, 1970.

Raven, Charles E. *Science, Religion, and the Future.* 1943. Reprint, Cambridge, England: Cambridge University Press, 1953.

Reining, Conrad. "A Lost Period of Applied Anthropology." In *Applied Anthropology: Readings in the Uses of the Science of Man,* ed. James A. Clifton. Boston: Houghton Mifflin, 1970.

Ro, Bong Rin, ed. *Christian Alternatives to Ancestor Practices.* Taichung, Taiwan: Asia Theological Association, 1985.

Ro, Bong Rin, and Ruth Eschenaur, eds. *The Bible and Theology in Asian Contexts.* Taichung, Taiwan: Asia Theological Association, 1984.

Sanneh, Lamin O. *Translating the Message: The Missionary Impact on Culture.* Maryknoll, N.Y.: Orbis, 1989.

Schilling, Harold K. *The New Consciousness in Science and Religion.* London: SCM, 1973.

Schreiter, Robert J. "Anthropology and Faith: Challenges to Missiology." *Missiology: An International Review* 19.3 (July 1991): 283–94.

Shedd, W. G. T. *Dogmatic Theology.* 3 vols. Edinburgh: T & T Clark, 1888–94.

Shenk, Wilbert. "The Changing Role of the Missionary: From 'Civilization to Contextualization.'" In *Missions, Evangelism, and Church Growth,* ed. C. Norman Kraus. Scottdale, Penn.: Herald, 1980.

Simon, Francis. *The Neglect of Science.* Oxford: Basil Blackwell, 1951.

Smedes, Lewis B., ed. *Ministry and the Miraculous: A Case Study at Fuller Theological Seminary.* Pasadena, Calif.: Fuller Theological Seminary, 1987.

Smith, Huston. *Beyond the Post-Modern Mind.* New York: Crossroad, 1982.

Stoll, Robert R. *Set Theory and Logic.* San Francisco: W. H. Freeman, 1963.

Stott, John R. *The Authentic Jesus: The Certainty of Christ in a Skeptical World.* Downers Grove, Ill.: InterVarsity, 1986.

Strong, Augustus H. *Systematic Theology.* 1886. Reprint, Philadelphia: Judson, 1973.

Sukenick, Ronald. "Upward and Juanward: The Possible Dream." In *Seeing Castaneda: Reactions to the "Don Juan" Writings of Carlos Castaneda,* ed. Daniel Noel. New York: Putnam, 1976.

Swidler, Leonard. *After the Absolute: The Dialogical Future of Religious Reflection.* Minneapolis: Fortress, 1990.

Taylor, John V. *The Growth of the Church in Buganda: An Attempt at Understanding.* London: SCM, 1958. Reprint, Westport, Conn.: Greenwood Press, 1979.

Tillapaugh, Frank R. *The Church Unleashed: Getting God's People Out Where the Needs Are.* Ventura, Calif.: Regal, 1982.

Tracy, David. *The Blessed Rage for Order: The New Pluralism in Theology.* New York: Seabury, 1975.

Turner, Victor. *The Ritual Process: Structure and Antistructure.* Chicago: Aldine, 1969.

Useem, John, Ruth Useem, and John Donoghue. "Men in the Middle of the Third Culture: The Rites of American and Non-Western People in Cross-Cultural Administration." *Human Organization* 22 (Fall 1963): 169–79.

Wagner, C. Peter, and F. Douglas Pennoyer. *Wrestling with Dark Angels: Toward a Deeper Understanding of the Supernatural Forces in Spiritual Warfare.* Ventura, Calif.: Regal, 1990.

Wakeman, Mary K. *God's Battle with the Monster: A Study in Biblical Imagery.* Leiden: E. J. Brill, 1973.

Walter, J. A. *Need: The New Religion.* Downers Grove, Ill.: InterVarsity, 1986.

Warner, Timothy. *Spiritual Warfare: Victory over the Powers of This Dark World.* Wheaton, Ill.: Crossway, 1991.

Weaver, Edwin, and Irene Weaver. *From Kuku Hill: Among Indigenous Churches in West Africa.* Scottdale, Penn.: Herald, 1975.

Weber, Max. *The Protestant Ethic and the Spirit of Capitalism.* Trans. T. Parsons. New York: Scribner's Sons, 1958.

———. *The Theory of Social and Economic Organization.* New York: Free Press, 1964.

Whitehead, Alfred North. *Science and the Modern World.* Cambridge, England: Cambridge University Press, 1926.

Wiley, H. O. *Christian Theology.* 1940. Reprint, Kansas City, MO: Beacon Hill, 1969.

Williams, Zella M. "Testimony of Christian Science Healing." *Christian Science Sentinel* 88.34 (1952).

Willimon, William. "A Crisis of Identity." *Sojourners* 15 (May 1986): 24–28.

Wink, Walter. Conference plenary address, Seminary Consortium for Urban Pastoral Education (SCUPE), Chicago, 1989.

———. *Engaging the Powers: Discernment and Resistance in a World of Domination.* Minneapolis: Fortress, 1992.

———. *Naming the Powers: The Language of Power in the New Testament.* Philadelphia: Fortress, 1984.

Yager, R. R., et al., eds. *Fuzzy Sets and Applications: Selected Papers by L. A. Zadeh.* New York: Wiley, 1987.

Zadeh, Lofti Asker. "Fuzzy Sets." *Information and Control* 8 (1965): 338–53.

Zimmerman, Hans-Jurgens. *Fuzzy Set Theory and Its Applications.* Boston: Kluwer-Nijhoff, 1985.

Index